International Perspectives on Social Policy, Administration, and Practice

Series Editors

Sheying Chen
Jason L. Powell

For further volumes:
http://www.springer.com/series/007

Zitha Mokomane
Editor

Work–Family Interface in Sub-Saharan Africa

Challenges and Responses

Springer

Editor
Zitha Mokomane
Population Health, Health Systems
and Innovation Programme
Human Sciences Research Council
Pretoria
South Africa

ISBN 978-3-319-01236-0 ISBN 978-3-319-01237-7 (eBook)
DOI 10.1007/978-3-319-01237-7
Springer Cham Heidelberg New York Dordrecht London

Library of Congress Control Number: 2013950719

Printed on acid-free paper

Springer is part of Springer Science+Business Media (www.springer.com)

To

Em'dee, Fifi and One
for constantly providing a supportive
family environment
to fulfill my work commitments

Preface

Among the most striking labour market trends of recent times has been the growing proportion of women in the labour force and the narrowing of the gap between male and female labour force participation rates. Despite this, the expectations of women as the primary careers of minor children, older persons, and the firm in their households and families remain the same. This often leads to competing demands between labour market and family roles and, in turn, to considerable stress, conflict and loss in the quality of life of working women with care responsibilities—all with significant social cost. Although this trend is global, much of the research and policy dialogue in this area have been taking place in Western countries, resulting in the paucity of cross-cultural and comparative work on the subject, and limiting the extent to which generalisations can be made based in conclusions by Western studies.

This book is one of the first systematic efforts to bridge this research gap by focusing on sub-Saharan Africa—one of the least studied regions in terms of the relationship between workers' family responsibilities and paid work, or work–family interface. The book is divided into four parts each dealing with a different aspect of the subject: (i) Work–Family interface as a policy issue in Sub-Saharan Africa; (ii) factors underlying Work–Family conflict in Sub-Saharan Africa; (iii) impact of Work–Family conflict on families; and (iv) current and plausible coping strategies. All chapters end with policy recommendations to enhance the reconciliation of the demands of paid work and family responsibilities. Together therefore, the chapters: (i) offer critical theoretical perspectives and empirical insights into the opportunities and constraints that workers with family responsibilities have in sub-Saharan Africa and (ii) provide a roadmap for future research and policymaking in the area of work–family interface in the sub-region.

The book will be of primary interest to graduate students, academics and researchers in social policy, family studies, sociology, social work and other social sciences. To the extent that each chapter concludes with recommendations for interventions, the book will also be of value to socio-economic policymakers in Sub-Saharan Africa. The book is timely and relevant against the United Nations Economic and Social Council's Resolution 2011/29 of 2011 on the "Preparations for an observance of the twentieth anniversary of the International Year of the Family" which will be in 2014. Among other things, the resolution encourages Member States to continue their efforts to develop appropriate policies to address family poverty, social exclusion and work–family balance and share good practices in those areas.

Contents

Contributors

Francis Annor St John's College, University of Cambridge, Cambridge, UK

Lisa Dancaster University of Cape Town, Cape Town, South Africa

Chantal Epie Lagos Business School, Victoria Island, Lagos State, Nigeria

Afam Ituma The Federal University Ndufu Alike Ikwo (FUNAI), Abakaliki, Ebonyi State, Nigeria

Virginia Mapedzahama School of Rural Medicine, University of New England, Armidale, NSW, Australia

Francine Masson Department of Social Work, University of Witwatersrand, Johannesburg, South Africa

Zitha Mokomane Population Health, Health Systems and Innovation, Human Sciences Research Council of South Africa, Pretoria, South Africa

Gladys Muasya Hugh Downs School of Human Communication, Arizona State University, Tempe, USA

Ndangwa Noyoo Social Policy Programme, National Department of Social Development, Pretoria, South Africa

Dolly Ntseane Department of Social Work, University of Botswana, Gaborone, Botswana

Ejike Okonkwo Enugu State University of Science and Technology, Agbani, Enugu State, Nigeria

Eleanor Ross Centre for Social Development in Africa, University of Johannesburg, Johannesburg, South Africa

Part I
Work–Family Interface as a Policy Issue in Sub-Saharan Africa

Chapter 1
Introduction

Zitha Mokomane

Background to the Book

With particular focus on sub-Saharan Africa, the purpose of this book is to contribute to cross-cultural research on the subject of work–family interface by giving an African perspective to it. The book has, to a large extent, being influenced by the steady increase in interdisciplinary academic and applied interest in the nexus between work and family life over the past 3 decades. Propelled by socioeconomic transformations such as increased employment of women; rising hours of work; today's service-intensive globalising economy and changes in family composition and structure, this interest—which spans "the boundaries of disciplines such as sociology, psychology, organisational behaviour, human development, labour economics, industrial relations, management, demography, and women's studies" (Bardoel et al. 2008:318)—has resulted in a substantial strand of literature showing that the interacting trends in the labour market and structure of families are making it increasingly difficult for employees in many countries to provide ordinary attention needed for the wellbeing of family members, including themselves (Bailyn et al. 2001). This literature shows that the 'time-money squeeze' between family responsibilities and work demands often leads to considerable stress and conflict for employees, a phenomenon generally known as 'work–family conflict'.

It is important to recognise the difference between work–family interface and other commonly used concepts in the literature such as 'work–life', 'work–life balance', 'work–care', 'work—care integration', etc. According to Dancaster (2012:21) work–life "includes the ability to integrate work into one's whole life and may include issues unrelated to family and care considerations, such as the ability to take time off work to pursue personal interests or self-development goals

Z. Mokomane (✉)
Population Health, Health Systems and Innovation, Human Sciences Research Council, 134 Pretorius Street, Pretoria, Gauteng 0001, South Africa
e-mail: zmokomane@hsrc.ac.za

Z. Mokomane (ed.), *Work–Family Interface in Sub-Saharan Africa*, International Perspectives on Social Policy, Administration, and Practice,
DOI: 10.1007/978-3-319-01237-7_1,

or to be involved in community issues". Work–care, on the other hand, refers to "the management of one's dependent-care responsibilities ... in addition to the responsibilities of the job and excluding more general 'work–life' issues that are unrelated to the need to care" (Dancaster 2012:22). This book is specifically focused on the challenges of combining the roles of paid work—in either the formal or informal sector—and family (however defined) as well as on the response that can enhance work–family balance, whereby the right balance between the commitments of work and those of the family is achieved.

Defining Work–Family Conflict

Defined as "a form of inter-role conflict in which the roles pressures from work and family domains are mutually incompatible in some respect" (Greenhaus and Beutell 1985:77), work–family conflict arises when time devoted to the requirements of one domain makes it difficult to fulfil requirements of the other; when the strain from participation in one domain makes it difficult to fulfil requirements of the other or when specific behaviours required by one domain make it difficult to fulfil the requirements of the other (Greenhaus and Beutell 1985).

To the extent that it arises from factors within the work and family domains, work–family conflict is conceptually bi-directional: there can be family-to-work conflict and work–to-family conflict. The former occurs when experiences in the family (for example, the presence of young children, primary responsibility for children, elder care responsibilities, interpersonal conflict within the family unit and unsupportive family members) interfere with work life (Frone et al. 1996). Work–family conflict on the other hand occurs when experiences at work (such as irregular or inflexible work hours; work overload and other forms of job stress; extensive travel and unsupportive supervisors or organizations) interfere with family life (Netemeyer et al. 1996).

Although these two types of interference are strongly correlated, research has found that work roles are more likely to interfere with family roles than vice versa. This is often a result of extended working hours; lack of policies that increase the quality or availability of flexible or alternative working arrangement; lack of workplace social support such as child care support and lack of care-related workplace policies such as paid maternity, paternity and parental leaves (Glass and Estes 1997; Earle et al. 2011; Hegewisch and Gornick 2011).

Impact of Work–Family Conflict

The different conclusions that have been drawn from the research literature on work–family conflict can be encapsulated by considering two main contradictory perspectives: the expansion and the role-conflict hypotheses (Hãrenstam and

Bejerot 2001). The expansion hypothesis (also called the social causation or role-accumulation hypothesis) generally posits that participation in multiple roles provides a greater number of resources—such as better financial situation, greater social integration, improved social support and higher self-esteem—that can be used to promote personal growth, general health and wellbeing and better functioning in other life domains (Hãrenstam and Bejerot 2001; Geurts et al. 2005). Oomens et al. (2007), for example, argue that the availability of alternative roles may serve as a buffer against distress experienced in one role. In other words, the difficulties or demands in one role may be offset by the positive attributes of the other roles.

The most dominant perspective, however, is the role-conflict hypothesis which argues that time and personal energy are two conflicting resources and of limited quantity. According to this perspective, people who occupy multiple social roles inevitably experience conflict which, in turn, may lead to considerable strain and stress on them, their families and their work. For instance, if one's paid job requires frequent overtime work, this limits the available time at home, which may conflict with family demands. Similarly, if one's child is sick this may put strain on work demands (Oomens et al. 2007). Indeed, work–family conflict has attracted the attention of researchers and policymakers because of its implication for, *inter alia,* workplace productivity; child care, health and development; gender equality; and family life. The conflict has, for example, been associated with workplace problems such as high turnover; increased absenteeism; tardiness and decreased job satisfaction, work quality, productivity and competitiveness (Wolcott 1994; International Labour Organisation 2004). According to Wolcott (1994:2):

> Concerns about child care, sick children, elderly parents, marital and family problems can increase absenteeism, coming to work late or leaving early, [affect] concentration and safety on the job. ... Family responsibilities can influence a worker's willingness to take on additional tasks, training, travel or relocate, Other employees' efficiency can be affected, especially in teamwork situations, when colleagues and workmates are absent or preoccupied with family concerns. Skilled employees many not be retained because of inadequate child care or inflexible hours are not available after maternity leave. Cost of recruitment, training and 'down time; before new employees are up to par can increase in these circumstances.

Work–family conflict can also lead workers to adopt less than satisfactory childcare solutions such as leaving children alone at home; enlisting the help of an older sibling, often a girl removed from school or taking children to work with them (International Labour Organisation 2004). It is well-documented, however, that having children at work not only takes away from the time and investment (such as training or business development) that women can put into paid work, but it also places children in hazardous environments and at risk of child labour (Cassirer and Addati 2007; International Labour Organisation 2010a). Leaving children alone, in the care of older siblings also has clear implications for the health and development of young children and for the long-term educational and employment opportunities of those children who withdraw from school to provide care.

In terms of child health and development, the failure to reconcile work and family demands has been associated with negative child outcomes, including being less likely to have regular medical check-ups in the first year of life, less likely to receive childhood immunisations, and less likely to breastfeed (Berger et al. 2005; Kamerman 2006; Kusakabe 2006). On the other hand, a 2-decade study done in 16 European countries found that after controlling for per capita income, the availability of technology and other factors related to child health, the availability of paid parental leave policies was associated with lower infant and child mortality rates as well as lower maternal stress (Ruhm 2000). Furthermore, to the extent that parental active involvement in their children's education is associated with children's improved behaviour, greater academic persistence and lower school dropout rates (Heymann and Earle 2000; Ruhm 2000), work–family conflict can affect parental involvement in their children's education, and eventually the children's scholastic performance.

While work–family conflict can also limit men's ability to be involved in family matters, research has shown that the pressures and stresses of this conflict are particularly higher for women who, despite their increasing entry into wage employment, continue to be primarily responsible for the general management of their households and for the care of minor children and elderly members in their households and families (UNECA 2001). It has been consistently noted that combining personal and occupational roles tend to induce physical and psychosomatic symptoms (such as fatigue, anxiety, migraines, hypertension and depression) among women than among men (Oomens et al. 2007; Blin 2008). The International Labour Organisation (2004) also posits that family responsibilities and their conflict with work demands are major factors contributing to: women's disadvantage in the labour market; the prevention of the attainment of equal opportunity and treatment for men and women in employment and the constraining of women's ability to maximise income generation opportunities and/or career prospects.

For society in general, work–family conflict can perpetuate poverty and the societal inequities through, for instance, reducing the number of adults who can participate in paid work; restricting the range of jobs that people are able to take up; and making it difficult to participate in leisure and social activities—which can limit social networks, opportunities and quality of life (International Labour Organisation 2004; Cassier and Addati 2007). This conflict has also been associated with negative impacts in the quality of relations between spouses, and increased risk of family dysfunction (Macewen and Barling 1994; Matthews et al. 1996; Duxbury and Huggins 2003). The "absence effect" hypothesis, for example, posits that women's participation in income generating activities outside the home has the potential to increase stress and conflict within a marriage, particularly when demands associated with both paid work and family roles are high (Greenstein 1995 cited by Reddy 2010). This can be partly attributed to the resultant decrease in the quality and quantity of time couples spend together, increased feelings of role conflict and overload among women and, in some instances, women's increased awareness of the inequity in the household division of labour (Reddy 2010).

Getting the work–family balance right is therefore not only vital to enhance the wellbeing of workers and their families but it can also have a positive impact on employee motivation, satisfaction and commitment, as well as on business performance and better labour market outcomes (OECD 2001; Pavalko and Henderson 2006). It is largely because of this that many western and industrialised countries have introduced several arrangements that may assist employees to better coordinate their work and domestic obligations. These 'family friendly policies' include, among others, working hour arrangements (for example, flexibility in work schedules, part-time work, working from home and telecommuting), subsidies for childcare, as well as statutory and on-statutory leave such as rights to parental leave, and allowing temporary leave periods for employees to take care of children and other dependent family members (Pavalko and Henderson 2006; Oomens et al. 2007).

While some contend that these policies have no or little significant effect (see Stier et al. 2012), many studies and evaluations of these policies have associated them with reduced individuals' perceived work–family conflict (for example, Crompton and Lyonette 2006) and with better labour market outcomes, work commitment and productivity (Commonwealth of Australia 2002). According to the International Labour Organisation (2004), family-friendly policies can also improve the potential for equity of opportunity between men and women by reducing the interruption of careers that are most often lost to women due to caring responsibilities. Decades of research have also shown that children's health and general development outcomes improve when there are supportive policies that allow parents to participate in their children's health care and scholastic activities (Earle et al. 2011). To this end, work–family interface is an important aspect of social policy because:

> while there are often complex and, at times, contradictory effects of different social policies and employment arrangements on the perception of work–family conflict among women and men … taken together …' national policies and institutional arrangements do make a difference and enhance to some extent the life balance of employed women and men (Stier et al. 2012:278).

Why Sub-Saharan Africa?

The concepts of work and family have varied significance and importance in different countries and cultures. In the West, for example, people tend to emphasise personal accomplishment and achievement through work, where individuals often perceive time spent at work as time spent fulfiling personal ambition. To this end, a Westerner will tend to view the needs of the self and the family as distinct, and will experience conflict when there are demands made by both

(Poelmans et al. 2003). In developing societies, on the other hand, people's focus is typically on the family's welfare, and work is seen not as a means of enhancing the self, but as a means of supporting the family, and as contributing to family welfare instead of competing with it (Yang et al. 2000 cited in Spector et al. 2004). It is also important to recognise that many developing societies have diverse family structures that are "complex, fluid, with wide boundaries and definitions as to what constitutes 'my family' …" (Dancaster 2012:22). It can therefore be expected that the conflicts between work and family will be experienced differently in different societies.

Against this background, a major limitation of the current research and literature on work–family interface is its decidedly Western focus, with the majority of the studies having been done in Anglo countries (such as Canada, the United Kingdom and the United States) and other western countries that share comparable cultural values and economic circumstances (Poelmans et al. 2003; Spector et al. 2004). However, "given that societies differ in the degree of importance attached to work and family, and therefore, the extent to which they are perceived to be compatible" (Aryee et al. 1999), the Western bias of the work–family interface literature means that very little is known about the extent to which employees from different cultures perceive the antecedents and outcomes of work–family conflict (Aryee et al. 1999). According to Shaffer et al. (2011:222) this bias has also "resulted in a disparate and fractured understanding of the dynamic interplay between work and family for those who live and work beyond the borders of [western countries]". Furthermore:

> Given the predominant western permeation of conceptualizations, methods, and operationalizations in [work–family] studies, the results are often inappropriate to the cultures involved in the studies and not easily interpretable (Shaffer et al. 2011:252).

There has, as a result, been emerging calls for more cross-cultural exploration of both the risk factors for the onset of work–family conflict, and its consequences. Proponents of this type of research have argued, among other things, that with the globalisation of the world economy, where managers around the world are being increasingly confronted with real and virtual employees and teams with diverse cultural and socio-demographic backgrounds there is need to document valuable lessons on suitable approaches to address the varying needs of employees (Poelmans et al. 2003; Ishii-Kuntz 1994 cited in Spector et al. 2004).

Given that the few studies that have been done in non-western contexts focused mainly on Asia (for example Abe et al. 2003; Kim and Kim 2004; Kusakabe 2006) and Latin America (for example, Sorj 2004; Reddock and Bobb-Smith 2008), sub-Saharan Africa provides an interesting investigation or case study of the broader issue of work–family interface in developing countries because some of the prevailing socio-economic and demographic transformations currently taking place in the sub-region have important implications for the reconciliation of work and family responsibilities. These changes include an increase in the proportion of older people (Konkolewsky 2008; Makoni 2008); increasing labour force participation of women (United Nations 2009); increased migration and urbanisation

(African Union 2009); increased job insecurity (Aryee 2005); changing marriage patterns and the increasing proportion of female-headed households and the high prevalence of HIV and AIDS (Mokomane 2012).

Increasing Proportion of Older People In the sub-Saharan African context where older persons have virtually no social security or social welfare programmes to cater for their everyday socioeconomic needs (Bigombe and Khadiagala 2003; Taylor 2008), and where nursing homes and homes for the aged remain a foreign concept (Aryee 2005), adult children (particularly daughters) are culturally expected to take responsibility for the care and maintenance of their elderly parents (Bigombe and Khadiagala 2003; Aryee 2005). It is thus not uncommon for working children to live with their parents in urban areas so as to provide this care. Even when children live apart from their elderly parents, they are still expected to visit frequently to provide support and care. This intergenerational caregiving in sub-Saharan Africa therefore contributes a unique type of work–family conflict relative to the West (Aryee 2005).

Increasing Labour Force Participation of Women While increasing labour force participation rates of women in sub-Saharan Africa are a commendable trend, the socioeconomic relations that relegate unpaid family responsibilities to women (Cassirer and Addati 2007) mean that the women are working longer hours than men when both market and non-market activities are taken into consideration (UNECA 2001) and they face the challenges of balancing work and family demands as much as their counterparts in the West (Aryee 2005; Mapedzahama 2008).

Increased Migration and Urbanisation The resultant physical separation of family members due to increased migration in the sub-region has, among other things, reduced household sizes and weakened traditional kinship mode of residential settlement. Together with increased urbanisation this has diminished the strength of traditional extended family networks (Miller et al. 2006) and, as a result, the traditional family support for care roles and domestic tasks, while still frequent, is becoming less available, and many workers can no longer rely on it (International Labour Organisation 2004; Cassirer and Addati 2007).

Increased Job Insecurity The widespread retrenchment of employees in many sub-Saharan African public and private entities that followed the implementation of structural adjustment and economic liberalisation programmes in the 1980s and the 1990s, and the recent global economic crisis has instilled a high sense of job insecurity among many workers in the sub-region (Aryee 2005). While job insecurity is not unique to sub-Saharan Africa, the sub-region's high employment rates and lack of comprehensive social protection programmes such as unemployment benefits (Aryee 2005; Taylor 2008) makes the threat of job insecurity much more stressful for its people. One of the main consequences of this job insecurity has been the ethic of long working hours that many workers have developed in an effort to guard against job losses. In the context of work–family conflict, the long hours spent in formal employment can be broadened to include the time spent in other income generating activities such as petty trading that many sub-Saharan

African workers undertake to augment the inadequate or low pay often associated with the sub-region's labour market (Aryee 2005).

Changing Marriage Patterns and Increasing Proportion of Female-Headed Households From the 1970s a large part of sub-Saharan Africa began to experience significant transformations in marriage patterns reflected in, among others, the increase in age at first marriage for women, and the increase in the amount of time spent out of marriage during adult years (van de Walle 1993; Hertrich 2002). This suggests that many women in the sub-regions are less likely to have a spouse available to help with household responsibilities, and are assuming responsibility alone as the economic provider and caregiver for their children (Cassirer and Addati 2007).

High Prevalence of HIV and AIDS With sub-Saharan Africa being the region most heavily affected by HIV and AIDS (UNAIDS 2008), the most evident social impact of this epidemic has been the great strain on the care-related activities of families, often with critical implications for gender inequality. In particular, to the extent that the HIV and AIDS 'care economy'[1] is performed primarily by women, many working women in sub-Saharan Africa have the extra burden of providing care and support for family and household members infected and affected by the epidemic (Ogden et al. 2004; Miller et al. 2006). Overall, research evidence (see for example, International Labour Organisation 2004; Heymann et al. 2007) shows that the work–family conflict experienced by the many women who provide HIV and AIDS-related care severely restricts their options, often forcing them to choose between employment and care or to combine them, all of which require difficult trade-offs in terms of quality of employment and/or quality of care and has long-term consequences for escaping poverty (International Labour Organisation 2010a).

Despite the foregoing many countries in sub-Saharan Africa, as in many parts of the developing world, do not seem to perceive the work–family conflict as a problem. Similar to what Kusakabe (2006) observed in Thailand, care responsibilities are not placed on the same pedestal as, say, pay and job-security. Overall, workplaces and conditions continue to be structured around an assumption that all workers have a source of unpaid labour to care for their families, or that they will somehow be able to manage their responsibilities. As Dancaster (2008) observed in South Africa, "the notion of the ideal worker as essentially male and free of domestic responsibilities still permeates the thinking of many employers". Furthermore, while many countries of the region provide maternity leave provisions, other 'family friendly' workplace policies such as paternity or parental leave are either non-existent or extremely limited (International Labour Organisation 2010b; Smit 2011). However, the current socioeconomic and demographic changes in sub-Saharan Africa suggest that the development and adoption of mechanisms that

---

[1] This is described as the unremunerated work undertaken within the home, which ensures the physical, social and psychological maintenance and development of family members, as well as 'volunteer' activities in the community that keep the social fabric in good order (Ogden et al. 2004).

will allow participation in paid employment for those women with caring responsibilities will increasingly become a key policy issue in many countries of the sub-region. Overall, the situation is succinctly described by the following statement:

> The lack of collective measures and support for balancing paid work and family responsibilities constrains many households to turn to 'individual reconciliation strategies', often with adverse consequences to families' wellbeing and decent work objectives. This situation hits poor and vulnerable families the hardest, as they have the weakest economic capacity to purchase goods (processed foods, labour saving devices) or services (private childcare, health services for the ill, domestic help) that can free up time for paid work (International Labour Organisation 2010a:4).

There is, against this backdrop, an urgent need for public and private workplaces in the sub-region to adapt to the socioeconomic and demographic transformations, and put in place explicit mechanisms that will allow workers to adequately reconcile the demands of work and family. It is however imperative that all policies and programmes aimed at achieving a work–family balance should be evidence-based. As Korenman and Kaester (2005) caution, considerable care is needed before assuming that the more "family friendly" institutional arrangements present on western countries would be desirable for developing countries. In addition, given the often-advanced argument that governments in developing countries cannot adequately deliver family support because of limited human and technical resources, undertaking context-specific research will highlight the most appropriate support mechanisms for the region, including the most feasible modes of delivery of those mechanisms.

To contribute to cross-cultural research on work–family interface, the remaining 11 chapters of this book use a variety of evidence—primary and secondary—to highlight various aspects of work–family interface in sub-Saharan Africa, including the antecedents and consequences of work–family conflict; its impact on workers and their families; workers' current coping strategies and their limitations and plausible future support and coping mechanisms.

In the next chapter Francis Annor uses the case of employed parents in Ghana to illustrate the lived experiences of African parents who combine paid work with family commitments. His chapter is complemented by that of Virginia Mapedzahama who uses the lived experiences of working mothers in Australia and Zimbabwe to show a cross-cultural comparative perspective on the subject. The second part of the book discusses some of the key factors underlying work–family conflict in sub-Saharan Africa. In the first chapters by Chantal Epie and Afam Ituma it is shown that long working hours and the number and age of children are important contributory factors in Nigeria. Ejike Onkonkwo's chapter explores the extent to which the number and age of children can be an additional factor in Nigeria. In Chap. 6 sexual harassment is identified as contributory factors in South Africa by Francine Masson and Eleanor Ross.

The two chapters that make up the third part of the book explore some of the impacts of work–family conflict on families. The lead chapter by Dolly Ntseane shows how the government's job transfer policy in Botswana aggravates the conflict among dual-career families, and the impact of these on spouses and other interfamily relationships. The chapter by Francine Masson and Eleanor Ross, on the other hand, highlights the impact of work–family conflict on gender roles in South Africa. Chapters in the fourth and last part discuss the current coping strategies used by workers with family responsibilities in sub-Saharan Africa and some of the plausible coping strategy that are worthy of consideration by policymakers. Gladys Muasya uses Kenya as an example to show how house helps or domestic workers are a common and valuable coping strategy for many working parents. This is followed by two chapters in which Ndangwa Noyoo and Lisa Dancaster, with a focus on Zambia and South Africa, respectively, advocate for explicit family policies and state measures as mechanisms to enhance work–family balance in sub-Saharan Africa. The book concludes with a chapter in which Desire Chilwane and I assess the current state of work–family research in sub-Saharan Africa and use this, and the conclusions of the preceding ten chapters to propose a future research agenda to inform both academic interests and policymaking in this area.

References

Abe, M., Hamamoto, C., & Tanaka, S. (2003). *Reconciling work and family: Issues and policies in Japan*. ILO Conditions of Work and Employment Series No. 5. Geneva: International Labour Organisation.

African Union. (2009). *Social policy framework for Africa*. Addis Ababa: African Union.

Aryee, S., Fields, D., & Luk, V. (1999). A cross-cultural test of a model of the work-family interface. *Journal of Management, 25*(4), 491–511.

Aryee, S. (2005). The work–family interface in urban Sub-Saharan Africa: A theoretical analysis. In S. Y. Peilmans (Ed.), *Work and family: An international research perspective* (pp. 261–286). Mahwah: Lawrence Erlbaum Associates.

Bailyn, L., Drago, R., & Kochan, T.A. (2001). *Integrating work and family life: A holistic approach. Sloan Work-Family Policy Network*. Retrieved June 4, 2010, from http://lsir.la.psu.edu/workfam

Bardoel, E. A., De Cieri, H., & Santos, C. (2008). A review of work–life research in Australia and New Zealand. *Asia Pacific Journal of Human Resources, 46*(3), 316–333.

Berger, L., Hill, J., & Waldfogel, J. (2005). Maternity leave, early maternal employment, and child outcomes in the US. *The Economic Journal, 115*, 29–47.

Bigombe, B. & Khadiagala, G. M. (2003). Major trends affecting families in sub-Saharan Africa. New York: United Nations. Retrieved May 2, 2013, from http://social.un.org/index/LinkClick.aspx?fileticket=3VvV_mL8oMw%3d&tabid=282

Blin, M. (2008). Export-oriented policies, women's work burden and human development in Mauritius. *Journal of Southern African Studies, 34*(2), 239–253.

Cassirer, N., & Addati, L. (2007). *Expanding women's employment opportunities: Informal economy workers and the need for childcare*. Geneva: Conditions of Work and Employment Programme, International Labour Organisation.

Commonwealth of Australia. (2002). *OECD Review of family friendly policies: Australia's background report*. Canberra: Department of Family and Community Services.

Crompton, R., & Lyonette, C. (2006). Work–life balance in Europe. *Acta Sociologica, 49*(4), 379–393.

Dancaster, L. (2008). Mom at work. *Mail&Guardian Newspaper*, September 12–18 Issue, 24.
Dancaster, L.A. (2012). *State and employer involvement in work-care integration in South Africa*. Unpublished PhD Thesis, University of Sydney, Sydney, Australia.
Duxbury, L., & Higgins, C. (2003). *Work–ife conflict in Canada in the new millennium: A status report*. Health Canada: Heath Communities Division.
Earle, A., Mokomane, Z., & Heymann, J. (2011). International perspectives on work–family policies: Lessons from the world's most competitive economies. *Future of Children, 21*(2), 191–210.
Frone, M. R., Russell, M., & Barnes, G. M. (1996). Work–family conflict, gender and health related outcomes: A study of employed parents in two community samples. *Journal of Occupational Health Psychology, 1*, 57–69.
Geurts, S., Kompier, M., Dikkers, J., Van Hooff, M., & Kinnunen, U. (2005). Work–home interaction from a psychological perspective: Development and validation of a new questionnaire, the SWING. *Work and Stress, 19*(4), 319–339.
Glass, J. L., & Estes, S. B. (1997). The family responsive workplace. *Annual Review of Sociology, 23*, 289–313.
Greenhaus, J. H., & Beutell, N. J. (1985). Sources of conflict between work and family roles. *Academy of Management Review, 10*, 76–88.
Greenstein, T. N. (1995). Gender ideology, marital disruption and the employment of married women. *Journal of Marriage and the family, 57*, 31–42.
Hãrenstam, A., & Bejerot, E. E. (2001). Combining professional work with family responsibilities—a burden or a blessing? *International Journal of Social Welfare, 10*, 202–214.
Hegewisch, A., & Gornick, J. C. (2011). The impact of work–family policies on women's employment: A review of research from OECD countries. *Community, Work & Family, 14*(2), 119–138.
Hertrich, V. *Nuptiality and gender relationships in Africa: An overview of first marriage trends over the past 50 years*. Paper presented at the annual meeting of the Population Association of America, Atlanta, Georgia. May 9–11 , 2002.
Heymann, J., & Earle, A. (2000). Low-income parents: How do working conditions affect their opportunity to help school-age children at risk. *American Educational Research Journal, 37*(4), 833–848.
Heymann, J., Earle, A., Rajaraman, D., Miller, C., & Bogen, K. (2007). Extended family caring for children orphaned by AIDS: Balancing essential work and caregiving in a high prevalence nation. *AIDS Care, 19*(3), 337–345.
International Labour Organisation. (2004). *Work and family responsibilities: What are the problems?* (Information Sheet No. WF-1). Geneva: International labour Organisation.
International Labour Organisation. (2010a). *The way to care is to share*. Retrieved July 28, 2010, from www.ilocarib.org.tt/portal/images/stories/contenido/pdf/Gender/Brochure%20Final%20 EN.pdf
International Labour Organisation. (2010b). *Maternity at work: A review of national legislation*. Geneva: International Labour Organisation.
Kamerman, S.B. (2006). Parental leave policies: The impact on child well-being. In *International review of leave policies and related research 2006*. (pp. 2–4). London: Department of Trade and Industry.
Kim, T.H. & Kim, K.K. (2004). *Reconciling work and family: Issues and policies in the Republic of Korea*. ILO Conditions of Work and Employment Series No. 6. Geneva: International Labour Organisation.
Konkolewsky, H.H. *Keynote address*. Paper presented at the ISSA International Conference on Comprehensive Social Security, Cape Town, South Africa, March 10–14, 2008. Geneva, International Social Security Association.
Korenman, S., & Kaester, R. (2005). Work–family mismatch and child well-being: A review of the economic research. In S. M. Bianchi, L. M. Casper, & R. B. King (Eds.), *Work, family, health and wellbeing* (pp. 293–308). Mahwah: Lawrence Erlbaum Associates.

Kusakabe, K. (2006). *Reconciling work and family: Issues and policies in Thailand.* ILO Conditions of Work and Employment Series No. 14. Geneva: International Labour Organisation.
Macewen, K. E., & Barling, J. (1994). Daily consequences of work interference with family and family interference with work. *Work and Stress, 8*(3), 244–254.
Makoni, S. (2008). Aging in Africa: A critical review. *Journal of Cross-Cultural Gerontology, 23*(2), 199–209.
Mapedzahama, V. (2008, November). *Work and family in a cross cultural context: a comparative review of work/life experiences of working mothers in Adelaide (Australia) and Harare (Zimbabwe).* Paper presented at the African Studies Association of Australasia and the Pacific (AFSAAP) Annual Conference, Monash University, Melbournew.
Matthews, L. S., Conger, K. A., & Wickrama, S. (1996). Work–family conflict and marital quality: Mediating processes. *Social Psychology Quarterly, 59*(1), 62–79.
Miller, C. M., Gruskin, S., Subramanian, S. V., Rajaraman, D., & Heymann, S. J. (2006). Orphan care in Botswana's working households: Growing responsibilities in the absence of adequate support. *American Journal of Public Health, 96*(8), 1429–1435.
Mokomane, Z. (2012). Social protection as a mechanism for family protection in sub-Saharan Africa. *International Journal of Social Welfare.* doi: 10.1111/j.1468-2397.2012.00893.x.
Netemeyer, R. G., Boles, J. S., & McMurrian, R. (1996). Development and validation of work–family conflict and family-work conflict scales. *Journal of Applied Psychology, 81*(4), 400–410.
OECD, *Balancing work and family life: Helping parents into paid employment* (2001). Retrieved March 10, 2008, from www.oecd.org/dataoecd/11/12/2079435.pdf
Ogden, J., Simel, E. & Caren, G. (2004).*Expanding the care continuum for hiv/aids: bringing carers into focus. Horizons report.* Washington, DC: Population Council and International Center for Research on Women.
Oomens, S., Geurts, S., & Scheepers, P. (2007). Combining work and family in the Netherlands: Blessing or burden for one's mental health? *International Journal of Law and Psychiatry, 30*, 369–384.
Pavalko, E. K., & Henderson, K. A. (2006). Combining care work and paid work: Do workplace policies make a difference? *Research on Aging, 28*(3), 359–374.
Poelmans, S., Spector, P. E., Cooper, C. L., Allen, T. D., O'Driscoll, M., & Sanchez, J. I. (2003). A cross-national comparative study of work/family demands and resources. *International Journal of Cross Cultural Management, 3*(3), 275–288.
Reddock, C., & Bobb-Smith, Y. (2008). *Reconciling work and family: Issues and policies in Trinidad and Tobago.* Geneva: International Labour Organisation.
Reddy, K. (2010). *An investigation into work-family conflict in females occupying lower-level jobs.* Unpublished MA Dissertation, Nelson Mandela Metropolitan University, Port Elizabeth, South Africa.
Ruhm, C. (2000). *Parental employment and child's cognitive development.* Cambridge MA: National Bureau of Economic Research, 2000 (NBER Working Paper 7666).
Shaffer, M .A ., Joplin, J. R. W., & Hsu, Y. (2011). Expanding the boundaries of work—family research: A review and agenda for future research. *International Journal of Cross Cultural Management, 11*(2), 221–268.
Smit, R. (2011). Family-related policies in Southern African countries: Are working parents reaping any benefits? *Journal of Comparative Family Studies, 42*(1), 15–36.
Sorj, B. (2004). *Reconciling work and family: Issues and policies in Brazil.* Geneva: International Labour Organisation.
Spector, P. E., Cooper, C. L., Poelmans, S., Allen, T. D., O'Driscoll, M., Sanchez, J. I., et al. (2004). A cross-national comparative study of work–family stressors, working hours, and well-being: China and Latin America versus the Anglo world. *Personnel Psychology, 57*(1), 119–142.

Stier, H., Lewin-Epstein, N., & Braun, M. (2012). Work–family conflict in comparative perspective: The role of social policies. *Research in Social Stratification and Mobility, 30*, 265–279.

Taylor V. (2008). *The study on social protection systems in Africa: An overview of the challenges.* Paper prepared for the First Session of the AU Conference of Ministers in charge of social development held from 27 to 31 October 2008 in Windhoek, Namibia

UNAIDS. (2008). *AIDS Epidemic Update of December 2008.* Geneva: UNAIDS.

UNECA. (2001). *5 years after Beijing: Assessing women and poverty and the economic empowerment of women.* Addis Ababa: United Nations Economic Commission for Africa (UNECA).

United Nations. (2009). *The Millennium Development Report: 2009.* New York: United Nations.

van de Walle, E. (1993). Recent trends in marriage ages. In in K.A. Foote, K.H. Hilland L.G. Martin (Eds.), *Demographic Change in sub-Saharan Africa* (pp.117-152). Washington DC: National Academy Press.

Wolcott, I. (1994). *Achieving family supportive workplace and community.* Retrieved July 24, 2009, www.aifs.gov.au/institute/pubs/fm1/fm37iw.html

Chapter 2
Managing Work and Family Demands: The Perspectives of Employed Parents in Ghana

Francis Annor

Introduction

The interconnection between work and family has been a subject of great deal of interest over the past 3 decades due to the influx of women in the workforce, as well as the increase in the proportion of dual-earner families and single-parent households (International Labour Office 2009). Following the notion that individuals have limited time and energy to devote to multiple roles (Goode 1960), much of this research has focused on conflict experienced when meeting competing demands from work and family domains. In essence work–family conflict occurs when pressures associated with the work and family roles are incompatible (Greenhaus and Beutell 1985). Extant research has provided ample evidence of work–family conflict as a pervasive phenomenon with negative consequences for individuals, families and organisations (for example, Allen et al. 2000; Frone 2000; Shockley and Singla 2011).

Despite the global nature of the socio-demographic changes that precipitated research on work–family conflict (Aryee 1992), past research in this area has been conducted mainly in Western countries, most notably the United States, United Kingdom and Canada. Given the comparable socio-economic circumstances in these countries (Poelmans et al. 2005), models developed from this body of research might appear as though they are generalisable. However, as argued by Bagger and Love (2010), work–family experiences might vary across countries due to differences in cultural values, national policies, employment opportunities and family structures. Thus, participation in work and family roles might have different meanings and implications to individuals in different societies (Yang 2005). As such, it cannot be assumed that models developed on work–family conflict based on Western data can be readily generalised. A major limitation in the work–family literature has thus been the lack of research from non-Western

F. Annor (✉)
University of Cambridge, Cambridge, UK
e-mail: fa285@cam.ac.uk

Z. Mokomane (ed.), *Work–Family Interface in Sub-Saharan Africa*, International Perspectives on Social Policy, Administration, and Practice,
DOI: 10.1007/978-3-319-01237-7_2,

contexts. The few studies conducted in non-Western societies have focused on Asian countries (for example, Aryee et al. 2005; Lu et al. 2009). Conspicuously absent in the work–family discourse has been research on sub-Saharan Africa. Despite this, and as in most Western countries, the increasing labour force participation of women has been well noted across different countries in sub-Saharan Africa (International Labour Office 2009). In addition, cultural endorsement of marriage and procreation (Oheneba-Sakyi and Takyi 2001), an ageing population, high prevalence of HIV (Mokomane 2012), and the virtual absence of support from government and private organisations pose a great challenge to individuals, particularly women, who have to juggle paid work and caring responsibilities.

The purpose of this chapter is to understand the lived experiences of parents who combine paid work with family commitments in Ghana. The objectives are to (i) examine incidences of work–family conflict; and (ii) identify sources of demands and support resources within the work and family domains, and the role these might play in impeding or facilitating participation in the work and family roles. The research reported in this chapter is part of a larger study examining antecedents and consequences of the work–family interface among individuals in dual-earner relationships in Ghana. The chapter begins with a brief review of previous research on work–family conflict, followed by an overview of the economic and socio-cultural context of the work–family interface in Ghana. This is followed by a description of the research approach, the findings on experiences of work–family conflict, as well demands and support resources in the work and family domains in the country. To conclude, the implications of the findings in the light of previous research on work–family conflict, and the socio-cultural and economic context of Ghana are examined.

Antecedents and Consequences of Work–Family Conflict: A Review of the Literature

The linkage between work and family roles has classically been studied from the perspective of role stress theory. An underlying assumption of this perspective is that individuals have a finite amount of physiological and psychological resources to expend on multiple role obligations (Goode 1960). Consequently, involvement in work and family roles depletes these resources and inevitably results in role conflict (Kahn et al. 1964). Based on the perspective of role stress theory, Greenhaus and Beutell (1985:77) defined work–family conflict as "a form of interrole conflict in which role pressures from the work and family domains are mutually incompatible in some respect". In other words, participation in one domain (for example, work) precludes participation in the other (for example, family). They suggested three forms of work–family conflict: time-based conflict, strain-based conflict and behaviour-based conflict. According to Greenhaus and Beutell, time-based conflict occurs when time pressures associated with involvement in one role make it physically impossible to meet competing demands in another role, or produce preoccupation with one role when an individual is physically attempting to fulfil demands in another role. Strain-based conflict occurs when strain created by involvement in one role makes it difficult to meet demands in another role. Behaviour-based conflict occurs when specific behaviour patterns developed in one role are incompatible with expectations regarding behaviour in another role. Although several researchers (for example, Carlson et al. 2000) have emphasised investigation of the three forms of work–family conflict there is little evidence to support behaviour-based conflict, perhaps due to difficulties in operationalisation (Dierdoff and Ellington 2008).

Earlier research in this area considered work–family conflict as a unidirectional construct, with the direction of conflict emanating from work to family domain (for example, Kopelman et al. 1983). However, consistent with Frone et al. (1997) and as stated in Chap. 1, recent research embraces a bidirectional conceptualization of work–family conflict. Thus, it is recognised that participation in the work domain can interfere with participation in the family domain (i.e. work-to-family conflict); and similarly, participation in the family domain can interfere with participation in the work domain (i.e. family-to-work conflict). There is ample evidence to show that both directions of work–family conflict are conceptually distinct (Byron 2005).

Antecedents of both directions of work–family conflict include within domain variables that make excessive demands on one's limited time and energy. Within the work domain job time demands have frequently been studied as antecedents of work–family conflict. It is assumed that the amount of time expended in a role is directly proportional to the amount of conflict an individual would experience (Gutek et al. 1991). In this regard, several studies have found that long working hours and inflexible work schedules are associated with increased work-to-family conflict (Byron 2005; Michel et al. 2010). The impact on work–family conflict is higher among employees who perceive greater misfit between job time demands and family-related responsibilities (Barnett et al. 1999). In addition to job time demands, other work stressors such as work ambiguity, work overload, lack of autonomy and job insecurity have been shown to be positively related to work-to-family conflict (see Byron 2005; Michel et al. 2010).

Within the family domain parental demands have been the most commonly studied antecedent of work–family conflict. Parental demands are thought to be highest among parents with preschool children and lowest among those with older children (Parasuraman and Simmers 2001) because younger children typically require more attention from caregivers. However, evidence on the relationship between age of children and work–family conflict is not conclusive. Some studies found that having a child below the age of six was positively related to work–family conflict (for example, Byron 2005; Parasuman and Simmers 2001). Other researchers found no relationship between age of children and work–family conflict (for example, Boyar et al. 2008). Yet, Wallace (1999) found that having preschool children was associated with decreased interference from family to work. Wallace suggested that the mere presence of a young child might not be perceived as demanding, if there is enough support at home. Some studies also suggest that the number of children in the family, regardless of their ages, is positively related to family-to-work conflict (for example, Grzywacz and Marks 2000). Additionally, the number of hours expended on housework has been related to increased family-work conflict (for example, Gutek et al. 1991; Parasuraman and Simmers 2001). Other demanding aspects of the family role such as family role conflict, family ambiguity, and high level of spousal disagreement have been found to impact employees' ability to accommodate family responsibilities with work demands (e.g., Grzywacz and Marks 2000; Michel et al. 2010).

In addition to domain-specific demands, studies have also examined resources within the work and family roles that might reduce work–family conflict. A key resource most frequently studied in the literature is social support. Social support is an interpersonal transaction that involves emotional concern, instrumental assistance, information, or appraisal (House 1981). Within the work and family literature, social support is typically studied as either a moderator, buffering the effects of work and/or family demands on work–family conflict; or as an antecedent, having a direct influence on work–family conflict (Carlson and Perewe 1999). Supervisors and colleagues represent informal sources of social support within the work domain. Thomas and Ganster (1995) demonstrated that having a supportive supervisor was related to increased sense of control over work and ultimately decreased work–family conflict. Recent studies have also found that emotional and instrumental support from supervisors and colleagues was negatively related to work–family conflict (Dolcos and Daley 2009; Kossek et al. 2011). Formal sources of social support within the workplace include family-supportive policies such as flexitime, telecommuting, job sharing, childcare, referral services, and eldercare services provided by organisations with the aim of helping employees manage family responsibilities. Formal workplace support has been found to decrease stress involved in combining work and family demands, thereby reducing work–family conflict (Frye and Breaugh 2004). Within the family domain, spouses have been the most frequently studied sources of social support. Matsui et al. (1995) found that husband support buffered the impact of parental demands on work–family conflict among working women in Japan. Several recent studies have also found that emotional and instrumental support from one's spouse was associated with lower levels of family-to-work conflict (for example, Aycan and Eskin 2005; Lapierre and Allen 2006). However, only a few studies (for example, Lapierre and Allen 2006) have examined social support from kin or extended family relations, with mixed findings.

Aside from antecedents, research has extensively examined myriad consequences of work–family conflict. These can be categorised under individual outcomes, work-related outcomes and family-related outcomes (Allen et al. 2000). Among individual outcomes, research has found that increased work–family conflict was associated with poor physical health (for example, van Steenbergen and Ellemers 2009) and greater odds of depression, anxiety and substance use (for example, Frone et al. 1993; Wallace 2005). Negative work consequences of work–family conflict include lower job satisfaction, organisational commitment and job performance; and increased withdrawal behaviours such as absenteeism and turnover (Allen et al. 2000; Shockley and Singla 2011). Within the family-related outcomes category, work–family conflict has been associated with lower marital satisfaction, marital adjustment, family satisfaction and family performance (Allen et al. 2000; see also Eby et al. 2005).

In summary, this section provided a brief overview of previous research on work–family conflict, noting that conflict may originate from either the work role or the family role. The review suggests that within-domain demands are associated with increased levels of work–family conflict, whilst social support helps decrease work–family conflict. It was also noted that work–family conflict has serious influences on individuals' wellbeing.

The Ghanaian Context

The Work Context

Ghana's economy has for the past 2 decades seen steady and significant growth, with Gross Domestic Product (GDP) and per capita GDP growth rates averaging 4.9 and 2.9 %, respectively (Aryeetey and Kanbur 2008). A key factor in this economic transformation has been the implementation of a series of economic reforms commencing in 1983 under the International Monetary Fund and World Bank's Structural Adjustment Program. These reforms included the abolition of price controls, the opening of capital markets, reductions in import tariffs and privatisation of many state-owned enterprises (Aryeetey and Kanbur 2008).

In spite of the substantial improvements in economic performance, there has been a lack of corresponding improvements in social conditions and labour market outcomes in Ghana (Aryeetey and Kanbur 2008). Much of these stems from lack of structural transformation in the economy. Ghana's economy still depends largely on agriculture, which accounts for about 36 % of GDP and 51 % of employment (Aryeetey and Baah-Boateng 2007). The significance of formal sector employment declined following the implementation of the neo-liberal economic policies that underpinned the structural adjustment program (Aryeetey and Baah-Boateng 2007), which saw large-scale retrenchment of public sector workers in the 1990s.[1] Consequently, much of the non-agricultural labour force participates in the informal sector of the economy. In addition to declining employment opportunities in the formal sector, there have been low levels of wages in both absolute and relative terms (Otoo et al. 2009). The daily minimum wage in Ghana for the past decade has averaged under US$2.00, with majority of workers earning below the minimum wage, particularly in the informal sector. Real earnings continue to

[1] It is estimated that about 15% of public sector workers were retrenched during the Structural Adjustment Program (Otoo et al. 2009).

decline with increasing level of inflation and depreciation of the Ghana cedi against major international currencies such as the US dollar and pound sterling (Otoo et al. 2009). Consequently, a significant proportion of working class people find themselves trapped in poverty (Aryeetey and Kanbur 2008). Applied to the work–family interface, Aryee (2005:272) argued that: "inadequate pay is not only a potential source of stress in urban sub-Saharan Africa but also motivates an increased investment of time and energic resources into income generating activities".

In addition to these labour market conditions, there is a lack of conscious efforts on the part of government and organisations in Ghana to enact or implement family-friendly policies to support employed parents. Whilst some regulations exist regarding working time limits and leave entitlements, such regulations have not been very helpful in enabling employees manage work and family responsibilities. Although the Ghana Labour Act, Act 651 of 2003 stipulates a maximum of 40 h of work a week (8 h a day)[2] for workers the enforcement of this working time limit is very weak. Close to 48 % of workers have average work hours of 40–70 per week.[3] (Ghana Statistical Service 2008). In addition, further provisions regarding annual leave and periods of absence from work due to sickness are subject to the discretions of employers. For example, Act 651 of 2003 permits employers, "in case of urgent necessity, ... [to] require a worker to interrupt his or her leave and return to work" (Section 25). Furthermore, women are entitled to 12 weeks of paid maternity leave, which may be extended by two additional weeks. However, the absence of paternity leave in particular makes it difficult for employed fathers to contribute to childcare, and thereby perpetuates existing gender inequalities in division of household labour. Family friendly policies such as flexible working arrangements and employer-provided childcare are largely non-existent. Privately run childcare centres, for example, remain the preserve of a small proportion of middle-class parents because these institutions are relatively expensive. In the absence of family-supportive programs from government and employers, workers in Ghana increasingly rely on supervisors and co-workers as sources of support for balancing work and family responsibilities.

The Family Context

In Ghana, the term 'family' invokes the notion of "male-headed units of extended families consisting of one or several wives and their children and often extended with unmarried or elderly relatives" (Brown 1996:21). Within the traditional

---

[2] This excludes overtime hours. The Act further establishes that any extra hours beyond the 40-hour statutory limit be considered as overtime, which may be paid or unpaid. The Act is, however, silent on the maximum number of overtime hours an employer can request from a worker.

[3] About 45 % of workers in this category work average of more than 49 h a week.

family structure men were regarded primarily as breadwinners whilst women took care of household responsibilities. Women's participation in income generating activities was mostly restricted to the informal sector, which offered the needed flexibility and geographical proximity to enable them meet their obligations in the household (Ardayfio-Schandorf 2001). However, this traditional family arrangement has undergone considerable changes in the past few decades. One of the most dramatic of these changes has been the increased involvement of women in wage employment, following better educational opportunities and economic transformations in Ghana. Although relatively low, the proportion of women involved in wage employment doubled between 1960 and 2008 (Ghana Statistical Service 2005, 2008). Complementing the changing nature of female work and family roles are the changes occurring in the work and family roles of men. Though women continue to bear much of household responsibilities, various rounds of the Ghana Living Standards Survey (GLSS) point to a slow but gradual increase in male involvement in household chores and childcare, particularly in urban settings (Ghana Statistical Service 1995, 2000, 2008). In addition, although fertility rate in Ghana has declined over the past 2 decades consequent upon urbanisation and economic hardship, average family size remains relatively high.[4] Thus, given the cultural premium on large family size in Ghanaian society, the gradual changes in gender roles pose a challenge to employed parents in meeting parental demands.

In addition to heavy parental demands posed by large family sizes, eldercare presents another challenge to individuals combining work and family responsibilities in Ghana. Couched in the adage "the one who cares for you when you are cutting teeth must be cared for by you till all that person's teeth fall out in old age" (Mensa-Bonsu and Dowuona-Hammond 1996:16), caring for aged parents is regarded a moral obligation to adult children. This obligation is particularly important given that government-sponsored social security benefits for old age in Ghana are limited and mainly cover the small number of people who worked for governmental organisations or in the formal sector of the economy (Oheneba-Sakyi and Takyi 2001). Traditionally, the responsibility to provide support to the elderly and less privileged relatives was that of the entire extended family. However, due to economic difficulties and migration, and the consequent weakening of extended family ties, the burden of providing care for the elderly has shifted from the extended family towards the nuclear family (Oheneba-Sakyi and Takyi 2001), usually one's own children and spouse. Thus, providing care for the elderly can be additional burden to adult children, especially where such children are involved in paid work and have their own families to care for. In addition to elder care, participation in extended family activities such as funerals and weddings, which are considered very important social events, contribute to time demands on workers.

[4] Total fertility rate (TFR) declined from 6.4 children per woman in 1988 to 4.4 in 1998 and then stabilized until 2003. As of 2008 the TFR in Ghana stood at 4.0 (GSS, GHS, and ICF Macro 2009).

Although extended family relations may constitute a source of demand, they also serve as an important source of social support for working parents. In the absence of family-supportive services from government and organisations, extended family relatives play a critical role in caring for young children. As a practice in most sub-Saharan African societies, grandmothers are often involved in providing childcare beyond the period of statutory maternity leave (Aryee 2005). Domestic helpers (commonly described as house helpers) also serve as an alternative source of instrumental support for employed parents when support from relatives is not feasible. Domestic helpers are often hired to assist in performing household tasks such as cleaning, washing, cooking and running errands, and sometimes to provide childcare. However, reliance on paid domestic helpers might increase financial burdens on workers. Hence, only a small proportion of (middle class) workers are able to afford the services of paid domestic helpers.

Methods

As mentioned earlier, this chapter is informed by data derived from a larger study on antecedents and outcomes of the work–family interface in Ghana. Given the scarcity of research on work–family conflict in Ghana, a qualitative approach was considered appropriate for an in-depth exploration of the "lived reality" of individuals combining paid work with family commitments in this context. As Poelmans (2001) noted, one advantage of qualitative studies is that they provide rich data to illustrate the complex interdependencies between variables. Data were collected through face-to-face semi-structured interviews. The use of semi-structured interviews was informed by its flexibility in allowing respondents to initiate issues that had previously not been anticipated (Kvale and Brinkmann 2009).

Participants comprised 18 university staff consisting of both lecturers and non-teaching staff, employed full-time at the University of Ghana—a public university. The sample was recruited through a combination of purposive, convenience and snowball sampling strategies. The sample included 10 women and eight men. Efforts were made to include different categories of employees within the university. Almost two-thirds of the participants were in administrative and clerical jobs; the remaining were academics, comprising a professor, two senior lecturers, three lecturers, and an assistant lecturer. The participants had worked in the university for periods ranging from 1 to 35 years. Finally, all the participants were married and were, with exception of one, in dual-earner relationships, and had at least one child living at home.

Prior to the interviews an interview guide was developed to ensure that participants were guided towards discussing the same topic areas. The interview guide was semi-structured, containing a series of open-ended questions with additional probes to ensure flexibility and to help the flow of interactions and encourage respondents to explore some topics in greater depth. The interview guide was based on a review of the relevant work and family literature, and my knowledge and experience of the work and family contexts in Ghana. The questions were developed to explore participants' experiences of conflict between work and family roles, with a series of probes to seek clarifications or more information on particular issues raised by participants. For example, participants were asked: "could you describe any situation when you felt your work and family roles interfered with each other?" Questions relating to sources of demands and support were also included in the interview guide. Participants were contacted individually at their places of work to schedule the interview, assuring them of confidentiality and anonymity of participation and data. The interviews were audio-recorded with the consent of the participants.

The recorded interviews were transcribed verbatim, with all references to interviewees removed to ensure anonymity. Data were analysed using thematic analysis. "Thematic analysis is a method for identifying, analysing, and reporting patterns (themes) within data" (Braun and Clarke 2006:6). It minimally organises data set in rich detail, and interprets various aspect of the research topic (Braun and Clarke 2006:6). To begin with, I familiarised myself with the data by actively reading and re-reading interview transcripts. The data were subsequently coded with the aid of qualitative analysis software—*Atlas.ti*. This involved assigning codes to meaningful chucks within the data set, which could be a phrase or series of sentences. Coded extracts of the data were collated to identify key patterns within and across codes, and to identify potential sub-themes. Themes that emerged from the data include work–family conflict, work stressors, family demands, work support and non-work support. Detailed explanations of these themes are provided in the next section under various sub-headings.

Findings

Work–Family Conflict

One of the aims of this chapter is to identify forms of interference experienced by employed parents juggling demands in the work and family domains. In line with the scarcity argument that participation in multiple roles leads to strain and role conflict (Goode 1960), majority of participants discussed pervasive conflicts or strains experienced as they fulfilled responsibilities in the work and family roles. Supporting the bidirectional conceptualization of work–family conflict, it was evident that demands associated with the work role interfered with the family domain; and similarly, demands associated with the family role spilled over to the work domain. From the work-to-family direction, a number of participants expressed dissatisfaction with the amount of attention they could give to their family due to high time demands of the job. For example, as one man noted, ... *the unfortunate bit is you don't have much time for your family because you're most of the time at work.* In several instances, tight work schedules coupled with long commuting time between home and work meant that employees had to arrive home late, leaving little time to perform household responsibilities. The following quote from a father of two children illustrate participants' experiences of work–family conflict resulting from time demands from the work domain:

> I was always with the kids, taking them to school, walk with them from school, and go out with them. But this time, the times I leave for work and get home, these things are no longer there.

In addition, participants discussed how pressures from heavy workloads impacted negatively on their family obligations. Several respondents mentioned that the pressure to be productive at work made them exhausted thereby limiting their ability to perform effectively in the family domain. For example, one woman stated: *when I get home I am already exhausted. Sometimes I do not even bath; I feel too tired.* For academics in particular, the pressure to get published put enormous strain on family relationships. For example, a male lecturer talked extensively about how his home had literally become an extension of his workplace:

> So I work at the office and I work at home. I don't have home life. When I'm at home and the children want to play I shut the door. I always shut the door. I can tolerate them for 5 to 10 min then I shut the door and let someone take care of them. I guess it's a phase. When I get more accomplished I will get the better balance, but at the moment my life is skewed towards work.

Furthermore, three of the academics interviewed indicated that in addition to teaching and examination, they were also required to take up administrative duties. One lecturer discussed how stress associated with serving on boards and committees interfered with his ability to meet family responsibilities. He noted that:

> For me the committee work [and] the faculty board ... are huge interruptions. Fatigue-wise, you'll be tired; you come and you can't do anything. You need to go and sleep. That is all, you simply need to go and sleep.

From the family-to-work direction, a number of participants mentioned time spent on family responsibilities as major constraints on their work. Interference resulting from family-related time demands was more pervasive among women, who were more involved in the family domain. For parents with young children (under age 10) in particular, taking children to and from school, and taking time off work to attend to sick children were major interruptions on performance at work. For example, one man shared his experience as follows:

> What I do at home is that from Monday to Friday I pick the children to school and go and pick them back. So it means that even if I'm in the middle of something I have to stop so I can pick them from school. And this is big interruption. It takes me not less than one hour to go and pick them and return to the office.

Another woman also said:

> The kids are always falling ill. And when you take them to the hospital you have to sit in the queue and wait your turn... You end up spending the whole day at the hospital and may not be able to return to work.

Additionally, family responsibilities placed considerable strain on parents, which spilled over to the work domain. A few participants mentioned that excessive household demands meant they had little amount of sleep at night, often resulting in feelings of fatigue and dizziness at work and reduced productivity. For example, one woman shared her experience as follows:

> Sometimes I feel dizzy, especially on Monday mornings. Sunday I have to go to church; after church I have to iron and prepare food for Monday morning. So I go to bed around 10.pm to 11 pm. Meanwhile, I have to wake up very early in the morning, 4 am. So when I come to work I have to sit down for a while before I start working.

In a minority of cases, participants shared their experiences in which their thoughts about unfulfilled family-related responsibilities hindered their engagement in the work role. One man described how his inability to meet his wife's request for assistance with domestic chores sometimes resulted in misunderstanding. Feelings of guilt resulting from this experience were transferred to the work domain:

> You quarrel with your wife before leaving the house to the office. ... It worries a lot; you feel down. It makes you think the more because it's your responsibility and you couldn't do that and it starts disturbing your mind.

Work Stressors

Participants mentioned different forms of stressors they encountered in the work domain. These stressors were grouped under job time demands, workload and insufficient pay. Job time demands include working hours, overtime, and weekend work. In terms of working hours both men and women worked average of 42 h per week. Generally, formal weekend work and overtime work were less frequent although a few participants were apparently willing to work paid overtime for additional income. Some participants worked occasional unpaid overtime as a strategy to avoid taking work home or piling up work for the next the day. A few participants, on the other hand, described overtime work as a routine in their jobs. These participants often worked over 10 h a day and usually without taking annual leave.[5] One participant lamented feeling "crippled" by the amount of time his job had taken, making it almost impossible to attend important social functions such as funerals: *at times you have to tell lies before you can sneak.*

---

[5] Two participants said they deliberately refused to take annual leave because they could not afford to forgo the addition income they would get from paid overtime work.

Heavy workload emerged as a significant stressor within the work role. Majority of participants described their workloads as emotionally and physically exacting. The most common examples participants gave about heavy workloads were related to lack of institutional capacity in terms adequate number of personnel to match the enormous student population of the university. One participant described her work as "very tedious", noting that she was sometimes forced to return from leave because there was no one to take over her work. She said: *my work is tedious; one person manning 30,000 students at a particular time is very tedious*. For academics in particular, heavy workloads were a combination of class sizes and the number of scripts they needed to assess after examinations. One lecturer showed me a backlog of scripts from a previous semester he needed to assess *because you cannot use 3 weeks [or] 4 weeks to finish marking about 900 papers*. To meet these heavy workloads, workers often had to double up their efforts, and as one participant noted, *in the end you have to split yourself into four individuals; you teach like two people and you work for your research like two people*.

In addition to long working hours and heavy workloads, some participants talked about insufficient pay as an issue of great concern in their job. A number of participants, especially those in lower level positions, lamented the fact that their salary could not adequately provide their family needs. One participant commented that *my take-home pay can't take me home*, to suggest he could barely survive on his monthly salary. To make ends meet, some workers were involved in petty trading and other forms of income generating activities outside their regular work schedules. One of these workers said: *the pay is not good. It is the extra job that helps*. Two participants who were not involved in any extra income-generating activity expressed interest in moonlighting as traders to support their income.

Family Demands

Participants were engaged in various forms of household chores such as cooking, cleaning, shopping for groceries, fetching water, and washing. Consistent with previous research, child caring also emerged as another form of demand in the household particularly for parents with young children. In line with traditional gender roles espoused by the Ghanaian culture, women showed greater involvement in household chores and childcare relative to men. All the women interviewed mentioned household chores as their sole responsibilities. One woman remarked: *I don't have a house help; I'm alone. … And the children are young. So I have to do most of the things on my own*. On the other hand, less than half of the men indicated sharing household work with their spouses. Men's contribution to household work was mostly limited to transporting children to and from school. In instances where men were actively involved in household work, they did so in the absence of their spouses. Even so, that was considered an "extra job" as reflected in the following comment:

> I have to wake up very early because I need to take care of the child, make sure she takes her bath and take her to school with me because my wife is also in school. She is studying so I have to do that extra job as well.

In addition to household demands, a number of participants described their responsibility for extended family members. Mostly, extended family responsibilities were in the form of financial contributions toward caring for less privileged or elderly relatives. More than half of the participants mentioned that they were responsible for the care of their parents. In a minority of cases, participants also mentioned the need to provide financial support to their siblings. For example:

> Being the eldest son in my family—I've lost my mother and my father—I extend my hand to my younger brothers as well. So I have to double whatever I'm doing to make sure I am not found wanting when they're in need.

Another woman also described being a "mother figure" to her three siblings following the demise of their mother:

> I have both financial [and] kind of big sister role because now I'm like the mother figure in the family for them because mum is gone. So I give them pocket money.

Work Support

Participants mentioned various forms of support resources within the work domain that helped in dealing with tensions in balancing work and family responsibilities. Informal support was the most dominant source of support in the work role. A number of participants, particularly non-teaching staff received instrumental and emotional support from their supervisors. One woman described her immediate boss as "more of a senior brother". She further noted: *we discuss our family problems together, we discuss the work*. One participant, on the other hand, described his supervisors as unsupportive particularly in sharing information that may be useful to his career. He noted: *here our bosses hide information from us. There is some information, when you go and ask they would not even like to give you*. In addition to supervisors, co-workers emerged as another important source of social support for a number of participants. Four participants cited instances in which advice they received from colleagues at work proved useful in dealing with important issues at home. However, a few participants were not comfortable about discussing personal problems with co-workers perhaps due to mistrust.

With respect to formal support at work, most participants were unfamiliar with any policies aimed at helping employees manage work and family demands beyond annual leave and statutory maternity leave. For example, when asked about policies in the university that facilitate combining work and family responsibilities, one woman noted:

> I don't think there is a facilitating policy here that says that because you're a mother, you're a woman let's give you this space". ... There isn't any conscious effort by the university to give working mothers space and time; you have to create it yourself.

Maternity leave, though relatively generous in terms of duration,[6] was limited to nursing mothers. Some participants, particularly academics, considered annual leaves as "mere window dressing" because they needed to work through the period of leave to avoid piling up work. Although the university had a nursery this was meant for children of school–going age (age four and above). Some participants with pre-school children mentioned that privately owned crèches were the only alternative though such facilities are mostly exorbitant. Indeed, some participants acknowledged that the university had provisions for payment of family medical bills, which might help alleviate the burden of health care cost on families.

Non-Work Support

Participants also described different forms of support they received from sources outside the work role. Immediate family members, usually spouses and older children, provided the greatest amount of support. Most of the participants discussed emotional and instrumental support they received from their spouse. One participant shared that the emotional support he received from his wife encouraged him about his work despite having tight schedule:

> When you tell her about what is happening at work she gives you the moral support and encourages you, and sometimes go to the extent of giving you some biblical quotations. Then you're compelled to realize there is somebody behind you who appreciates what you're doing, even if you're not appreciated at work.

A few participants mentioned that their older children provided instrumental support in the form of running errands, helping with household chores such as cooking, cleaning and washing. One participant described her children as her main source of emotional support, noting *we sit to converse; we talk about problems, issues, and crack jokes. That keeps me, but when they are away it makes me lonely.*

In addition, a number of participants also mentioned friends and extended family relatives as important sources of instrumental support especially in regards to childcare. Some of the participant reported receiving childcare assistance from elderly parents. This form of instrumental support relieved employed parents of stress involved in taking care of young children. One parent shared her experiences of the extensive childcare assistance she received from her mother and mother-in-law:

[6] In addition to the statutory 12 weeks of maternity leave, the university permits nursing mothers to work half day till the child turns 1 year.

> When I had my first child my mother came to live with us for five years and then she left… And then when I had the second child my mother was with me for 1 year and then my mother-in-law was also with me for five years. So I would say that I have not had problems with who to take care of my children.

Finally, some parents also relied on house helpers including paid domestic assistants and unpaid relatives for support in performing various household tasks and childcare. In most cases, house helpers performed most of the household chores, which helped alleviate the stress of working parents. However, some participants considered the presence of paid house helpers as invasion on their privacy and as such were reluctant to hire their services.

Conclusion

This chapter sought to examine employees' experiences of work–family conflict as they navigate the multiple roles of work and family. The chapter also sought to identify factors that may impede or facilitate participation in work and family roles. This section discusses the implications of the findings reported in the previous sections with reference to past research and the socio-cultural and economic context of Ghana.

Findings from interviews with parents employed full-time at a public university in Ghana showed similarities in experiences in the work–family interface relative to previous research. The findings suggest that, for majority of these parents, boundaries between the work and family domains were permeable. Thus, negative experiences and strains experienced in one role impacted negatively on performance in the other role. Consistent with the role scarcity argument (Goode 1960; Kahn et al. 1964), it was evident that for many employed parents in Ghana participation in multiple roles of work and family was a source of strain and conflict. Participants' descriptions of work–family conflict were reminiscent of Greenhaus and Beutell's (1985) notion of time-based and strain-based conflict. Participants reported time-based conflict in the form of role-related time demands such as long working hours, weekend work, overtime work and time spent on household work that limited their ability to meet obligations in another domain. Strain-based conflict occurred in the form of stress produced in one role having a negative spillover effect on performance in another role. However, no incidence of behaviour-based conflict was reported. This could be due to the fact that participants were not specifically probed for instances of behaviour-based conflict. Another possible explanation could be the nature of occupations in which the participants were engaged. A recent study by Dierdorff and Ellington (2008) suggests a high degree of diversity in behaviour-based sources of work–family conflict across occupations. Behaviour-based conflict tends to be higher in occupations characterised by high levels of interdependence and responsibility for others (Dierdorff and Ellington 2008).

Findings from the interviews also supported the bidirectional conceptualization of work–family conflict (Frone et al. 1997). In most cases, participants were able to distinguish whether interference was due to experiences in the work domain or the family domain. These findings suggest that the conceptualization of work–family conflict in Western based studies is largely applicable to the Ghanaian context.

As noted previously, several studies have examined within-domain demands as antecedents of work–family conflict. Within-domain demands are characteristics of one domain that are associated with processes that limit the ability of individuals to meet obligations in another domain (Voydanoff 2005). Evidence presented in the previous section suggests that the nature of within-domain demands is shaped by contextual factors. In the Ghanaian context stressors in the work domain were not limited to the physical or emotional aspect of the job (such as time demands and quantitative workload), which have been shown to have direct impact on combining work and family commitments, but also included the amount of financial rewards the job could provide. Several participants lamented low levels of pay, and were forced to increase the amount of time they devoted to extra income generating activities, which negatively impacted the amount of time they devoted to family activities. This finding supports Aryee's (2005) proposition that inadequate pay represents a major source of stress for employees in sub-Saharan Africa. Furthermore, it was found that family demands also goes beyond presence of children at home and time devoted to the family. In traditional Ghanaian society, as noted previously, 'family' connotes both nuclear family and extended family. As such, caring for relatives in the extended family, particularly elderly parents and siblings, was considered a legitimate concern among a number of participants. This finding points to a major limitation in conceptualization of 'family demands' in the work and family literature.

It was also evident that despite the absence of formal family-supportive practices, employed parents in Ghana were not completely bereft of support for managing work and family responsibilities. The family served as an important source of support for majority of working parents. It was found that instrumental and emotional support received from spouses helped eased the burden of meeting family demands. However, support in the family domain was not limited to spouses. Older children were also found to be a vital source of emotional and instrumental sustenance to working parents. This is in sharp contrast to the existing literature, which portrays children entirely as a source of stress to parents. Moreover, extended family relatives and house helpers were other important sources of support for some participants. It is therefore important that researchers incorporate these diverse sources in measures of family support, especially in the Ghanaian context. Within the work domain employees often relied on social support from colleagues and supervisors in balancing work and family responsibilities.

It is worth noting that the findings reported in this chapter are not without limitations. The purposive nature of the sample prohibits generalisation of the findings. In addition, the university employees used in the study may not be typical of the average worker in Ghana. Moreover, although in-depth interviews are useful in obtaining a rich descriptive data, this method is not amenable to testing causal relationships. Consequently, studies using quantitative approaches would help to understand how the role demands and support resources identified relate to work–family conflict. To do this, there would be the need to develop comprehensive measures that incorporate the various aspects of work/family demands and support identified in this chapter. Such studies would also benefit from examining work–family interactions beyond the individual level.

Notwithstanding the above limitations, the findings have illuminated important aspects of the work–family interface in the Ghanaian context. The findings reported in this chapter have practical implications for the design of human resource practices in Ghana. An important consideration is that work–family conflict is not unique to only women; men are equally affected. Thus, introduction of paid parental and paternal leaves would enable employed fathers in particular to contribute effectively to family obligations. This could help minimise gender inequality in the allocation of household labour, and reduce the burden of household work on women. Considering the increasing strain on kin solidarity (Ardayfio-Schandorf 2001) in Ghana, it remains to be known how long employed parents can continue to depend on extended family relatives for support in managing work and family demands. As such, it behoves organisations to consider assisting employees with such policies as flexible working arrangements and childcare services for increased productivity of their employees.

In conclusion, this chapter has provided an empirical examination of the phenomenon of work–family conflict in a non-Western context: Ghana. Furthermore, it has identified different forms of role demands and support resources that can exacerbate or reduce work–family conflict. More importantly, it has also demonstrated that while the experience of work–family conflict might be considered universal, some underlying factors may be context-specific. To this end, this chapter has responded to Aryee's (2005) call for examination of the subjective experience of work–family conflict in a sub-Saharan African context using a qualitative research approach.

References

Allen, T., Herst, D., Bruck, C. S., & Sutton, M. (2000). Consequences associated with work-to-family conflict: A review and agenda for future research. *Journal of Occupational Health Psychology, 5*(2), 278–308.

Ardayfio-Schandorf, E. (2001). The family in Ghana: Past and present perspectives. In Y. Oheneba-Sakyi & B. K. Takyi (Eds.), *African families at the turn of the 21st century* (pp. 129–152). Westport, CT: Praeger.

Aryee, S. (1992). Antecedents and outcomes of work–family conflict among married professional women: Evidence from Singapore. *Human Relations, 45*(8), 813–837.

Aryee, S. (2005). The work–family interface in urban sub-Saharan Africa: A theoretical analysis. In S. A. Y. Poelman (Ed.), *Work and family: An international research perspective* (pp. 261–286). Mahwah, NJ: Lawrence Erlbaum Associates Inc.

Aryee, S., Srinivas, E. S., & Tan, H. H. (2005). Rhythms of life: Antecedents and outcomes of work–family balance in employed parents. *Journal of Applied Psychology, 90*(1), 132–146.

Aryeetey, E., & Baah-Boateng, W. (2007). *Growth, investment and employment in Ghana. Working Paper No. 80.* Geneva: Policy Integration Department, International labour Organisation.

Aryeetey, E., & Kanbur, R. (2008). Ghana's economy at half-century: An overview of stability, growth and poverty. In E. Aryeetey & R. Kanbur (Eds.), *The economy of Ghana: Analytical perspectives on stability, growth and poverty* (pp. 1–19). Accra: Woeli Publishing Services/ James Currey.

Aycan, Z., & Eskin, M. (2005). Relative contributions of childcare, spousal support, and organizational support in reducing work–family conflict for men and women : The case of Turkey. *Sex Roles, 53*(7/8), 453–471.

Baggar, J., & Love, J. (2010). *Methodological considerations in conducting cross-national work–family survey research.* Retrieved February 2, 2011 from http://wfnetwork.bc.edu/ encyclopedia_entry.php?id=17169&area=Al.

Barnett, R. C., Gareis, K. C., & Brennan, R. T. (1999). Fit as a mediator of the relationship between work hours and burnout. *Journal of Occupational Health Psychology, 4*(4), 307–317.

Boyar, S. L., Maertz, C. P, Jr, Mosley, D. C, Jr, & Carr, J. C. (2008). The impact of work/family demand on work–family conflict. *Journal of Managerial Psychology, 23*(3), 215–235.

Braun, V., & Clarke, V. (2006). Using thematic analysis in psychology. *Qualitative Research in Psychology, 3*, 77–101.

Brown, C. K. (1996). Gender roles and household allocation of resources and decision-making in Ghana. In E. Ardayfio-Schandorf (Ed.), *The changing family in Ghana* (pp. 21–41). Accra: Ghana Universities Press.

Byron, K. (2005). A meta-analytic review of work–family conflict and its antecedents. *Journal of Vocational Behaviour, 67*(2), 169–198.

Carlson, D. S., & Perrewé, P. L. (1999). The role of social support in the stressor-strain relationship: An examination of work–family conflict. *Journal of Management, 25*(4), 513.

Carlson, D. S., Kacmar, K. M., & Williams, L. J. (2000). Construction and initial validation of a multidimensional measure of work–family conflict. *Journal of Vocational Behaviour, 56*(2), 249–276.

Dierdorff, E. C., & Ellington, J. K. (2008). It's the nature of the work: Examining behaviour-based sources of work–family conflict across occupations. *Journal of Applied Psychology, 93*(4), 883–892.

Dolcos, S. M., & Daley, D. (2009). Work pressure, workplace social resources, and work–family conflict: The tale of two sectors. *International Journal of Stress Management, 16*(4), 291–311.

Eby, L. T., Casper, W. J., Lockwood, A., Bordeaux, C., & Brinley, A. (2005). Work and family research in IO/OB: Content analysis and review of the literature (1980–2002). *Journal of Vocational Behaviour, 66*, 124–197.

Frone, M. R. (2000). work–family conflict and employee psychiatric disorders: The national comorbidity survey. *Journal of Applied Psychology, 85*(6), 888–896.

Frone, M. R., Russell, M., & Cooper, M. (1993). Relationship of work–family conflict, gender, and alcohol expectancies to alcohol use/abuse. *Journal of Organizational Behaviour, 14*(6), 545–558.

Frone, M. R., Yardley, J. K., & Markel, K. S. (1997). Developing and testing an integrative model of the work–family interface. *Journal of Vocational Behaviour, 50*(2), 145–167.

Frye, N., & Breaugh, J. (2004). Family-friendly policies, supervisor support, work–family conflict, family-work conflict, and satisfaction: A test of a conceptual model. *Journal of Business and Psychology, 19*(2), 197–221.

Ghana Statistical Service. (1995). *Ghana living standards survey: Report on the 3rd round (GLSS 3).* Accra: Ghana Statistical Service.

Ghana Statistical Service. (2000). *Ghana living standards survey: Report on the 4th round (GLSS 4).* Accra: Ghana Statistical Service.

Ghana Statistical Service (2005). *Population data analyses report* (Vol. 1)*: Socio-economic and demographic trends.* Accra: Ghana Statistical Service.
Ghana Statistical Service (2008). Ghana living standards survey: Report on the 5th round (GLSS 5). Retrieved December 12, 2012 from www.statsghana.gov.gh/docfiles/glss5_report.pdff. Accessed .
Goode, W. J. (1960). A theory of role strain. *American Sociological Review, 25*(4), 483–496.
Greenhaus, J. H., & Beutell, N. J. (1985). Sources of conflict between work and family roles. *Academy of Management Review, 10*(1), 76–88.
Grzywacz, J. G., & Marks, N. F. (2000). Reconceptualising the work–family interface: An ecological perspective on the correlates of positive and negative spillover between work and family. *Journal of Occupational Health Psychology, 5*(1), 111–126.
Gutek, B. A., Searle, S., & Klepa, L. (1991). Rational versus gender role explanations of work–family conflict. *Journal of Applied Psychology, 76*(4), 560–568.
House, G. S. (1981). *Work stress and social support.* Reading, MA: Addison-Wesley.
GSS, GHS, & ICF Macro (2009). *Ghana Demographic and Health Survey 2008.* Accra, Ghana: GSS, GHS, and ICF Macro.
International Labour Office. (2009). *Global employment trends for women: March 2009.* Geneva: International Labour Organisation.
Kahn, R. L., Wolfe, D. M., Quinn, R. P., Snoek, J. D., & Rosenthal, R. A. (1964). *Organizational stress: Studies in role conflict and ambiguity.* New York: John Wiley & Sons, Inc.
Kopelman, R., Greenhaus, J., & Connolly, T. (1983). A model of work, family, and interrole conflict: A construct validation study. *Organizational Behaviour and Human Performance, 215*, 198–215.
Kossek, E. E., Pichler, S., Bodner, T., & Hammer, L. B. L. B. (2011). Workplace social support and work–family conflict: A meta-analysis clarifying the influence of general and work–family-specific supervisor and organizational support. *Personnel Psychology, 64*(2), 289–313.
Kvale, S., & Brinkmann, S. (2009). *Interviews: Learning the craft of qualitative research interviewing.* CA: Sage Thousand Oaks.
Lapierre, L. M., & Allen, T. D. (2006). Work-supportive family, family-supportive supervision, use of organizational benefits, and problem-focused coping: Implications for work–family conflict and employee well-being. *Journal of Occupational Health Psychology, 11*(2), 169–181.
Lu, J., Siu, O., Spector, P. E., & Shi, K. (2009). Antecedents and outcomes of a fourfold taxonomy of work–family balance in Chinese employed parents. *Journal of Occupational Health Psychology, 14*(2), 182–192.
Matsui, T., Ohsawa, T., & Onglatco, M. L. (1995). work–family conflict and the stress-buffering effects of husband support and coping behaviour among Japanese married working women. *Journal of Vocational Behaviour, 47*, 178–192.
Mensa-Bonsu, H. J. A. N., & Dowuona-Hammond, C. (1996). The child within the Ghanaian family. In E. Ardayfio-Schandorf (Ed.), *The changing family in Ghana* (pp. 5–20). Accra: Ghana Universities Press.
Michel, J. S., Kotrba, L. M., Mitchelson, J. K., Clark, M. A., & Baltes, B. B. (2010). Antecedents of work–family conflict: A meta-analytic review. *Journal of Organizational Behaviour.* doi: 10.1002/job.695.
Mokomane, Z. (2012). Social protection as a mechanism for family protection in sub-Saharan Africa. *International Journal of Social Welfare,* 1–12.
Oheneba-Sakyi, Y., & Takyi, B. K. (2001). Introduction to the study of African families: A framework for analysis. In Y. Oheneba-Sakyi & B. K. Takyi (Eds.), *African families at the turn of the 21st century* (pp. 1–23). Westport, CT: Praeger.
Otoo, K. N., Osei-Boateng, C., & Asafu-Adjaye, P. (2009). *The labour market in Ghana: A descriptive analysis of the labour market component of Ghana living standard survey (V).* Labour Research Institute, Research Paper (No. 2009/01)
Parasuraman, S., & Simmers, C. A. (2001). Type of employment, work–family conflict and well-being: A comparative study. *Journal of Organizational Behaviour, 22*(5), 551–568.

Poelmans, S. (2001). *A qualitative study of work-family conflict in managerial couples*. IESE Research paper, 445.

Poelmans, S. A. Y., O'Driscoll, M., & Beham, B. (2005). An overview of international research on the work–family interface. In S. A. Y. Poelmans (Ed.), *Work and family: An international research perspective* (pp. 3–46). Mahwah, NJ: Lawrence Erlbaum Associates Inc.

Shockley, K. M., & Singla, N. (2011). Reconsidering work–family interactions and satisfaction: A meta-analysis. *Journal of Management, 37*(3), 861–886.

Thomas, L. T., & Ganster, D. C. (1995). Impact of family-supportive work variables on work–family conflict and strain: A control perspective. *Journal of Applied Psychology, 80*(1), 6–15.

van Steenbergen, E. F., & Ellemers, N. (2009). Is managing the work–family interface worthwhile? Benefits for employee health and performance. *Journal of Organizational Behaviour, 30*(5), 617–642.

Voydanoff, P. (2005). The differential salience of family and community demands and resources for family-to-work conflict and facilitation. *Journal of Family and Economic Issues, 26*(3), 395–417.

Wallace, J. E. (1999). Work-to-nonwork conflict among married male and female lawyers. *Journal of Organizational Behaviour, 20*(6), 797–816.

Wallace, J. E. (2005). Job stress, depression and work-to-family conflict: a test of the strain and buffer hypothesis. *International Relations, 60*(3), 510–539.

Yang, N. (2005). Individualism-collectivism in work–family interfaces: A Sino-US comparison. In S. A. Y. Poelmans (Ed.), *Work and family: An international research perspective* (pp. 287–218). Mahwah, NJ: Lawrence Erlbaum Associates, Inc.

Chapter 3
Work and Family in a Cross-Cultural Context: A Comparative Review of Work–Family Experiences of Working Mothers in Australia and Zimbabwe

Virginia Mapedzahama

Introduction

Recent years have seen a growth in research and literature, as well as policy interest in the interface between work and family domains. In particular, this interest has been in women's subjective experiences of the work–family interface, specifically on how they negotiate the demands of their paid work and family. Much of the resultant research evidence has been used as a base for family and employment policies targeted at facilitating women's labor force participation. A major limitation of this work, however, is that it has been carried out in predominantly affluent countries of the West such as the United States, Europe and Australia, and in highly industrialised Asian societies like Japan. It is also based primarily on studies conducted with (oftentimes, largely) white, middle-class workers. Relatively little research, has been done with or in other regions of the world, especially those that are still developing (Poster and Prasad 2005). Yet, as O'Brien (2012, p. 8) notes, "across developing countries and emergent economies, the reconciliation of work and family responsibilities is increasingly becoming an important phenomenon with high policy relevance…" Therefore by ignoring developing countries in Asia, Africa and Latin America the current research on work–family interface is also ignoring a range of global variation (Poster and Prasad 2005).

By exploring the work–family experiences of working mothers in Zimbabwe therefore, this chapter addresses a significant gap in African-based research on work–family interface. As Maerten (2004, p. 3) pointed out, while it can no longer be taken for granted that the public and private spheres do not "necessarily hold a contradiction" for African women the nexus between women's economic and familial roles is still rarely thought about in the region, and it remains neglected in

V. Mapedzahama (✉)
School of Rural Medicine, University of New England, Unit 5 163 Dangar St, Armidale, NSW 2350, Australia
e-mail: vmapedza@une.edu.au

Z. Mokomane (ed.), *Work–Family Interface in Sub-Saharan Africa*, International Perspectives on Social Policy, Administration, and Practice,
DOI: 10.1007/978-3-319-01237-7_3,

analyses women's working lives. All in all, sub-Saharan African scholars have typically studied work and family domains separately. In Zimbabwe, neither feminist literature nor literature on the status of working women have considered the experiences or patterns of working women's work and family life intersection. In consequence very little is known about the work–family experiences of working women in the country. However, given that Zimbabwean women, like most of their counterparts in other parts of the world (see for example Aluko and Alfa 1985; Di Domenico et al. 1987; Fapohunda 1982; Lewis 1982) are traditionally the primary care givers who seek to raise children while earning an income, it is inevitable that like their Western counterparts, they experience the strain of negotiating between work and familial roles (see, Industrial Psychology Consultants 2010; Mapedzahama 2007).

This chapter draws on findings from qualitative interviews conducted with women in Harare, Zimbabwe and Adelaide, Australia to analyse how working women in the two cities negotiate the 'borderlands' between the various work sites of paid work and unpaid familial work. The aim of the study on which the chapter is based was to reveal not only the commonality and diversity of the women's experiences, but also the commonalities that can exist within a diversity of experiences. Bearing in mind the distinct cultural contexts of the two countries, the rationale for comparing the two groups of women drew partly from theories arguing that restricting cross-national comparative research to 'most similar' countries constrains the usefulness of comparative research while selecting countries that differ as much as possible makes it possible for theories and social phenomena to be checked and compared under the most 'unfavourable' conditions at differing stages of economic, political and social development.

While some of the research findings discussed herein confirm and contribute to research undertaken into women's workforce experiences over the past 30 years or so in Australia, the study sheds *new* light on the work–family experiences of working women in Zimbabwe. Perhaps more importantly then, the findings provide an overview of hitherto unknown qualitative data on the nature, consequences, challenges and opportunities presented by the synchronisation of work–family roles by working mothers in Zimbabwe. In that respect, the discussion herein is not only exploratory, but also theory-building for the study of work and family research in Zimbabwe and sub-Saharan Africa in general. The main contention in this chapter is that while negotiating work and family life may not necessarily (re)present the same magnitude of burden or conflict for the Zimbabwean working mothers interviewed for the research (as it does for their Australian counterparts), it still presents them with significant challenges which point to a need for more in-depth sociological investigations.

The chapter progresses in three overlapping sections. The first section: "Data Set" presents an overview of the data sources and a brief overview of the study from which this chapter draws. The Second section: "Work and Family policy context in Zimbabwe and Australia" provides a brief overview of the work and family policy context within which the working mothers in the two sites are located. This section contextualises the discussions presented in this chapter.

Thereafter, two main study findings are presented in the third section: "Findings". The first theme (The Everyday Context) discusses the strategies that women in the two sites employ in negotiating paid work and family: employing paid domestic workers for employed mothers in Harare, and part time work for women in Australia. The second theme (How the women feel about negotiating work and family) discusses how the participants talk about their own perceptions of work–family negotiations, highlighting the similarities and diversity of women's everyday work–family realities and demonstrating that what can appear as diversity at first can have underlying commonalities. The chapter concludes by (re)articulating the significance of cross-cultural analyses in work–family research for family policy

Data Sources

The data are derived from an exploratory study undertaken between 2004 and 2005 with the aim to uncover the routine, commonplace, day-to-day activities of women's work–family negotiations in a cross-cultural context: Zimbabwe and Australia. The central focus was the women's everyday contexts and everyday experiences, specifically the daily challenges and opportunities the women face as they cope with the demands of paid work and family. Smith's (1987) notion of interpreting the "everyday as problematic" (discussed in detail later in the chapter), provided the framework for focus.

In total, 30 women (15 in each research site) whose ages ranged from 20 to 50 years were interviewed. The target population for the study was employed married or cohabiting women who work no less than 20 h per week and have at least one child of pre-school age (5 years or below). The decision to limit the criteria to married or cohabiting women was made to enable the exploration of questions related to household gender division of labour among spouses or partners. On the other hand, the decision to focus on women with at least one preschooler was made against the background of earlier research (see for example, Spitze and Ward 1995, cited in Tsuya and Bumpass 2004; Carlson et al. 1995) showing that relative to older children, the presence of younger children increases the amount of housework to be done and hence as greater demands on parents' time and energy.

The study was located across various sectors: retail industry; hospitality; teaching; nursing; call centre utility industry. In Zimbabwe women engaged in various informal sector activities were also studied. Semi-structured, open-ended, conversational style interviews were used to collect data. According to Reinharz (1992, p. 18), an open-ended interview research "explores people's views of reality and allows the researcher to formulate theory"; it thus maximises discovery and description. The interviews ranged from 45 to 90 min in duration, with the average time being one hour. The interviews in Harare tended to be longer than those in Adelaide. This can be attributed to the fact that the women in Harare were talking about, and reflecting on, aspects of their work–family experiences in ways they had not done before. While all of the interviews in Adelaide were conducted in English, all of the interviews in Harare were conducted mainly in the vernacular, Shona. These were later transcribed and translated to English. It is for this reason that all the excerpts herein are in English.

Findings

Work and Family Policy Context in Zimbabwe and Australia

This section outlines three interventions which can have significant implications for the reconciliation and work and family responsibilities—parental leave policies, flexible work arrangements and childcare—and their availability in Zimbabwe and Australia.

Parental Leave Policies

It is widely agreed that existence of comprehensive parental leave provisions (the paid or unpaid time that parents get off, or are entitled to get off, to care for a child) have a substantial impact on women's labour force participation and work–family balance. It emerged from this study that there are significant differences in the parental leave policies in Zimbabwe and Australia. Like most other sub-Saharan African countries (Mokomane 2011; Smit 2011), Zimbabwe does not have any paternity leave provisions. The only parental leave available is the employer-funded maternity which entitles working pregnant women to at least 21 days before their due date, and 98 days off after the birth of a child, paid at 100 % of their normal pay (see Smit 2011). The paid maternity leave scheme in Zimbabwe also includes a "right to nursing breaks" provision where:

> A female employee breastfeeding her child has the right take at least one hour or two 30 minutes periods for each working day, as she may choose during normal working hours, to nurse her child. However, the grant of such break shall be done without disrupting the normal production processes (Mywage.com/Zimbabwe 2012).

It is noteworthy, however, that since a the large proportion of working women in Zimbabwe are employed in the informal sector (Ngwenya and Luebker 2009), a significant proportion of them do not have access to paid maternity leave as it is typically employer-funded. Conversely, while Australia was, until recently one of only two OECD (Organization for Economic Cooperation and Development) countries without any parental leave scheme (Broomhill and Sharp 2012) this changed in 2011 when a national, government funded parental leave scheme was introduced. According to Broomhill and Sharp (2012, p. 1):

> The new Australian arrangements comprise an industrial relations provision for an extended period of unpaid parental leave available for the majority of workers and a separate legislative provision of government financial support equal to the minimum wage for working parents for a lesser period up to 18 weeks.

Worthy to note also is that Australia's national parental leave policy incorporates paternity leave. As the Department of Education, Employment and Workplace Relations (2009, p. 1) explains:

> If a primary carer [for example the mother] returns to work before they have received all of their PPL [parental paid leave] entitlement, they may be able to transfer the unused part of their PPL to another caregiver (for example the father) who meets eligibility requirements.

Prior to the introduction of this national scheme, most employees in Australia had access to parental leave "through industrial awards, workplace agreements, company policies or legislation covering public sector employees" (Broomhill and Sharp 2012, p. 4). As such employee entitlements varied significantly. For example, maternity leave conditions were variable with some paid and some unpaid depending on the sector. Employees such as casual workers who were not covered under such agreements had no access to paid maternity leave (Ochiltree 1991).

Flexible Work Arrangements

Flexible work arrangements allow employees to adapt the way they work as well as how and when they work, with the aim to accommodate non-work responsibilities. These arrangements include, for example, job sharing; flexitime; telework or telecommuting; flexible or reduced hours such as part-time or casual work; and compressed work-week (working longer hours for fewer days in the week). While the availability of flexible work arrangements in Zimbabwe is almost non-existent, workers in Australia have access to several flexible work arrangements. For example, the National Employment Standards) introduced by the Labour Government in 2010, "includes a right for certain employees to request flexible working arrangements (such as changes in hours of work) from their employer. "An employer can only refuse such a request on 'reasonable business grounds'" (Fair Work Ombudsman Australia 2012). It is largely because of the availability of flexible work arrangements that women in Australia often choose part time work as a strategy for balancing work and family responsibilities as shall be discussed later in the chapter.

Childcare Centres

Out-of-home childcare in Zimbabwe is not only limited but it is also privatised and there are essentially no government funded childcare centres. As such, out-of-home childcare is very expensive and out of reach for many employees, particularly those in the low-income bracket. It follows then, that use of out-of-home childcare centres is generally limited to those in the middle or upper classes who can afford the high costs involved. Cheaper, more sustainable childcare practices for most working parents in Zimbabwe involve utilising live-in paid domestic workers or live-in unpaid kin-care. Although in 2005 the Government of Zimbabwe introduced a mandatory early childhood education and care (ECEC) programme with the aim to enable ordinary working parents avoid the high fees in private early childhood development centres, while still making sure their children are cared for, this programme is generally viewed in the country as an "extension of formal education, not childcare" (Johnson et al. 1997, p. 199). Indeed, in their study, Johnson and colleagues found that most Zimbabwean working parents with children in pre-schools reported that they utilised other forms of childcare such as paid domestic workers or kin-care, more than they did with the national ECEC programme.

Conversely, in the Australian context out-of-home childcare is not only the norm but it is also crucial for working parents. Childcare centres in the country are "seen as both a mechanism to support labour force participation and as an important form of early learning and education" (Department of Education, Employment and Workplace Relations 2010, p. 2). To this end, the Australian government plays a major role in the provision of childcare, as the Department of Education, Employment and Workplace Relations (2010, p. 2) further asserts:

> There has been a long history of the Commonwealth [central] Government providing funding to assist families to access early childhood education and child care. The Commonwealth Government first provided financial assistance for child care in 1972. Today, the majority of Commonwealth funding assists families with their child care costs. Early childhood education and child care funding has more than doubled in the last five years, increasing from $1.7 billion in 2004–05 to $3.7 billion in 2008–09 and is expected to further increase to $4.4 billion in 2012–13. During the next four years, the Commonwealth will invest $16.1 billion in early childhood education and child care.

While the "childcare fee relief" that is provided on a sliding scale—with those on the lowest incomes having full entitlement (Ochiltree 1991)—is available to most parents in Australia, the State does not fund all childcare centres. Rather, childcare is provided publicly by the government; by private organisations; or by community or not-for-profit organisations. Irrefutably, therefore, childcare is widely used in Australia and, indeed, the last few decades have seen an increase in the number of children in formal childcare centres (Department of Education, Employment and Workplace Relations 2010).

The Everyday Context

As earlier stated, the central focus of the study on which this chapter is based is the everyday contexts and experiences of work and family negotiations of working mothers in Harare and Adelaide. Particular interest was on their routine, commonplace, day-to-day activities of moving between the 'worlds' of paid work and family. According to Smith (1987, p. 89):

> The everyday world is the world we experience directly. It is the world in which we are located physically and socially. Our experience arises in it as conditions, occasions, objects, possibilities, relevancies, presences and so on, organized in and by the practices and methods through which we supply and discover organisation. It is necessarily local—because that is how we must be—and necessarily historical.

In the study, interpreting the "everyday" was significant not only because it located the women in their "bodily and material existence" (Smith 1987, p. 97) but it also provided an interconnection between their 'public' and the 'private' worlds. This facilitated the in-depth analyses of the struggles and resistance that the women encounter on a daily basis. Thus, the experiences presented in this section provide a deeper understanding of the complexities of the women's everyday work and family experiences.

An important finding of the study reaffirmed other findings on women's work and gendered household division of labour in both Zimbabwe and Australia. In essence it was evident that women in both countries are still responsible for the major share of housework. While most of the women in Adelaide reported that their husbands did some share of the housework, they also reported that it was still the women who, in the words of Hochschild (1989, p. 20) did the "lion's share of work at home, do most of the daily chores and take responsibility for the running of the home" The women in Harare on the other hand, reported that men virtually did not do *any* share of the housework and/or childcare.

Despite of the similarity in the burden of care, the women in both sites use different strategies to negotiate the demands of work and family life. Three strategies particularly stood out in the two study sites: reliance on paid domestic workers and on unpaid kin help in Zimbabwe, and part-time work in Australia.

Paid Domestic Workers

For all the participants in Harare, negotiating between paid work and family was facilitated by the presence of a live-in paid domestic worker who assisted with household chores and childcare. This is consistent with previous research showing that in many developing countries couples are more likely to outsource domestic tasks to assist them in their work–family negotiations if both spouses or partners work full-time (see for example, Venn 2003). This is made particularly feasible by the fact that in most of these countries labour is relatively cheap and the high unemployment levels tend to force people into poorly paid, unregulated jobs such as domestic work. In their work on women's work and child-bearing in Ghana, for example, Blanc and Lloyd (1994) noted that child-bearing and child-rearing are not necessarily synonymous, and that the opportunities for cash available to women as domestic workers make paid domestic work a readily available source of childcare. It is not surprising then, that for most working mothers in Zimbabwe paid domestic workers were found to be the most common strategy used to negotiate the demands of paid work and family life.

All in all, in contemporary Zimbabwe where urbanisation has significantly changed the extended family structure, working mothers no longer have ready access to traditional sources of help. Thus unlike their counterparts in the more industrialised countries who devise childcare arrangements from a limited range of out-of-home, privatised childcare facilities, many Zimbabwean women often left their children—including infants—at home with a female helper who would care for the children while the mother was away. Sometimes, as in the case of informal sector cross-border trading women (see Mapedzahama 2007, 2009), the time away can be several weeks:

> When I left him [the son] the first time he wasn't quite two months old, yes, two months… There was nothing else I could do; I had to go across the border to Botswana for trade. Luckily the paid domestic worker I had, actually she is the same one that I still have … She is a mature woman and she very competent with children. So she took good care of him for me (Mother of five, informal sector cross-border trader, Harare).

All in all the employment of live-in paid domestic workers is a phenomenon that has been normalised within Zimbabwean culture. Having another female in the household who can take care of some of the household chores seems to suggest that women in Zimbabwe can engage in full-time labour force participation, perhaps because the women are relieved of some domestic duties.

Nevertheless, a closer analysis of the relationship between the women in the Harare group, their paid domestic workers, and the implications for the participants' work family interface exposes two important paradoxes. The first is that of the additional responsibilities of 'supervisor' inherent in the employment of a domestic worker. While all of the participants in Harare acknowledged that their work–family negotiations would be virtually unmanageable without assistance from paid domestic workers, they still did not think of paid domestic workers as competent enough to manage the household without constant supervision. The women's narratives of how paid domestic workers assist in their work–family negotiations suggest that as much as employing paid domestic workers helps ease the burden of negotiating work and family, it also adds to the burden of housework by adding another role: that of 'supervisor'. One woman in Harare explained her situation as follows:

> When I come home from [my paid] work I have to check everything in the house, so I am starting another job. Even though the domestic worker is doing some of the work, I am also working because when I get home I have to inspect [what the domestic worker has done] as well. Checking if she has done her job, the duties for the day, I check that everything has been done properly. What about this or that? Has the laundry been done properly? … So I am doing some work too, it is work as well (Mother of four, teacher, Harare).

The above mother's statement seems to imply that she does not see her role of 'supervising' the paid domestic worker as any different from supervising staff in more formal workplaces. In this way, supervising the paid domestic worker constitutes the "second shift" that Hochschild (1989) discussed in relation to Western women's paid work and familial responsibilities. Moreover, given that the "stalled revolution"[1] that Hochschild proposed in the 1980s seems to still persist, working mothers in Zimbabwe are still expected to do housework, and when they cannot fulfil this expectation due to paid work commitments, the role of supervising paid domestic workers falls to them. This role, as the interviewed women concurred, adds to their burden of the second shift. Hence, while it could be argued that the presence of an additional adult female helper means that the women in Harare are able to utilise a strategy which reduces anxiety and distress, it also means additional responsibilities for the women.

The second paradox relates to the perceived implications of having a paid domestic worker for one's image as a wife and mother. The women admitted that while having doemstic help was instrumental in their ability to participate in paid work, they also felt that employing a domestic worker to do what are societal expectations of them as women, mothers and wives has negative implications for their socio-cultural images:

> It does help a lot (having a live-in domestic helper); it's just that as a married woman you don't want the helper to do all the work for you; it seems like you are shifting your responsibilities to her. So whatever you can do yourself when you are home, you do (Mother of one, teacher, Harare).

The above mother's statement not only highlights the strength and persistence of gender roles, it also exposes the contradiction of societal expectations and change. There is a slow but emerging shift in societal expectations that if a mother is in the paid workforce she can enlist the help of paid domestic workers to assist with housework. At the same time, however, there is still a sense of the stigma attached to not fully meeting traditional gender role expectations of motherhood, wifehood and womanhood. The mother in the above quotation, for example, is fully aware of the persistence of cultural constructs and expectations of motherhood, womanhood and wifehood that still construct women as responsible for housework, hence the feeling that getting someone else to help with the housework is "like shifting responsibilities". It is largely for this reasons that many Zimbabwean working mothers still endeavour to adhere to cultural expectations: they continue to strive to do household chores and provide care for their family members even when participating in full time paid work. The following statement by another mother illustrates:

> It is a mother's duty to teach her children the norms, morals and values of our culture. Like here in the cities it's very tricky because it is easy for children to pick up on lots of other

[1] According to Hochschild (1989) a 'stalled' gender roles and gender behaviour revolution refers to the disjuncture between the rate at which women have entered the (full time) labour market (the increase in female labour force participation) and men's participation in unpaid household and care work that still leaves women overburdened with paid work and familial responsibilities. Even though men are taking on more responsibility for domestic work than before, women still do the bigger share, even when engaged in full time work.

> bad values and norms, so a mother has to make sure that the children grow up with proper values and are well-mannered… But it's like when you are not there most of the time—like in my case I go out of the country—it becomes difficult. You leave the children with the domestic worker and that is when they (the children) misbehave a lot, because they can say that the domestic worker is only just a worker, "so she cannot tell us (to do) anything because she is not our mother"… Some things a father can do like teaching his son men's duties such as cattle herding… or chopping firewood… but for a lot of the things, it is still expected that as the mother, you are the one who is with the children most of the time (looking after them), so you should teach them the cultural values, women's duties and men's duties.

This mother believes that it is a key role of a mother to socialise her children in the norms and morals of their culture, and she does not think that either her husband or the domestic worker who looks after her children while she is away can do so adequately in her absence. In a way this finding also exposes a division of labour in the socialisation of children in many African societies, which reinforces 'mother' as the primary carer regardless of her economic responsibilities.

Unpaid Kin Help

Where a working mothers' salary or wage does not allow for the employment of a paid domestic worker—as if often the case due to the increasing costs associated with hiring such help in light of the economic crisis in the country—the help of relative is often sought. The relative is typically a young girl who, like a domestic worker, "lives-in" with the family. This is in line with the customary practice in Zimbabwe, as in many other countries in sub-Saharan Africa where women were helped with household chores by their older daughters and younger female relatives. This is even more so in contemporary Zimbabwe, with "the absence of well-developed and established formal social support systems to help the … [working mothers], the … family has become the main provider of these services" (Takyi 2011, p. 1). Somewhat similarly, some of the women in the Adelaide group also mentioned that they regularly receive help from extended family, particularly their own mothers. This finding is consistent with other research in Australia (for example, Australian Bureau of Statistics 2005; Goodfellow 2003; Goodfellow and Laverty 2003) that points to an increase in 'grand caring' or grandparent care. According to the Australian Bureau of Statistics (2005) for example, in 2002 grandparents provided 31 % of the total hours of childcare provided in the week the survey was conducted.

The key difference between the participants in the two groups of women, however, is that those in Harare typically provided food and board in exchange for their relatives' assistance with domestic chores and childcare. Conversely, for the women in the Adelaide group grandparent help was provided at no cost, whatsoever, to the women. Indeed, none of the women interviewed spoke of paying (or giving gifts to) their mothers for the childcare. Another difference is that the historic low use of domestic help by working women in Australia (Wolcott and Glezer 1995) seems to continue even though the majority of women are now likely to be in paid work. Evidence shows that there is still little indication that working mothers are employing household help to assist with domestic and caregiving chores and fact, none of the women expressed any wish to employ or even to look for paid domestic workers. Only after being prompted on the topic did some of the women say that it would be a 'nice' thing to do, and that it could make their role juggling easier. However, the women cited the expenses involved in employing a paid domestic helper as the major deterrent and many explained that they would not be able to justify employing a domestic helper since they worked part-time. One of the participants commented that:

> I do all that (household chores) myself. I would [get paid domestic help] if I worked full-time. I'd get someone into do it ... like basically if I worked 5 days a week, I'd get someone into do my washing and that ... Yeah, coz I could afford it ... Also if I worked full-time I would not have the time to do all that sort of stuff ... (Mother of two, call centre worker, Adelaide).

Part-Time Work

Due to relatively strict labour laws (governing wages and working conditions for paid domestic work) the employment of domestic workers is rare in Australia. Indeed, none of the women interviewed in Adelaide reported that she had a paid domestic worker. Rather, an important strategy that the women employ to confront their challenges of combining work and family roles challenges is part time work. Most women (13 of the 15 interviewed) worked part-time, ranging from a minimum of 20 h to a maximum of 30 h per week. In contrast, all of the women interviewed in Harare worked full-time. Explaining why part-time work was her option, a mother of two in Adelaide responded as follows:

> I just find that working part-time is really a good compromise for me at the moment. I guess it just means that I can look after my family, my kids, but at the same time continue to work. I love my job, I love working in customer service (Mother of two, call centre worker, Adelaide).

While part-time work seems to offer women the "best of both worlds" (Higgins et al. 2000; Pocock 2001) some of those in this type of employment lament the hectic pace involved in balancing work and family life:

> Yeah, the only thing about working part-time is that it seems there is never enough time. I mean I go to work in the morning, finish up, say at 3 p.m., pick up the kids from school or after school care or day care or whatever, start on tea as soon as I get home and stuff like that... so there's really no time in there for anything else, it's always either work or kids' stuff. So it's like you are working part-time but you are even busier ... (Mother of three, nurse, Adelaide).

The above statement affirms the view of some commentators such as Higgins, et al. (2000, p. 19) who state that when women work part-time, they "figure ... they can do *everything* (my emphasis)... yet, looking at their everyday lives, they were never not working". In the same vein, Watson et al. (2003, p. 49) argued that, the "mere existence of reduced hours in a job does not mean that part-time work… can fully meet the needs of the workers who seek reduced hours". Overall, therefore, it is noteworthy that while part-time work can, in some cases, facilitate easier work–family negotiations, it can also enhance time-poverty and increase burnout among working women.

Furthermore, many part-time jobs are characterised by routine tasks, employment insecurity and negative perceptions that "part-time [workers] are committed primarily to their families rather than to their work … [and therefore] lack career ambition" (Charlesworth and Whittenbury 2007, p. 39). Such negative perceptions result in part-time work being characterised by limited advancement opportunities that "threaten to ghettoise the women who work these schedules" (Higgins et al. 2000, p. 18). Linked to this is the financial disadvantage or inadequate income associated with working part-time. Women with family responsibilities "are forced to make trade-offs when taking up part-time employment" (Watson et al. 2003, p. 149), trading off the reduced hours they seek for poorer wages and poorer conditions.

In the African context, informal sector work has been cited for providing a somewhat similar level of flexibility as part-time work. Some scholars argue that by doing informal sector work located in the home or close to the home, women are better able to combine economic work with childcare; care of old, disabled or sick family members; as well as other domestic responsibilities (Elder and Schmidt 2004; Lingam 2005; Loewenson 1998). However, the findings from this study do not seem to full support this notion and as I have reported elsewhere (Mapedzahama 2007, p. 201):

> The reality for women in the informal sector is that their roles cannot be easily compartmentalised into domestic and public lives, instead, they are constantly intertwined … Women in the informal economy also perform a juggling act that is constantly changing. In fact … the dilemma of work and family can be "serious for women… [in the informal sector] as they are responsible for the success of their own…" (Kim & Ling 2001, p.204) as well as the welfare and survival of their families.

How Women Feel About Negotiating Work and Family

The interviews in both Adelaide and Harare probed the women to talk about how they felt about the way they negotiated between work and family. The women generally reported feeling that their day is divided into specific blocks of time units: dropping off children at school or childcare; picking them up; rushing them to some extra-curricular activity; doing the shopping or being at work. They felt that they always had to rush to be somewhere or that they were doing something all the time. The overall feeling was that negotiating work and family responsibilities was difficult. The following statement summarises the women's sentiments in this regard:

> It is a very hard thing to do [negotiating paid work and family] I won't lie. It is very hard. And it will never be easy doing this work that we do. But there is nothing else you can do. Because as mothers, the reason we work is to try and meet the cost [of living], but even that is still difficult to do, the prices for everything keep going up. But if you put in more time at work so that you can earn more money, the home front suffers, and then sometimes you just have to take some time off work to concentrate on your family responsibilities [sighs]. Raising a family is very hard; you have to be strong as a mother to sustain both sides [paid working and family responsibility]. (Mother of five, informal sector cross border trader, Harare).

Additionally, the women in both sites talked about the burden of feeling like they were always in "thinking mode … planning the next move" (mother of two, Adelaide), and (re)arranging the lives of their families, figuring out who needs what, who needs to go where and what the family will eat. Hence, even though women in both sites felt the effects of engaging in paid work were more positive than negative for them (especially for financial purposes), they still spoke of the negatives in terms of work–family interaction. An important similarity in the way the women in both sites talked about this challenge is the management of time. Most of the women spoke of the importance of 'managing' their time well so that they could perform daily tasks or duties. For example, one woman in Adelaide explained that:

> You have to be organised: I think every mum is a time manager to the maximum. You've gotta be always thinking about things in advance: always thinking, making lists. That's what I have got to do. (Mother of one, retail worker, Adelaide).

The women in Harare echoed similar sentiments. They explained that, in spite of the support they got from extended family and paid domestic workers, they were still solely responsible for all the planning for the household, particularly in terms of the day-to-day management including the supervision of domestic workers. As one participant pointed out:

> You have to be good at planning. Even with the paid domestic worker you still have to lay out what needs to be done for the day while you are at work, otherwise nothing really gets done. (Mother of one, data capturing clerk, Harare).

Another Harare participant concurred:

> Aah, the situation (working motherhood) really needs for you to be a good time planner because the paid domestic worker does not plan anything; that is the mother's role. Her [the domestic worker] role is to carry out whatever you have planned for her … It's hard … making sure that things don't turn into chaos when you are not there. (Mother of three, receptionist, Harare).

The women in Harare felt that the role of 'household planner' added to the burden of everyday negotiations. Some women even talked about regularly calling their homes from work to either advise the paid domestic worker about tasks that need completing, or to confirm that tasks have been performed. One could argue that this is an important example of the blurring of the boundaries between familial responsibilities and paid work, or what Western literature on work–family interface cites as family interference with work.

Interestingly, while the mothers in both Harare and Adelaide talk about time-management, only mothers in Adelaide reported 'feeling rushed'. A notable number (ten) of the women in Adelaide, but none in the Harare group, talked of feeling that they were 'always in a rush' or 'in a hurry' to be somewhere or to get things done, as one explained:

> Oh, you know working as well, it's like running here and running there … sometimes I think oh, it's all too much, running here and running there. But … I'm a pretty organised person as well … when you are a working mum and you've got kids, and you're running here and there, you've gotta be organised (Mother of two, call centre worker, Adelaide).

The difference in 'time-poverty' between the two groups of women can be attributed to the availability of *live-in* paid domestic workers or *live-in kin* to women in Harare. The extended family networks in Zimbabwe, and the relative ease with which childcare is outsourced or obtained (for example when grandmothers, other relatives and older children take care of the young), provide mothers with additional help that eases feelings and experiences of time-poverty. One could speculate here that it is because African mothers do not present as 'time-poor' as their western counterparts, that some scholars argue that childcare and paid work are compatible and that the work–family debate is a non-issue for African women. Clearly, the availability of paid and unpaid household assistance makes it easier for the Zimbabwean women to *better* manage paid work and family responsibilities compared to their Australian counterparts. However, this cannot be taken to imply that paid work and family in Zimbabwe are easily compatible or that they do not present a problem for the women.

Conclusion

The data presented and discussed in this chapter reaffirms debates that "the reconciliation of work and family responsibilities is increasingly becoming an important phenomenon with high policy relevance in many sub-Saharan Africa" (Mokomane 2011, p. 5), as it has been in most Western contexts. The comparative approach in the broader study highlighted that regardless of their socio-economic status, or the degree of hardship they endure, working mothers in developing and developed countries experience surprisingly similar everyday work–family realities, although they tend to employ different coping strategies. Overall the findings show that the "duality of [women's] roles is universal, [it is only] the *magnitude of burden* [that] distinguishes the woman of the south from her sister in the north" (Mbire-Barungi 1999, p. 438). Although some cultural and national differences may exist that result in differences in the way women juggle between work and family, there are still some elemental relationships between the 'worlds' of paid work and familial relationships across national boundaries that lead to similar outcomes in the way that women negotiate the two.

By drawing out the commonalities of work–family experiences of the Harare women and Adelaide women, the chapter reaffirms, as Bulbeck (1998, p. 6) argues, that "sometimes we find similarities where they are not expected", therefore, feminism's pre-occupation "with difference as a retort to the universalising claims of categories like 'sisterhood'... [can result]...in danger of losing sight of the commonalities and connections between women".

The similarity of the women's work–family experiences further exposes the complex nature of the work and family interface for women in Zimbabwe. It can no longer be unproblematically claimed for example, that the availability of live-in kin who can assist with domestic responsibilities, or a pool of cheap labour from which working mothers can employ live-in paid domestic workers, presents "societal mechanisms through which the conflict over time arising from women's multiple roles may be alleviated" (Blanc and Lloyd 1994, p. 124). Or that the possible conflict over time management could be lessened in a setting in which kin ties are strong and there exists a strong belief that costs and benefits of child-rearing are appropriately shared among kin groups.

Overall this chapter has underscored the need for attention to the Zimbabwean and sub-Saharan women's work–family realities as part of social-economic research on working women's lives in the sub-continent. The experiences of the Harare women further suggest that the issues of concern and research on women's working lives in sub-Saharan Africa should not be simply ones of survival because women's everyday contexts are also characterised by challenging work and family negotiations that warrant critical examination. Finally, the comparative analyses formulated in this chapter suggest that, notwithstanding the diversity of women as a result of socio-economic, political and cultural contexts, and significant differences in the ways in which women take on paid work and family responsibilities, there are sufficient commonalities among women and their work–family realities to warrant discussions at an international level. Though the results of this micro-level qualitative study do not claim to be representative of women's experiences in the West or in sub-Saharan Africa, they still point to the usefulness and need for global alliances on women, work and family. The aim in forming such global alliances is not to arrive at a universal definition of women's experiences, but to incorporate issues of relevance to under-researched, underrepresented, non-western women.

References

Australian Bureau of Statistics. (2005). *Australian social trends*, ABS Catalogue no. 4102.0. Canberra: Australian Bureau of Statistics.

Aluko, G.B., & Alfa M.O. (1985). Marriage and family in women in Nigeria today. In Women in Nigeria Organisation (Ed.), *Women in Nigeria Today*, (pp. 163-173). London: Zed Books.

Blanc, A. K., & Lloyd, C. B. (1994). Women's work, child-bearing and child-rearing over the life cycle in Ghana. In A. Adepoju & C. Oppong (Eds.), *Gender, work and population in sub-Saharan Africa* (pp. 112–131). London: James Currey Ltd.

Broomhill, R., & Sharp, R. (2012). *Australia's parental leave policy and gender equality: an international comparison*. Adelaide: Australian Workplace Innovation and Social Research Centre, University of Adelaide.

Bulbeck, C. (1998). *Re-orienting western feminisms: Women's diversity in a postcolonial world*. Cambridge: Cambridge University Press.

Carlson, D. S., Kacmar, K. M., & Stepina, L. P. (1995). An examination of two aspects of work—family conflict: Time and identity. *Women in Management Review, 10*(2), 17–25.

Charlesworth, S., & Whittenbury, K. (2007). Part-time and part-committed?: The challenges of part-time work in policing. *Journal of Industrial Relations, 49*(1), 31–47.

Department of Education, Employment and Workplace Relations. (2009). *Australia's paid parental leave scheme*. http://foi.deewr.gov.au/documents/australia-s-paid-parental-leave-scheme. Accessed 3 December 2009.

Department of Education, Employment and Workplace Relations. (2010). *State of child care in Australia*. http://foi.deewr.gov.au/node/3710. Accessed 3 December 2012.

Di Domenico, C. M., De Cola, L., & Leishman, J. (1987). 'Urban Yoruba mothers: At home and at work. In C. Oppong (Ed.), *Sex roles, population and development in West Africa: Policy related studies on work and demographic issues* (pp. 118–132). London: James Currey.

Elder, S., & Schmidt, D. (2004). *Global employment trends for women, 2004: Employment strategy papers No. 8*. Geneva: Employment Strategy Department, International Labour Organisation.

Fair Work Ombudsman Australia. (2012). *Requests for flexible working arrangements and the National Employment Standards*. www.fairwork.gov.au. Accessed 20 December 2012.

Fapohunda, E. R. (1982). The childcare dilemma of working mothers in African cities: The case of Lagos, Nigeria. In E. G. Bay (Ed.), *Women and work in Africa* (pp. 277–288). Colorado: Westview Press Inc.

Goodfellow, J. (2003). Grandparents as regular childcare providers: Unrecognised, undervalued and under-resourced. *Australian Journal of Early Childhood, 28*(3), 7–17.

Goodfellow, J., & Laverty, J. (2003). Grandparents supporting working families. *Family Matters, 66*, 14–19.

Higgins, C., Duxbury, L., & Johnson, K. L. (2000). Part-time work for women: Does it really help balance work and family? *Human Resources Management, 39*(1), 17–32.

Hochschild, A. R. (1989). *The second shift*. New York: Avon Books.

Industrial Psychology Consultants (2010). *Women in the workplace*. www.ipcconsultants.com. Accessed 15 December 2012.

Johnson, D. J., Dyanda-Marira, C., & Dzvimbo, P. K. (1997). Urban Zimbabwean mothers' choices and perceptions of care for young children. *Early Childhood Research Quarterly, 12*(2), 199–219.

Lewis, B. (1982). Fertility and employment: An assessment of role incompatibility among African urban women. In E. G. Bay (Ed.), *Women and work in Africa* (pp. 249–276). Colorado: Westview Press Inc.

Lingam, L. (2005). *Structural adjustment, gender and household survival strategies: Review of evidence and concerns*. Michigan: Centre for the Education of Women, University of Michigan.

Loewenson, R. (1998). *Health impact of occupational risks in the informal sector in Zimbabwe*. Geneva: International Labour Organization.

Maerten, M. (2004). *African feminism: RoSA Fact Sheet*, 34. www.rosadoc.be/site/rosa/english/pdf/factsheetsenglish/34.pdf. Accessed 29 November 2006.

Mapedzahama, V. (2007). Worlds apart? *A cross-national comparative study of employed mothers negotiating paid work and family in Australia and Zimbabwe*. Unpublished PhD Thesis, University of South Australia, Adelaide.

Mapedzahama, V. (2009). Weaving paid work, informal sector work and motherhood in Harare (Zimbabwe): A new arena for research? *The Australasian Review of African Studies, 30*(1), 64–82.

Mbire-Barungi, B. (1999). Ugandan feminism: Political rhetoric or reality? *Women's Studies International Forum, 22*(4), 435–439.

Mokomane, Z. (2011). *Work–family balance: Overview of policies in developing countries: Introductory remarks.* Paper prepared for the United Nations Programme on the family expert group meeting on assessing family policies: Confronting family poverty and social exclusion and ensuring work–family balance, 1–3 June 2011, New York.

Mywage.org/Zimbabwe. (2012). *Maternity leave.* http://m.mywage.org/zimbabwe/main/decent-work-check/maternity-leave/maternity-leave. Accessed 12 December 2012.

Ngwenya, L. & Luebker, M. (2009). *Gender and informal employment in Zimbabwe.* Paper presented at the Global Forum on Gender Statistics 26–28 January 2009 in Accra, Ghana.

O'Brien, M. (2012). *Work–family balance policies.* Background paper prepared for United Nations—Department of Economic and Social Affairs. New York: UNDESA.

Ochiltree, G. (1991). Child care: a contrast in policies. *Family Matters, 30*, 38–42.

Pocock, B. (2001). *Having a life: Work, family, fairness and community in 2000.* Adelaide: Centre for Labour Research, Adelaide University.

Poster, W. R., & Prasad, S. (2005). Work–family relations in transnational perspective: A view from high-tech firms in India and the United States. *Social Problems, 52*(1), 122–146.

Reinharz, S. (1992). *Feminist methods in social research.* New York: Oxford University Press.

Smit, R. (2011). Family-related policies in Southern African countries: Are working parents reaping any benefits? *Journal of Comparative Family Studies, 42*(1), 15–36.

Smith, D. E. (1987). *The everyday world as problematic: A feminist sociology.* Milton Keynes: Open University Press.

Takyi, B. K. (2011). *Transformations in the African family: A note on migration, HIV/AIDS and family poverty alleviation efforts in Sub-Saharan Africa (SSA).* Paper prepared for the United Nations expert group meeting on assessing family policies, 1–3 June, New York.

Tsuya, N. O., & Bumpass, L. L. (2004). Gender and housework. In N. O. Tsuya & L. L. Bumpass (Eds.), *Marriage, work and family life in comparative perspective: Japan, South Korea and the United States* (pp. 114–133). Honolulu: University of Hawaii Press.

Venn, D. (2003). *Coordinating work and family: Evidence from the Australian time use survey.* Paper presented at the Australian Institute of Family Studies conference, 12–14 February, Melbourne.

Watson, I., Buchanan, J., Campbell, I., & Briggs, C. (2003). *Fragmented futures: New challenges in working life.* Annandale: The Federation Press.

Wolcott, I., & Glezer, H. (1995). *Work and family life: Achieving integration.* Melbourne: Australian Institute of Family Studies.

Part II
Factors Underlying Work–Family Conflict in Sub-Saharan Africa

Chapter 4
Working Hours and Work–Family Conflict in the Institutional Context of Nigeria

Chantal Epie and Afam Ituma

Introduction

Recent years have witnessed a growing global interest in work–family and work–life issues and the topic has attracted considerable empirical and theoretical attention in the literature. Throughout the world, efficient and effective work–family and work–life balance programs have been upheld as measures that can contribute to societal productivity and well-being (Ransome 2007; Ten Brummelhuis and van der Lippe 2010; for a review of the literature, see Kelly et al. 2008). Harrington and Ladge (2009:148), point out that the topic of work–life or work–family interface "has evolved into one of the most significant business issues of the twenty-first century" and many firms are increasingly adopting some type of work–life and work–family balance program because of their potential to effectively contribute to employee well-being and positive organizational outcomes.

Although we are dealing with an issue of global concern, and considerable research has been conducted on a variety of work–family topics, there have, paradoxically, been few studies of these issues in diverse national contexts, particularly non-Western contexts. Those few studies have focused mostly on Asia (for example, Lee et al. 2011; Jyothi and Jyothi 2012). Comparative studies have also concentrated on American, European, and Asian populations (for example, Lu et al. 2010). Consequently, our knowledge has been largely informed by research and models developed in Western industrialized countries and may not truly reflect the situation in African national contexts. In this respect, the challenges confronting individuals and organizations in Africa constitute a relatively neglected

C. Epie (✉)
Lagos Business School, Pan-Atlantic University, Km 22, Lekki-Epe Expressway, Lagos, Nigeria
e-mail: cepie@lbs.edu.ng

A. Ituma
Federal University Ndufu-Alike Ikwo, 2 Ngboejeogu Crescent, Abakalike, Ebonyi, Nigeria
e-mail: afamituma@yahoo.com

Z. Mokomane (ed.), *Work–Family Interface in Sub-Saharan Africa*, International Perspectives on Social Policy, Administration, and Practice,
DOI: 10.1007/978-3-319-01237-7_4,

and little understood area of inquiry. This research gap is particularly problematic given that we live in an increasingly global economy. Moreover, it is necessary to gain deeper insights into the characteristics of the work, personal, and family life interface in Africa to guide social and business policy as there is undoubtedly a great socio-economic contrast between African countries and other national contexts in which most previous studies on work–family balance have been conducted (for example, Poelmans 2005; Houston 2005; Spector et al. 2004).

Most of the existing African research on work–family interface has been carried out in South Africa (recent examples include: De Klerk and Mostert 2010; Stey and Koekemer 2011). We should not assume that findings of these extant studies in Africa will necessarily generalize to all parts of the continent due to important cultural differences. It is logical to expect cultural differences in attitudes relating to work–family issues.

The overall objective of this chapter is, therefore, to contribute a West African perspective to the wider discourse on work–family interface and extend current conceptualizations in this area. The chapter specifically focuses on the work–family balance issues that individuals and organizations face in the context of Nigeria, nicknamed *the giant of Africa*, and more particularly in Lagos, the business capital and, with a population of 10.2 million (Central Intelligence Agency 2012), the largest and busiest city of the country. The overall aim of this chapter is to explore and analyze: (i) how much time Lagosians spend for working and commuting; (ii) in the case of those who spend much longer hours at work than those specified in their work contract, the reasons for doing so; (iii) the kind of work–family conflict Lagosians experience and its impact on their wellbeing; and, (iv) the impact of excessively long work hours on employees' stress and turnover intentions, both of which are bound to have an impact on productivity and employee costs. It is envisaged that the findings will: (i) provide valuable empirical data to help decision making on public policy; (ii) be useful to those with practical responsibility for the management of people in organizations in Nigeria; and (iii) stimulate further research on this topic.

The remainder of the chapter is organized as follows: Firstly, a brief review of the literature is presented. Secondly, the study is located within the Nigerian context. Thirdly, an overview of the research method adopted is discussed. The penultimate section presents our findings. The final section concludes with a discussion of the findings and a review of the implications for governmental and organizational policy makers.

Literature Review

It has been argued that a culture of long hours, heavy workloads, and lack of flexibility in the use of time provoke a stressful conflict between work and private life for many employees (Cooper 1998). It is generally accepted in the literature that hours of work are *excessive* if they add up to more than 48 h per week (Messenger 2006). In their meta-analytic review of research on hours worked and health, Sparks et al. (1997) noted small but significant correlations between the number of hours worked and psychological and physical health symptoms; they showed that long working hours are associated with increased errors, workplace injuries and health problems. Thus, long hours reduce workers' productivity as well as their well-being (Shepard and Clifton 2000). Summarizing previous research, Burke (2006) reports that long hours lead to: lower productivity, increased work place injuries and errors, increased levels of ill health, and work–family conflict. The bad business consequences of the first three items above are self-evident. By contrast, work–family conflict might be thought of as the exclusive concern of each employee. There is, however, abundant evidence of its negative impact on employee well-being and performance at work in Western contexts (for example, Grzywacz et al. 2005; Anderson et al. 2002). Poelmans and Sahibzada (2004) provide a thorough literature review showing that work–family conflict, defined by Greenhaus and Beutell (1985:77), as "a form of inter-role conflict in which the role pressures from the work and family domains are mutually incompatible in some respect," tends to lead to higher levels of stress, lower employee commitment, greater turnover intentions and lower job satisfaction, all of which have an impact on the quantity or the quality of work.

Work–family conflict can take two directions: work interfering with family (work-to-family conflict), and family interfering with work or family-to-work conflict (Frone et al. 1992). Work-to-family conflict has been found to be linked to turnover intentions, stress and lack of job satisfaction, while family-to-work conflict is correlated to absenteeism as well as stress (Anderson et al. 2002). Whatever the direction taken, work–family conflict affects employees' well-being and their work performance, with the natural consequences on organizational outcomes. Yet corporate culture tends to remain attached to the ideal of segmentation, meaning the strict separation of work and family, and to ignoring the reality of spill-over in the lives of very many people for whom the satisfactions or frustrations experienced in the work domain affect the family domain and vice versa (Guest 2001). The prevalent *face time* mentality at all management levels equates presence with commitment. Not surprisingly, employees fear that going home at the official close of work or showing reluctance to put in extra hours at weekends will stigmatize them in the eyes of their supervisors and co-workers (Fredriksen-Goldsen and Scharlach 2001). In Nigeria, two quantitative studies have looked at the relationship between organizational work–family culture, physical and psychological well-being, work–family conflict and other variables, concluding that employees of organizations with a more family-friendly culture tend to enjoy higher psychological wellbeing together with a lower level of work–family conflict. Turnover intentions are also lower than those of employees within a harsher type of culture (Epie 2007, 2010).

Work–family conflict can be time-based (lack of time to juggle between the work domain and the family domains, or timing clashes between both domains) or stress-based (high stress from one domain interfering with the ability to handle the other domain). Research among 11 organizations in Nigeria indicates that, within the same industry, organizations in which time-based or stress-based work-to-family conflict is higher register lower levels of organizational commitment and trust in management as well as higher levels of stress and turnover intentions (Epie 2011). It is clear therefore that the amount of extra time work absorbs to the detriment of one's family obligations has a negative impact on organisations. This is in harmony with the work of Poelmans and Sahibzada (2004).

Evbuoma (2007), in a survey of female employees from the most varied organizations in Nigeria including state ministries, secondary schools, universities, hospitals, manufacturing concerns, and banks, found that women workers who benefited from family-friendly support services achieved higher performance than those who did not (using a self-report measure of performance); these women were protected from the negative impact of excessively long work hours. Another interesting Nigerian study is that of Amah (2010) whose results confirmed that work–family policies have the potential to reduce the experience of work–family conflict if organizations provide a work environment favorable to their use. Abundant anecdotal evidence is available and some qualitative studies have been carried out to understand what Lagosians experience while juggling the various aspects of their lives (Epie 2009a, b) and the problems faced by bank employees in the management of their work–family interface (Mordi et al. work under review). There has, however, up to now, been no empirical quantitative study to examine the extent of the problem of long work hours in Lagos and to explain why employees agree to work much longer hours than those set by the law. Hence, the need to undertake research to better understand how long employees work each day and why. The following section examines the characteristics of the Nigerian context.

The Nigerian Context

A recurring theme in the literature on international management has been the impact of national context on management practices and individual behavior. As noted above there has, however, been a preponderance of Western-based work–family studies. It could be argued that the Anglo Saxon Western-based contexts (particularly the United States context in which most extant studies have been framed) are characterized by high levels of wealth, strong corporate governance, and government commitment to rule of law (Aguilera and Jackson 2003). Drawing from institutional theory (Scott 2008), it could be argued that companies and individuals operating in other national contexts are likely to be exposed to different sets of factors which affect their management practices (cf. Lee et al. 2011). Thus, analyzing the significant contextual characteristics that prevail in a country is important given that the unique history and socio-economic environment of a nation can produce disparate socially constructed realities which shape and constrain the behavior of individuals and firms in the country. Some of the key factors that are likely to affect the interface of work and other life domains in Nigeria are discussed below. Firstly, we provide a general overview of Nigeria.

The Federal Republic of Nigeria is a former British colony that obtained its independence in 1960. It is a West African coastal country that shares boundaries with Chad Republic and the Republic of Cameroon in the east, Niger Republic in the north, and the Gulf of Guinea in the south (Central Intelligence Agency 2012). The population is estimated at about 170 million (July 2012 estimate), with 40.9 % aged 0–14 years, 55.9 % between the ages of 15 and 64, and only 3.1 % over the age of 65 (Central Intelligence Agency 2012). While the average GDP per capita (PPP) is US$2,600 (2011 estimate), 70 % of the population lives below poverty levels, having steadily risen over the 34 % registered in 1992. The country is made up of 36 States and a Federal Capital Territory. In 1991, the capital was moved from Lagos to Abuja—a purpose-built city. Lagos, however, remains the largest commercial hub. Nigeria is a diverse society with over 250 ethnic groups, although the official language is English. The most widely spoken native languages are Yoruba, Igbo, and Hausa.

Like most African countries, Nigeria's culture is collectivist: an individual's identity is tied to a group (extended family, tribe). Nigeria constitutes a strongly male-dominated society (Omololu 1997). A gendered division of work prevails. Running one's own home is the woman's responsibility, even though she may employ male helpers to cook, do the laundry or clean the house (Gannon 2004). As many urban women are in some form of paid employment, they face a heavy workload on two fronts. Under the pressure of modern life, gender roles are slowly evolving. While more and more women occupy managerial positions alongside their male counterparts, few men are willing to assume a substantial share in household chores. Nigeria's culture is one of high status consciousness. Except in very modern, high-technology environments, the use of first names is not habitual and great care is taken to address senior people by the appropriate title (Ovadje and Ankomah 2001). High status people usually like to display their wealth or their status symbols (four-wheel drive vehicles, chieftaincy coral beads, etc.). The occupational distribution of the Nigerian people is, by and large, conjectural, as a high proportion of the population earns a living in the informal sector of the economy. It is estimated that, of a labor force of approximately 50.5 million (2010 estimate), 70 % are engaged in agriculture, 20 % in services, and 10 % in industry (Central Intelligence Agency 2012).

Conditions of employment are still regulated by the Labor Act (1974), although a revision of the legislation is foreseen in the near future. The provisions of this law concern mainly blue-collar workers and are very basic. Daily hours of work are to be fixed by mutual agreement or by collective bargaining (section 13, 1). If the working day is longer than 6 h, rest intervals of no less than 1 h in total must be allowed (section 13, 3). There must be 1 day of rest per week (section 13, 7). After 12 months of continuous service, every worker is entitled to an annual leave of at least 6 working days; this leave may be deferred by mutual agreement between the employer and the worker, but no longer than another 12 months (section 18). Women are entitled to 12 weeks maternity leave with no less than half pay. The customary benefits are more generous, with 2–3 weeks annual leave, full-pay maternity leave, and a 2-day weekend. Working conditions for white-collar employees at all levels are a matter of individual negotiation between employer and employee unless there is a union, in which case the union negotiates with the employer on behalf of its members. Collective agreements are intended to be binding on both parties. The Nigerian Supreme Court has, however, repeatedly ruled that collective agreements are enforceable only when their terms and conditions are incorporated into every employee's contract of employment.

There is no public social security because of the historical role of the extended family in providing for the old, the sick, and the needy; yet the extended family support system is being eroded through the influence of Western culture, rising consumerism and the dramatic reduction in real incomes over the past 30 years. The need for structural adjustment and the drive for privatization and recent government intervention in the governance of banks have led to large-scale retrenchment exercises. Oil companies are making growing use of contract work in a bid to reduce their employee-related costs and union demands. Unemployment is on the increase, having risen from 19.7 % in 2009 to 21.1 % in 2010, and 23.9 % in 2011, but it is lower in urban areas (17.1 %) particularly in Lagos State where only 8.5 % of the active population is affected (National Bureau of Statistics 2012). The overall implication of these factors is that the importance individuals attach to work–family balance is likely to be shaped by the prevailing economic conditions and the socio-cultural values embedded in this context.

As has been the case in the Western world for years, work intensification has become a widespread phenomenon in Nigerian cities, driven and controlled by technological developments. Cell phones not only *enable* employees to keep in touch with customers and bosses, but often *force* them to do so. Blackberries not only *enable* people to make good use of time outside the office but also *oblige* them to be *on duty* in any place and at any time. The 8 h working day has become in many organizations a fictional concept and the official work hours indicated in employees' conditions of service remain a dead letter.

The environment is another source of pressure. Bad roads make traffic chaotic. Road construction works bring the promise of a brighter future but also the immediate—albeit temporary—experience of frustrating bottlenecks. Add to all of the above the problems of power and water shortages, the financial and other demands from the extended family, and you get a picture of some of the pressures bearing upon Nigerians and the frustrations they may feel when trying to satisfy their legitimate aspirations to a happy, fulfilling personal and family life.

Research Methods

Survey Instrument

A survey methodology was deemed the most appropriate to collect data giving its usefulness in examining the frequency of occurrence of a phenomenon or variable, and also for testing the existence of relationships between variables of interest. The questionnaire used in this study began with questions to gather demographic information relevant to an African population (age, gender, industry, job level, marital status, number of children below the age of 18, number of relatives living with them, number of relatives being financially supported).

The survey instrument continued with open questions about the number of hours worked *per* week on average, and the time spent commuting daily. Then respondents who worked extra hours were asked to select their reasons for doing so on a list of 11 items such as "I do it by choice", "I am worried about losing my job" or "It is necessary to meet deadlines." They were also asked how their journey to and from work affected the stress of their day. One question enquired to what extent line managers were sympathetic when respondents needed time off or wished to reschedule work around their family and caring responsibilities.

With regard to stress, respondents were asked: (i) whether they experienced stress; and, (ii) whether they ever felt their working life was out of control, all of the time, almost all the time, sometimes, rarely or never. They were also asked whether they had, in the previous 12 months, suffered from ill health that they felt was related to stress at work; if the answer was positive, they were to indicate what this entailed on a list of 12 stress symptoms, such as anxiety or panic attacks, frequent or unexplained crying, increased smoking or drinking, or a life-threatening problem (such as stroke or heart attack). Further questions enquired whether respondents had ever sought help with these problems within or outside their organization and, if so, how they evaluated the effectiveness of the help received.

The work-to-family conflict scale (Carlson et al. 2000) contained eight questions and distinguished between time-based conflict (for example, "I wish I had more time to do things for the family" or "My time off work does not match other family members' schedule well") and stress-based conflict (for example, "I feel physically drained when I get home from work" or "Work makes me too tired or irritable to participate in or enjoy family life"); the two parts of the scale had a Cronbach Alpha of 0.85 and 0.84, respectively, which indicates a high level of reliability. Perceptions of organizational support—a scale derived from the work of Allen (2001) and Clark (2001), with a Cronbach Alpha of 0.79—were captured by five questions (for example "My organization really cares about my wellbeing" and "Help is available from my firm if I have a problem"). Ten questions derived from the work of Thompson et al. (1999) with a Cronbach Alpha of 0.89 investigated the organizational work-family culture; sample questions were "Long hours inside the office are the way to achieving advancement" and "It is assumed that the most productive employees are those who put their work before their family." The affective commitment scale (adapted from Ovadje 1996) included five questions and had a Cronbach Alpha of 0.72, which indicates an acceptable level of reliability; sample questions were "I feel very loyal to this organization" and "I am quite proud to be able to tell people who it is I work for." All these scales were of the Likert type, ranging from strongly disagree to strongly agree. Turnover intention was measured by two questions, "I am considering moving to a less stressful job" and "In the past 6 months I have been on the lookout for a better job elsewhere," derived from Poelmans et al. (2003) and designed to be answered on a 5-point Likert scale.

A questionnaire for spouses was designed on the same pattern as the work–family conflict scale administered to the principal respondents, but the questions were asked from the spouse's point of view (for example, "I wish my spouse had more time to do things for the family" and "I see my spouse emotionally drained when he/she gets home from work"). This would serve to validate the responses of the principal respondents. Two other questions were added: "I believe heavy job demands have a negative impact on the quality of our relationship" and "I wish we would spend more time together", in order to capture something of the impact of the respondent's work life on the couple's relationship.

Sample

Our sample was drawn from residents of Lagos—the financial capital of Nigeria. Lagos was selected because it is the business capital of Nigeria and has the largest concentration of working class people, which would facilitate data distribution and collection. Respondents consisted of lawyers, senior managers, and chief executives enrolled on a management training program of a top business school in Nigeria and some of their non-managerial staff. Participants in the management program took the survey instrument to fill in and return it 1 week later; some of them asked for additional questionnaires to distribute to some of their employees whom they thought would like to be part of the project. Participation was voluntary and questionnaires were to be filled in anonymously.

Of the 300 questionnaires distributed, only 156 usable questionnaires were returned, representing a response rate of 52 %, which can be considered good for this type of survey. Table 4.1 provides a summary of the demographic characteristics of the respondents. The sample included 19 chief executives officers, 113 managers (including lawyers with managerial responsibilities in their legal chambers), and 24 non-managerial white-collar workers from various sectors of the economy. The banking/finance/insurance sector was the largest single sector representing 35 % of the respondents, followed by shipping/logistics with 8 %, manufacturing with 7 %, information technology with 5 %, the health sector with 4.5 % and law, energy, and advertising with 4 % each, the remaining 28.5 % forming a miscellaneous category including education, real estate, and other areas of business activities. There were 115 men (74 %) and 41 women (26 %). The vast

Table 4.1 Demographic characteristics of respondents

Demographic characteristic	*N*	Percent (%)
Job level		
Chief executive officer	19	12
Managers and lawyers	113	73
Non-managerial, middle level staff	24	15
Industry		
Miscellaneous	44	28.5
Banking/finance/insurance	55	35.0
Shipping/logistics	12	88.0
Manufacturing	11	7.0
Information technology	8	5.0
Health	7	4.5
Law	6	4.0
Energy	6	4.0
Advertising	6	4.0
Gender		
Male	115	74
Female	41	26
Marital status		
Married	140	90
Widowed	4	2.0
Single	12	8.0
Number of children below 18 years		
3–6 Children	62	40
1–2 Children	72	46
No children	22	14
Number of relatives helped financially		
10–20	9	6.0
5–9	55	35.0
1–4	65	41.0
None	27	18.0

majority of them (90 %) were married, 12 % were single, and 2 % widowed. Only 14 % had no child below the age of 18; 40 % had one or two children, and 46 % had between three and six children. Most of them (82 %) provided financial help to relatives. Of the spouses, 132 returned usable questionnaires.

Data Analysis

The data were analyzed using the Statistical Package for Social Science (SPSS) software. This involved calculation of frequency scores and statistical tests of significance, namely Pearson correlation coefficient and paired-sample *t*-tests.

Research Findings

Nuclear and Extended Family Obligations

Respondents were asked about the number of their children below the age of 18. Responses therefore do not reveal specifically the size of the family but only the number and presence of small or adolescent children. Responses show that 40 % of the sample had three to six children below the age of 18. Another 46 % had one or two children in the specified age range, and 14 %—including married and single employees—had no children younger than 18. Nuclear family size seemed therefore moderate, considering the fertility rate (2010 estimate) of 5.6 children per woman in Nigeria (World Bank 2012). Apart from the expense and work involved in maintaining and educating their own children, Nigerians—like other Africans—have responsibilities toward the extended family. In the sample surveyed, 42 % had one or two relatives living with them and 12 % had three to seven relatives. The presence of relatives in a Nigerian home cannot, however, be evaluated merely as a financial load. It is also an important family resource as everyone is expected to help in the running of the household and less privileged relatives from the village are often brought to the city to serve as domestic assistants at the same time as they go to school or receive some vocational training. This is an instance of a mutual benefit between extended family members.

The fact that 46 % of respondents had no relative living with them does not mean that the extended family made no claim. Of all respondents, 41 % was financially helping one to four relatives, 35 % was helping five to nine relatives, and 6 % was helping 10–15 relatives. Only 18 % was not helping anyone financially; yet, this percentage seemed very high to a large group of Nigerian managers with whom these results were shared—it was believed that in reality it should be a much smaller proportion that would be free from financial obligations toward the extended family.

Hours Worked Per Week

The number of hours worked in a typical week ranged from 30 to 91 h, with a mean of 53.5 h. Only 14 % of respondents never or seldom worked more than the official hours. More than two-third of them (69 %) worked excessively long hours (i.e., more than 48 h per week). Of these, 44 % worked in the banking/finance/insurance sector, 10 % in manufacturing and the rest in a wide range of sectors such as telecommunications, shipping, education, services, information technology, and others.

Reasons for Working Long Hours

Respondents were asked to give, in order of priority, three reasons for working long hours. Of those who usually work 49 h or more per week (i.e., 107 respondents), 27 (25 %) stated they do so because they enjoy their job—though this is the *main* reason for only 4 of them (5 %). A larger number—46 (43 %) say they do it by choice. For most of them, however, this simply means that they are not compelled but freely decide to do it in view of the same circumstances that make many of their colleagues feel obliged to work long hours. What are those circumstances? For the majority, the volume of work is the main culprit (65 %), coupled with the necessity to meet tight deadlines (60 %). For 25 % of respondents, it is only after normal work hours that one has time to think. For many, long hours are also perceived as part of the organizational culture (21 %). While only 13 % feel pressurized by management, another 10 % think that working long hours is necessary to get ahead in their career and 4 % do it for fear of losing their job.

Impact of Commuting Time and Long Working Hours on Health and Wellbeing

Commuting time ranged from a few minutes to 6 h. Nearly, half of the respondents—63 (47 %)—spent 3–6 h in the traffic on a typical day, and only nine (7 %) spent less than an hour. As many as 35 % of respondents stated that their journey to and from work greatly added to the stress of their day, and another 42 % considered it added only slightly to the stress, while 23 % estimated it had no impact, or it even reduced their stress. Stress was defined as the difficulty to cope with work demands that endangered the person's health as a result. Only 4 % of respondents working *excessive* hours never or rarely experienced such difficulty. Another 74 % experienced it sometimes, 21 % almost all the time and 1 % all the time.

More than two-thirds (68 %) of respondents working excessive hours had suffered in the previous 12 months from ill health which they felt was related to stress at work. This entailed: fatigue (52 %), migraines (37 %), series of persistent minor ailments (31 %), irritability with colleagues, family, and/or friends (25 %), sleeplessness (20 %), anxiety attacks (19 %), lack of concentration (17 %), loss of appetite (12 %), and depression (12 %). Over 62 % had experienced from three to nine such problems in the previous 12 months. They were twice more likely to suffer from anxiety attacks and lack of concentration than those working more moderate hours, and 30 % more likely to suffer from fatigue, irritability, and persistent minor ailments.

Work-to-Family Conflict

Of all those working more than 48 h a week, 38 % had a high score in all four measures of time-based work–family conflict but only 9 % in the case of stress-based work-to-family conflict. The proportion rises to 59 and 37 %, respectively, when considering also those whose scores were high on at least three of the measures. Business leaders may shrug their shoulders when they are told that 80 % of respondents working excessive hours wish they had more time for their family and 77 % feel they do not have enough time for themselves: after all, they cannot expect to make a good living while spending lots of time at home. We get, however, a glimpse of an objective problem when we find out that, for as many as 48 %, their time off work does not match well with other family members' schedules. The fact that 74 % of them habitually feel physically drained and 43 % emotionally drained when they get home from work is worth noting because it is doubtful that they are able to recover overnight and return to work refreshed on the following day; surely fatigue, irritability, anxiety, and lack of concentration will have a negative impact on performance.

It is interesting to note that the *t*-tests revealed substantial agreement between spouses in their assessment of the employee's time-based work–family conflict. There was also substantial agreement as to whether the employee was physically or emotionally drained when returning from work, which validates employees' self-report assessments. On other points, the difference between spouses' perceptions was statistically significant. Employees generally saw themselves as less irritable and better able to participate in and enjoy family life than their respective spouses perceived them to be ($p < 0.02$), and had a more favorable estimation of the patience they manifested with their children ($p < 0.001$). Spouses also felt more strongly that the employee should perhaps work less and spend more time with the children ($p < 0.001$).

Supervisor Support

Fortunately, the vast majority of supervisors/managers (93 %) showed a level of sympathy when someone needed time off or wished to reschedule work around family and caring responsibilities.

Organizational Culture

Perceptions of organizational culture are positive in the majority of cases. It is encouraging to see that one-third of those working excessively long hours still perceive that their organization offers them some flexibility as a strategic way of doing business. Less than 25 % consider that they are, however, given ample opportunity to perform both their job and their personal responsibilities well.

Turnover Intentions

Of all respondents, 28 % have been seriously considering moving to a less stressful job, and 18 % have been on the lookout for a better job during the past 6 months.

Where Does Help Come From?

Of all respondents, only 29 % felt habitually in control of their life. Others feel out of control sometimes (29 %), often (38 %) or even most of the time (4 %). Do they seek help? Of those who felt out of control over their life at least sometimes, 51 % seek help from outside, mostly from their doctor, with a small minority turning to spouse, family, or spiritual advisors for support, and this help is generally considered effective. A few respondents (9 %) have looked for help within the organization, mostly from their line manager, or some other senior manager rather than from the human resources (HR) department, and this help is considered effective in a small majority of cases. The rest (40 %) do not seek help but simply try to draw on their own internal resources.

Impact of Work–Family Conflict on Turnover Intentions

Among those working more than 50 h per week, time-based, and stress-based work–family conflict are highly and significantly correlated to the feeling of loss of control over one's life ($r = 0.546$ and 0.646 respectively, $p < 0.001$), which is in turn significantly correlated to turnover intentions ($r = 0.491$, $p < 0.001$). These correlations are just as statistically significant, but lower in intensity, in the total sample, indicating that excessively long work hours trigger an escalation of the problem of work–family conflict and loss of control over one's life, inclining the employee to look for a better job.

Implications

The percentage of people working excessively long hours sends a danger signal. It is particularly important to recognize that an employee's productivity is likely to be affected by the law of diminishing returns toward the end of the official 8 h work per day. Add to this the time spent commuting daily in the Lagos traffic, and it becomes clear that the employees in our sample have little opportunity to recover from their work stress from 1 day to the next. Their personal and family life suffers, which further increases stress.

When considering employees' reasons for working long hours it is evident that the majority of respondents in our survey work long hours because of the volume of work and tight deadlines. Among other things this calls for strategies to address the perceived HR constraints in many companies and to enhance employees' ability to complete regular assignments during normal working hours and within set deadlines. While working overtime or taking on more work can, at times, be necessary and/or unavoidable, the problem arises when it becomes a permanent feature of a job or is perceived as part of the organizational culture. Essentially, long hours on the job are not a sign of high productivity and, indeed, organisations would do well to implement the well-known (but poorly applied) saying *"work smarter, not harder."* For example, intense work for 7 h a day would be more productive than moderate work for 5 h followed by sluggish work during the next 4, 5 or 6 h. A possible solution to the need to reduce commuting time would be the adoption of staggered working hours—a system implemented by only a very small number of organizations in Lagos. Commuting time tends to be very long, not so much because of distances as because of bottlenecks blocking traffic in the mornings and the evenings. With a critical mass of organizations implementing staggered work hours, roads would be less congested as traffic would be more evenly spread out throughout the morning hours, then again throughout the afternoon and evening hours. This system can, however, only work if the official number of hours per day is respected. Otherwise why should an employee agree to start work earlier—say, at 6.30 a.m.—if he or she will still be expected to remain late in the office?

Implications for Business Leaders

Can appropriate support be given to employees? It is noteworthy that less than one-third of respondents feel in control of their life, and that, out of the two-thirds who experience loss of control sometimes or often, only 9 % seek help from their organization, approaching their line manager or some other senior manager rather than the HR department. The HR function does not seem to be perceived as a defender of employee welfare but mostly as a representative of top management. It is therefore important for business leaders to take steps to make their HR managers know that they are expected to combine and reconcile both perspectives.

The high level of work–family conflict is a danger signal to organizational leaders, not only because of its direct negative impact on productivity, but also because of its relationship with turnover intentions. The survey indicates that excessive work hours escalate the problem of work–family conflict and loss of control over one's life, inclining the employee to look for a better job. It is noteworthy that replacing a good employee can be an expensive exercise considering recruitment and induction costs as well as learning curve characteristics. Even if the person does not actually leave the job, the desire for change and the search for better conditions entail considerable expenditure in terms of time and even materials, as employees browse the net for job offers, prepare their CVs and print them on office stationery—all during working hours—thus getting distracted from their assigned tasks. It is also well-documented, as revealed by the literature review section, that excessively long hours lead to lower productivity, more injuries, more errors, and higher levels of ill health. Thus, any attempt to boost productivity without the expense of higher technology and to lower employee-related costs needs to address the issue of work–family conflict if it is to be successful and sustainable. Unfortunately, business leaders are often impervious to this type of reasoning, and appropriate legislation would be helpful if substantial change is to take place.

Implications for Public Policy

As seen from the reviewed literature, individuals who effectively manage multiple roles are often effective at work, contribute to their firm's profitability and achieve satisfaction and fulfillment in personal life, which facilitates the sustained economic and social development of a nation. Thus, given the potential negative consequences of work–family conflict for individuals and firms, it can be argued that there is need for more proactive government intervention in ensuring a worker-friendly environment and the enactment of family-responsible policies that will help employees reduce and better manage their work and non-work role conflicts.

Socially responsible town planning should be high among the Nigerian government's concerns. There should be various residential areas within the reach of all purses around the main business districts of cities, in order to reduce distances between employees' work place and their home. Appropriate infrastructure, road maintenance, and public transport services should be provided to reduce excessively long commuting time.

The ability of parents to get personally engaged in their children's upbringing to form them as responsible and honest citizens who will constitute the next generation of active workforce should also be among the top concerns of governments. Essentially, the enhancement of the educational role of the family is, in the long term, more effective than a strong police force in ensuring peace and respect for the law throughout the country. Legislation is thus needed to protect employees at all levels from excessively long work hours. While one cannot guarantee that employees will effectively spend their new-found spare time with their family, at least one can ensure that they are all given the opportunity to do so. The encouragement of self-employment is another avenue that can be used to assist workers' integration of economic activities with family responsibilities.

Conclusion

This chapter reported the results of an empirical quantitative study on long work hours and work–family conflict in Lagos, the commercial capital of Nigeria. It is clear that a considerable percentage of employees in the Lagos metropolis spend a disproportionate amount of their time and energy in commuting to and from work, and in the work place. It is also clear that many experience disruptive levels of stress while few seek help from their organization. The reasons given for working long hours suggest problems related to the management style and the culture of organizations. Stress-related problems, work–family conflict, a feeling of loss of control over one's life, and a desire to leave the organization were all associated with excessively long work hours. Recommendations were made to business organizations, such as the introduction of staggered work hours, reasonable deadlines, and the recruitment of a sufficient number of people to habitually do the job within normal work hours, an effort to eliminate the long hour syndrome which forms part of the organizational culture in many places, together with effective time management training throughout the organization. An appeal is made to organizational leaders to provide the necessary support to their staff so that their organization may benefit from higher performance by distress–free employees. The chapter highlighted implications for public policy, such as appropriate legislation and town planning to ensure a more worker-friendly environment and protection of the family institution. Overall, we believe our study contributes to the development of a better understanding of the work–family and work–life issues that confront individuals in the Nigerian context, and possibly also in other major cities of the African continent.

References

Aguilera, R. V., & Jackson, G. (2003). The cross-national diversity of corporate governance: Dimensions and determinants. *Academy of Management Review, 28*(3), 447–465.

Allen, T. D. (2001). Family-supportive work environments: The role of organizational perceptions. *Journal of Vocational Behavior, 58*, 414–435.

Amah, O. E. (2010). Family-work conflict and the availability of work-family friendly policy relationship in married employees: The moderating role of work centrality and career consequence. *Research and Practice in Human Resource Management, 18*(2), 35–46.

Anderson, S. E., Coffey, B. S., & Byerly, R. T. (2002). Formal organizational initiatives and informal workplace practices: Links to work-family conflict and job-related outcomes. *Journal of Management, 28*, 787–810.

Burke, R. J. (2006). Work hours and work addiction. In R. J. Burke (Ed.), *Research companion to working time and work addition* (pp. 3–35). Cheltenham, UK: Edward Elgar.

Carlson, D. S., Kacmar, K. M., & Williams, L. J. (2000). Construction and initial validation of a multidimensional measure of work–family conflict. *Journal of Vocational Behavior, 56*, 249–276.

Central Intelligence Agency (CIA). (2012). *The World Factbook.* Retrived August 18, 2012, from https://www.cia.gov/library/publications/the-world-factbook/geos/ni.html.

Clark, S. C. (2001). Work cultures and work/family balance. *Journal of Vocational Behavior, 58*, 348–365.

Cooper, C. L. (1998). The 1998 crystal lecture: The future of work—A strategy for managing the pressures. *Journal of Applied Management Studies, 7*(2), 272–282.

De Klerk, M., & Mostert, K. (2010). Work-home interference: Examining socio-demographic predictors in the South African context. *South African Journal of Human Resource Management, 8*(1), 1–10.

Epie, C. (2007). *Company performance and employees' family time—Two case studies from Nigeria.* Paper presented at the IERA 15th Annual Conference on Working Lives, Working Choices, co-hosted by the International Employment Relations Association and Christ Church University, Canterbury

Epie, C. (2009a). Managing time-based conflict across life domains in Nigeria—A decision-making perspective. *Ife PsychologIA, 17*(1), 194–216.

Epie, C. (2009b). *Strategies for work-family balance and preferences for work-family policies in the Lagos metropolis.* Paper presented at the 3rd Colloquium of the Network of African Family Scholars, Nairobi.

Epie, C. (2010). Benefits of family-responsible management in Nigeria—A comparison of two breweries. *Gender and Behaviour, 8*(1), 2649–2665.

Epie, C. (2011). *The business case for family-responsible management—How an organizational culture favourable to work-family integration benefits employers and employees.* Doctoral thesis. Saarbrücken: Lambert Academic Publishing.

Evbuoma, I. K. (2007). Influence of women and family-friendly support services on women's work performance in organizations. *Gender and Behaviour, 5*(1), 1109–1128.

Fredriksen-Goldsen, K. I., & Scharlach, A. E. (2001). *Families and work—New directions in the twenty-first century.* New York: Oxford University Press.

Frone, M. R., Russell, M., & Cooper, M. L. (1992). Antecedents and outcomes of work-family conflict: Testing a model of the work-family interface. *Journal of Applied Psychology, 77*, 65–78.

Gannon, M. (2004). *Understanding global cultures—Metaphorical journeys through 28 nations, clusters of nations, and continents.* Thousand Oaks: Sage Publications.

Greenhaus, J. H., & Beutell, N. J. (1985). Sources of conflict between work and family roles. *Academy of Management Review, 10*, 76–88.

Grzywacz, J. G., Quandt, S. A., Arcury, T. A., & Marin, A. (2005). The work-family challenge and mental health. *Community, Work and Family, 8*, 271–279.

Guest, D. E. (2001). Human resource management: When research confronts theory. *International Journal of Human Resource Management, 12*, 1092–1106.

Harrington, B., & Ladge, J. J. (2009). Work-life integration: Present dynamics and future directions for organizations. *Organizational Dynamics, 38*, 148–157.

Houston, D. M. (Ed.). (2005). *Work-life balance in the 21st century.* Basingstoke: Palgrave MacMillan.

Jyothi, V. S., & Jyothi, P. (2012). Assessing work-life balance: From emotional intelligence and role efficacy of career women. *Advances in Management, 5*(6), 35–43.

Kelly, E. L., Kossek, E. E., Hammer, L. B., Durham, M., Bray, J., Chermack, K., et al. (2008). Getting there from here: Research on the effects of work-family initiatives on work-family conflict and business outcomes. *Academy of Management Annals, 2*, 305–349.

Lee, Eun-Suk, Chang, Jae Yoon, & Kim, Hyosun. (2011). The work-family interface in Korea: Can family life enrich work life? *International Journal of Human Resource Management, 22*(9), 2032–2053.

Lu, L., Cooper, C. L., Kao, S.-F., Chang, T–. T., Allen, T. D., Lapierre, L. M., et al. (2010). Cross-cultural differences on work-to-family conflict and role satisfaction: A Taiwanese-British comparison. *Human Resource Management, 49*(1), 67–85.

Messenger, J. C. (2006). 'Decent working time': Balancing the needs of workers and employers. In R. J. Burke's (Ed.) *research companion to working time and word addiction* (pp. 221–241). Cheltenham, UK: Edward Elgar.

National Bureau of Statistics (2012). *2011 Annual Socio-Economic Report—Unemployment*. Retrieved August 18, 2012 from www.nigerianstat.gov.ng.

Nigerian Labour Act. (1974). Retrieved September 23, 2002, from http://www.nigeria-law.org/LabourAct.htm.

Omololu, F. O. (1997). *Socio-cultural factors affecting occupational health in Nigeria. In Death by instalment: Occupational health and hazards in Nigeria*. Lagos: Friedrich Ebert Foundation.

Ovadje, F. O. (1996). *Employee organizational commitment: Its relationship with communication satisfaction and performance*. Barcelona: Doctoral thesis, IESE.

Ovadje, F. O., & Ankomah, A. (2001). Human resource management in Nigeria. In P. S. Budhwar & Y. A. Debrah (Eds.), *Human resource management in developing countries* (pp. 174–189). New York: Routledge.

Poelmans, S. (Ed.). (2005). *Work and family—An international research perspective*. London: Lawrence Erlbaum Associates.

Poelmans, S., & Sahibzada, K. (2004). A multi-level model for studying the context and impact of work-family policies and culture in organizations. *Human Resource Management Review, 14*, 409–431.

Poelmans, S. A. Y., Chinchilla, N., & Cardona, P. (2003). The adoption of family-friendly HRM policies—Competing for scarce resources in the labour market. *International Journal of Manpower, 24*, 128–147.

Ransome, S. (2007). Conceptualization boundaries between 'Ife' and 'work'. *International Human Resource Management Journal, 18*(3), 374–386.

Scott, W. R. (2008). *Approaching adulthood: The maturing of institutional theory*. Dordrecht: Springer Science Business Media B.V.

Shepard, E., & Clifton, T. (2000). Are longer hours reducing productivity in manufacturing? *International Journal of Manpower, 21*(7), 540–553.

Sparks, K., Cooper, C., Fried, Y., & Shirom, A. (1997). The effects of hours of work on health: A meta-analytic review. *Journal of Occupational and Organizational Psychology, 70*, 391–409.

Spector, P. E., Cooper, C. L., Poelmans, S., Allen, T. D., O'Driscoll, M., Sanchez, J. I., Oi Ling Siu, Dewe, P., Hart, P., Luo Lu, De Moraes, L.F.R., Ostrognay, G. M., Sparks, K., Wong, P., & Yu, S. (2004). A cross-national comparative study of work-family stressors, working hours, and well-being: China and Latin America versus the Anglo world. *Personnel Psychology*, 57 (1) 119-142.

Stey, B., & Koekemer, E. (2011). Conflict between work and nonwork roles of employees in the mining industry: Prevalence and differences between demographic groups. *South African Journal of Human Resource Management, 9*(1), 85–98.

Ten Brummelhuis, L. L., & van der Lippe, T. (2010). Effective work-life balance support for various household structures. *Human Resource Management, 49*(2), 173–193.

Thompson, C., Beauvais, L., & Lyness, K. (1999). When work-family benefits are not enough: The influence of work-family culture on benefit utilization, organizational attachment and work-family conflict. *Journal of Vocational Behavior, 54*, 392–415.

World Bank. (2012). Social Development Indicators. Retrived September 2, 2012, from http://data.worldbank.org/indicator/.

Chapter 5
Strain-Based Family Interference with Work: A Theoretical-Empirical Analysis from South-Eastern Nigeria

Ejike Okonkwo

Introduction

Recent decades have witnessed an increasing entry of women into the labour market, a trend that has stimulated much research on work–family interface (Grzywacz and Marks 2000) as women have, in many societies, traditionally being responsible for the management of their households and families. The Nigerian labour market has also followed the trend: in addition to being mothers and wives who are primarily responsible for family responsibilities, a growing number of Nigerian women are engaged in paid employment and other economic activities. In both rural and urban areas, women in the country are known to be the pillars of subsistence agriculture, trading, and cottage industries (Ekwe 1996). They are also increasingly engaged in policy making and management at various levels of the society and in several major sectors which were hitherto seen as male preserves. For instance, women have been able to distinguish themselves in ministerial positions at the Federal level, in major national corporations such as the Nigerian Stock Exchange, the National Agency for Food Drugs Administration and Control, the National Insurance Corporation of Nigeria, and in several banks and companies (Okiy 2002). Overall Nigerian women are found in different professions although the greater percentage is in human services professions such as teaching, nursing, clerical work and banking which are characterised by high levels of interpersonal involvement and exposure to emotionally demanding situations.

Despite this trend in the Nigerian labour market, the division of labour at home still falls along traditional lines where women are primarily responsible for overseeing household duties. In other words, women, irrespective of their involvement in paid work, are significantly more likely than men to bear primary responsibilities of home care and childcare (Lero 1992). In a bid to balance these

E. Okonkwo (✉)
Psychology, Enugu State University of Science and Technology,
Agbani, 400001 Enugu, Nigeria
e-mail: aejyke@yahoo.com

Z. Mokomane (ed.), *Work–Family Interface in Sub-Saharan Africa*,
International Perspectives on Social Policy, Administration, and Practice,
DOI: 10.1007/978-3-319-01237-7_5,

multiple roles many working women in Nigeria are caught between the cross-role demands of family responsibilities and work behaviour expectations (Ajaja 2004), which many a time precipitate work interference with family, and family interference with work. The interferences between work and family often result in work–family conflict which occurs when the employees extend their efforts to satisfy their work demands at the expense of their family demands or vice versa (Cole 2004).

With a focus on the experiences of female teachers in Enugu in the South-eastern Nigeria, this chapter explores the extent to which the number and age of children make it difficult to meet work responsibilities (Okonkwo 2011). As noted by Adebola (2005), family interference with work is primarily determined by family demands and predicts negative work outcomes. Thus, because of the traditional gender roles that place higher priority on domestic obligation for women, factors associated with family life are likely to exert greater influence on women's attitudes and behaviours (Voyandoff 1988). The number of children and ages of children are some of the key factors that influence the level of family demands (Rothausen 1999). In essence, given that childcare responsibilities normally rest on women, working mothers with relatively more or younger children are likely to experience greater family interference with work than their counterparts with no, fewer, or older children (Voyandoff 1988).

The interest of the chapter is particularly on strain-based family interference with work, a situation in which strain symptoms such as stress, pressure, tension, anxiety and fatigue, experienced within the family role intrudes into the work role and affects one's performance in that role (Okonkwo 2011). Being a developing society, Nigeria has been characterised by a marked sex division of labour both inside and outside the family (Adekola 2006) where, as already stated, roles such as childcare and other domestic responsibilities remain the primary responsibilities of women irrespective of their participation in paid employment. Considering this traditional sex-role obligation, role strain may occur more frequently among working women as a result of dual commitments to employment and to the family (Adekola 2010). However, in spite of these challenges, employers and the government in Nigeria do not have any explicit work–family policies which would support these working women. The chapter is also important in view of the paucity of research conducted in the area of strain-based work–family conflict in Nigerian and in sub-Saharan Africa as a whole.

Theoretical Review

There are a number of theories that can be applied to understand the relationship between the number and age of children, and strain-based family interference with work. These include the role strain theory, spill-over theory, the role identity theory, the ecological theory and the conservation of resources theory.

Role Strain Theory

This theory postulates that responsibilities from work and family domains compete for limited amount of time, physical energy and psychological resources (Greenhaus and Beutell 1985; Small and Riley 1990), leading to role strain which often results in negative consequences in both the workplace and family (Williams and Alliger 1994).

Considering this theory in relation to working mothers it can be argued that those with young and/or relatively more dependent children are likely to face a situation where childcare competes for limited amounts of time, physical energy and psychological resources with work responsibilities. The strain experienced as a result of childcare responsibilities might spill-over into work responsibilities causing strain-based family interference with work among working mothers with young and many dependent children. It can thus be concluded that it would be less stressful to care for fewer number of or older independent children.

Role Enhancement Theory

According to the role enhancement theory, participation in multiple roles provides a greater number of opportunities and resources that can be used to promote growth and better functioning in other life domains (Rozario et al. 2004). The theory thus suggests that whereas having young dependent children is likely to drain the resources of a working mother, the presence of older independent children who have the ability to take care of themselves and help the mother with her domestic chores will likely provide her with additional resources. If properly managed these additional resources could spill over positively into the mother's life by, for example, assisting her to recover from stressful working days (Repetti 1989), to better handle the pressure associated with her multiple roles at work and home and to, overall, perform better in both domains (Barnett 1996; Gattiker and Larwood 1990; Weiss 1990).

Spill-Over Theory

According to this theory, positive spill-over (work–family enhancement) refers to situations in which the satisfaction, energy and sense of accomplishment derived from one domain transfers to another (Frone 1992). Negative spill-over (work–family conflict), on the other hand, occurs when problems are carried over from one domain to another. An example is when increased dissatisfaction in the work domain leads to increased dissatisfaction in the family domain (Zedeck and Mosier 1990).

Overall this theory is of the view that work and family domains can either benefit or hamper each other. In line with the theory, the number and age of children can lead to either negative or positive spill-over. For example, if a working mother has large number of young dependent children, she might be forced to spend more time and energy at home and the strain associated with this will spill over into work thereby interfering with work responsibilities (negative spill-over). Conversely, if the mother has older independent children, they can take care of themselves as well as assist her in family responsibilities and other domestic chores. Thus, she will spend less time and energy on family responsibilities and more on work responsibilities. This invariably could lead to work–family enhancement (positive spill-over).

Role Identity Theory

Each role a person assumes (for example, mother, wife, care giver, employee, etc.) has its accompanying socially based behavioural expectations and identity. To this end the role identity theory postulates that when a person assumes any social role, he or she internalises the socially constructed behavioural expectations associated with that status as part of their role identity (Stryker 1980). The internalisation of these expectations and identity is the basis for the person's self. The theory hypothesises that the more competently and easily a person is able to fulfil all the internalised normative behavioural expectations coming from her or his social roles, the more likely the person will be to exhibit high self-esteem and psychological well-being (Stryker 1980).

Considering this view in relation to working mothers, their roles as wives, mothers and employees provide them with internalised socially constructed behavioural expectations which have the potential for introducing conflicting behavioural expectations leading to role conflict and strain. For example, if a mother's role expectation is that she has to be available to take her young-dependent sick child to hospital on a Monday morning and at the same time her employee (work) role expectation is to be available for a crucial office staff meeting, family responsibility (taking sick child to hospital) is likely to interfere with work responsibility (office meeting). As a result of such work–family role conflict, which can sometimes become chronic, the role identity theory would predict role pressure which could lead to role strain.

Ecological Theory

This theory postulates that work–family experience is a joint function of process, person, context and time characteristics (Bronfrebrener and Morris 1998). As a process, the theory suggests that each type of characteristic exerts an additive, potentially interactive effect on the work–family experience (Barnett 1996). This means that as a process, the other three characteristics (person, context and time) interact and additionally precipitate work–family conflict. The impact of gender as a specific person characteristic is a particularly important factor for understanding this interactive process and family interference with work. To this end, guided by traditional gender role socialisation, Pleck (1977) hypothesised that family factors (context) would spill over into work (context) more for women (gender) than men (gender). Thus, family responsibilities are more likely to make participation in work activities relatively more difficult for women than for men. This, if uncontrolled, can lead to chronic role strain resulting in strain-based family interference with work among women. In view of this, Nigerian women who are engaged in paid employment because of the importance they attach to family roles as a result of gender-role socialisation are more likely than men to experience family role strain interfering with their work responsibilities.

Family time component, often operationalised as the age of an individual's oldest child, has also been found to be associated with work–family conflict (Voyandoff 1988). This means that if a working mother has older independent children, they will be able to take care of themselves and other family responsibilities. This will give the working mother less pressure and enough time to take care of her job responsibilities. By contrast, if a working mother has young-dependent children, she is likely to spend more time at home giving care to them. This will not give her much time to take care of her job responsibilities. Consequently, role strain emanating from the family will likely interfere with work responsibilities.

Conservation of Resources Theory

This theory holds that individuals experience stress whenever they are threatened with resource loss or when their resources are actually depleted and, therefore, potentially inadequate to resolve any impending demands (Hobfoll 1998). According to Hobfoll, when resources are actually depleted the individual experiences *actual stress*; when resources are threatened they experience *anticipatory stress* (Hobfoll 1989).

In view of this theory, a working mother with older independent children could be likened to an individual with a greater pool of resources. That is, because the children are independent and capable of taking care of themselves, they give the mother less pressure and more time since she spends less time and energy taking care of them. To this end, she is less vulnerable to resource loss or depletion, and more capable of resource gain. This gain translates into more time and energy being given to work responsibilities, hence she can spend more time on her job and become more committed. Invariably, this will enhance her job performance, improve opportunities for promotion and growth on the job (more resource gain), and reduce both actual and anticipatory stress.

In contrast, a working mother with large number of young-dependent children is likely to spend more time at home and will lack enough resources (time and energy) to be spent on her work responsibilities. Thus, effort to share the weak resource pool between family and work responsibilities results in a continuous draw on resources, leaving her with depleted resources to combat the chronic strain situation. As this condition continues repeatedly, meeting family responsibilities exhausts the available resources thereby making it difficult for her to meet work responsibilities resulting in strain-based family interference with work, and experiences of both actual and anticipatory stress.

Methods

Sample

The study on which this chapter is based was conducted in 2010 among 304 female secondary school teachers drawn from 24 state government secondary schools within Enugu, the capital city of Enugu State in the South-eastern part of Nigeria. All the participants were qualified with 24 % holding a National Certificate of Education, 53 % had Bachelor's degree in Education and 10 % had Postgraduate diploma in Education and 13 % with a Master's degree in Education.

Criterion sampling, which involves selecting, cases (participants) that meet some predetermined criteria of importance (Patton 1990), was used to select the sample. Following the criteria set for the sample selection, the female teachers selected for the study were aged between 26 and 54 years, had spent at least a year as teachers in the schools, were married and living with their husbands, had at least one child and were living with at least one of their children. Widows and divorcees were not included. The principals of the selected schools facilitated the sample selection by examining the files of their teachers in order to identify those who met the set criteria.

A total of 177 (58.2 %) of the participants had children aged between 1 and 11 years, 87 (28.7) had children aged 12–17 years and 40 (13.2 %) had children aged 18 years and above. In addition, 198 (65.1 %) of the participants had at least one person assisting them with domestic chores while the remaining 106 (34.9 %) had no domestic help.

Data Collection Instrument

Data was collected through a self-administered questionnaire that had two components. The first was designed to collect the teachers' demographic information such as their age, educational qualification, rank, years of experience as a teacher, marital status, as well as the number and ages of their children. The second component, on the other hand, was designed to collect the teachers' experience of strain-based family interference with work using a scale designed to strain from family responsibilities interfering with work responsibilities (Okonkwo 2011). The scale had the following four items:

i. I worry much about my children that I find it difficult concentrating on my job.
ii. The pressure of family responsibilities makes me fail in my duties in the office that my boss (principal) complains.
iii. Worrying about financial problems at home makes me lose concentration in the office.
iv. The stress I experience at home hosting/attending to events like birthday/marriage/burial ceremonies stops me from giving proper attention to my students.

The four-item scale was in Likert form and had direct scoring for all the items. A response of 'Strongly Agree' attracted a score of 5 points; 'Agree' attracted 4 points; 'Undecided' attracted 3 points; 'Disagree' attracted 2 points; and 'Strongly Disagree' attracted 1 point. Scores below the mean (10.73) indicated low level of strain-based family interference with work while scores above the mean (10.73) indicated high level of strain-based family interference with work.

In all the 24 schools, the principals distributed the questionnaire to the identified teachers who met the study criteria and had volunteered to participate. Each participant was instructed to take a copy of the questionnaire home, study it carefully, complete and return it to her principal within one week. The researcher then collected the copies of the questionnaire from each principal. Of the 356 copies of the questionnaire distributed, 304 (85.4 %) copies were properly completed and returned, 43 were returned but were not properly completed and 9 were not returned at all. Therefore, the 304 copies properly completed and returned were used for the present analyses.

Data Analysis

The 2 × 2 Analysis of Variance F-test for unequal sample was used as statistical test for data analysis. Analysis of Variance (ANOVA) is a multivariate statistical technique used compare the means of three or more groups or variables in a population differ (Altman and Bland 1996). A 2 × 2 or two way analysis is one in which there are two factors or independent variables (in this case number of children and age of children). An ANOVA, F-test, on the other hand determines if the variation between the means is significant (Lee and Kuchroo n.d.).

Results

The overall finding from the study, using the four-item scale described above, was that the number and ages of children did not influence the experience of strain-based family interference with work among the teachers studied. The means in Table 5.1 for example show that teachers who had few number of children in the 1–11 years age bracket experienced the highest level of strain-based family interference with work (x = 11.69), while teachers that had few number with the children aged 12–17 years had the least experience of strain-based family interference with work (x = 10.03). All in all, teachers that had few number of children experienced higher level of strain-based family interference with work (x = 11.23) than teachers that had large number of children (x = 11.13). However these mean scores were found not to be significantly different.

By the same token, Table 5.2 shows that age of the teachers' children had no significant influence on the teachers' experience of strain-based family interference with work, $F\ (2{,}303) = 0.59$, $p > .05$. The number of children the teachers had, also did not have any significant influence on their experience of strain-based family interference with work $F\ (1{,}303) = 0.05$, $p > .05$. No significant interaction influence of age of the children and number on their experience of strain-based family interference with work, $F\ (2{,}303) = 1.30$, $p > .05$.

Number of Children

While the findings are contrary to previous research findings (e.g. Noor 1995; Eagle 1996; Ngo and Lau 1998), they support the positive spill-over hypothesis which postulates that satisfaction, energy and sense of accomplishment derived from one domain transfers to another (Frone 1992).

Table 5.1 Table of Means on number-age of children and strain-based family interference with work

Age	Number of Children	Mean	Std. deviation	N
1-11 years	Large number	11.0000	4.30946	36
	Few number	11.6950	4.73881	141
	Total	1.5537	4.65133	177
12-17 years	Large number	11.3226	4.05288	31
	Few number	10.0357	3.43757	56
	Total	10.4943	3.69750	87
18 years	Large number	11.0909	3.55781	22
	Few number	11.2778	3.21404	18
	Total	11.1750	3.36564	40

Note Dependent variable: strain-based family interference with work
Large number: (5 and above)
Small number: (4 and below)

Table 5.2 2×2 ANOVA table on number-age of children and strain-based family interference with work

Source	Type III sum of square	Df	Mean square	F	Sig	Partial Eta squared
Corrected model	112.571	5	22.548	1.249	.286	0.021
Intercept	23720.410	1	23720.410	1.314E5	0.000	0.815
Age	21.432	2	10.716	0.594	.553	0.004
Number of children	0.882	1	0.882	0.049	.825	0.000
Age family and number of children	46.984	2	23.492	1.302	0.274	0.009
Error	5378.019	298	18.047	–	–	–
Total	43629.00	304	–	–	–	–
Corrected total	5490.760	303	–	–	–	–

Despite being an oil producing country, Nigeria is one of the poorest nations in the world, ranking 178th out of 228 countries in Gross Domestic Product per capita because of ravages caused by bribery and corruption (Central Intelligence Agency 2010). Moreover, illiteracy and unemployment levels are very high. These together with the high levels of poverty, make domestic workers, (commonly known as house helps) readily available at a very affordable rate. The house helps are usually hired on permanent basis to take care of non-job responsibilities thereby giving working Nigerian mothers enough time to focus on work responsibilities by reducing the pressure and stress associated with the presence large number dependent children. This research evidence thus supports a tenet of the conservation of resources theory which holds that individuals must invest resources in order to limit loss of resources, protect resources or gain resources (Hobfoll 1998). By, hiring house helps on permanent basis to take care of domestic challenges enables these women to invest more time and energy in their teaching responsibilities, hence protecting their resources (time and energy) and gaining more resources in the workplace (efficiency, effectiveness and productivity).

Age of Children

Based on previous research findings (for example, Beutell and Greenhaus 1980) it was expected that those women with young dependent children would have experienced higher level of strain-based family interference with work because they ought to shoulder more family responsibilities coming from these young-dependent children. However, the results showed no significant difference in the experience of strain-based family interference with work of mothers who have young-dependent and those with older independent children.

The inconsistency between these present results and those that emerged from previous research can be partly accounted for by the kind of family system practiced in the South-eastern part of Nigeria. That is, while the family structure in

Nigeria, as in other parts of sub-Saharan Africa is definitely changing (Bigombe and Khadiagala 2003; Mokomane 2012) the South-eastern part of Nigeria is one of these areas where the extended family system is still predominant. This family system—which comprises the couple, their children, parents, siblings, in-laws, nephews, nieces, cousins and other extended family members living together—differs from the nuclear family system which is predominant in most Western countries where much of the literature linking age of children and strain-based family interference with work is located. To the extent that that social support is a highly effective intervention for coping with burnout (Pines et al. 1981). The social support and reciprocal care giving relations inherent in the extended family system means that many of the working women studied had, at least to some extent, assistance with domestic responsibilities and tasks such as childcare, cooking, washing, shopping, etc. This assistance from extended family members is likely to have cushioned family responsibilities (for example, caring for dependent young children) interfering with work responsibilities which ordinarily would have been related to elevated level of strain. To this end, it can be argued that social support does not only help women to take care of domestic chores but to also develop emotional stability which enhances their well-being.

This evidence supports another tenet of conservation of resources theory which suggests that individuals with greater resources are less vulnerable to resource loss and more capable of resource gain (Hobfoll 1998). This follows because individuals use those resources that they have to offset resource loss, to protect resources, and to gain other resources. To this end, the social support provided by the extended family system could have accounted for the greater resources which made these women less vulnerable to strain emanating from family responsibilities interfering with work responsibilities.

Summary and Recommendations

Although much of the related literature show that people who occupy multiple roles inevitably experience conflict which in turn may lead to considerable strain and stress on them, their families and their work (see for example Oomens et al. 2007), there is a segment that argues that it is the quality of roles rather than the quantity of roles that matters (see for example Barunch and Barnett 1987). The expansion hypothesis, for example, posits that participation in multiple roles can have positive effects on general health and well-being as it provides a greater number of resources—such as better financial situation, greater social integration, improved social support and higher self-esteem—that can be used to promote personal growth and better functioning in other life domains (Hãrenstam and Bejerot 2001; Geurts et al. 2005). Furthermore the availability of alternative roles may serve as a buffer against distress experienced in one role, that is the difficulties or demands in one role may be offset by the positive attributes of the other roles (Oomens et al. 2007).

In line with this latter view it is argued, based on the results of this study, that in South-eastern part of Nigeria the traditional gender-role orientation which designates domestic responsibilities the preserve of women irrespective of their participation in paid employment makes women view multiple roles as beneficial as it also provides adequate opportunities and resources which benefit both work and family, and lead to work–family enhancement. This is indeed consistent with the Okonkwo (2011) findings that many Nigerian women are happy and satisfied with combining work and family responsibilities because resources from paid employment (for example, salaries and wages) contribute immensely to the upkeep of their families by augmenting the meagre income of their husbands, especially in the context of the high levels of poverty and underemployment and unemployment in the country. The high enrolment of women in every stratum of education has also enabled Nigerian women to acquire the appropriate skills for competing with men in the world of work thereby precipitating the shift from the traditional one income family to a dual income family in contemporary society.

Against the above background, it can be concluded that the results presented in this chapter are vivid reflection of the resilience of Nigerian workers especially female teachers. Despite the general poor working conditions and remuneration, the results of this study suggest that the Nigerian workforce remain resolute in shouldering family and work responsibilities.

Therefore, in order to enhance the benefits accruing from engaging in multiple roles, social support from extended family members and contributions from house helps, the following are some of the policy recommendations that are worthy of consideration by Nigeria and other sub-Saharan African countries:

- Policies that strengthen resilience of African workers and the care giving roles of the traditional African family support system.
- Policies that can enhance and provide adequate support for personal growth and accomplishment in workers' fulfilment of work and family roles.
- Policies supported by adequate laws that protect and promote traditional African extended family system such as adequate provision of family allowance and other support by the public and private sectors to workers which will enable them to support other extended family members living with them. This is necessary because it will help the few employed to cushion the burden of supporting many dependent unemployed extended family members who provide social support to this working segment. This will reduce strain; strengthen the family tie and harmony among extended family members.
- Policies that will regulate the engagement of house helps. Such policies among other things will regulate the minimum age and educational qualification for one to become a house help in order to avoid child labour, child abuse and trafficking. Moreover, such policies supported by adequate laws will regulate the minimum salaries and other benefits to be received by house helps in order to avoid exploitation.
- Considering the immense contributions of house helps to the growth of the economy of societies, policies supported by enforced laws are necessary in order

to prevent negative and illegal use of this indispensable workforce. Such policies will strengthen workforce and also reduce human trafficking in Nigeria and sub-Saharan Africa.

- Policies that support the traditional African family practice of having large number of children should be sustained since having many children as shown in this study had no negative influence. This will contribute to the benefits derived from large population such as adequate human resources and reduced chance of African race facing extinction.

References

Adebola, H. E. (2005). Emotional expression at workplace: Implications for work-family role ambiguities. *Journal of Applied Social Psychology, 32*(21), 102–115.

Adekola, B. (2006). *Job and personal factors in work-family conflict and work burnout among University Employees in South-western Nigeria*. Unpublished Ph.D Thesis, Olabisi Onabanjo University Ago Iwoye-Nigeria.

Adekola, B. (2010). Interference between work and family among male and female executives in Nigeria. *African Journal of Business Management, 4*(6), 1069–1077.

Ajaja, A.A. (2004). *Gender factors as determinants of managerial efficiency in work organizations in Oyo State, Nigeria*. Unpublished Ph.D Thesis, University of Ibadan: Nigeria.

Douglas G Altman, D.G. & Bland, J.M. (1996). Statistics notes: Comparing several groups using analysis of variance. *BMJ, 312:1472.* doi: http://dx.doi.org/10.1136/bmj.312.7044.1472.

Barnett, R. C. (1996). *Towards a review of work/family literature: Work in progress: Boston.* MA: Wesley College Centre for Research on Woman.

Barunch, G., & Barnett, R. (1987). Social roles, gender and psychological distress. In R. Barnett, L. Biner, & G. Barunch (Eds.), *Gender and stress* (pp. 122–143). New York: Free Press.

Beutell, N. J., & Greenhaus, J. H. (1980). Some sources and consequences of conflict among married women. *Proceedings of the Annual Meeting of the Eastern Academy of Management, 17*, 2–6.

Bigombe, B., & Khadiagala, G. (2003). Major trends affecting families in sub-Saharan Africa. New York: United Nations. http://social.un.org/index/LinkClick.aspx?fileticket=3VvV_mL8oMw%3d&tabid=282 Accessed 2 May 2013.

Bronfenbrener, U., & Morris, P. A. (1998). The ecology of development processes. In W. Damon (Ed.), *Handbook of child psychology* (pp. 993–1028). New York: John Wiley & Sons.

Central Intelligence Agency (2010). *The World Fact Books*. www.eia.gov/library/publications worldfact/geos/ni.html.website. Accessed 02 Oct 2012.

Cole, D. W. (2004). Social reflection on women playing dual roles: An assessment of women in leadership positions. *Journal of Gender Studies, 7*(2), 126–132.

Eagle, B. W. (1996). Interrole conflicts and the permeability of work-family domains. Are there gender differences? *Journal of Vocational Behaviour, 50*, 168–184.

Ekwe, S.N. (1996). Women's role in agricultural production in Nigeria. In Oruwain Yomi (Ed), *Women, development and the Nigerian environment* (pp. 148-155). Ibadan: Vantage Publishers.

Frone, M. R. (1992). Antecedent and outcomes of work-family interface. *Journal of Applied Psychology, 77*(1), 65–78.

Gattiker, U. E., & Larwood, L. (1990). Predictors of career achievement in the corporate hierarchy. *Human Relations, 43*, 703–726.

Geurts, S., Kompier, M., Dikkers, J., Van Hooff, M., & Kinnunen, U. (2005). Work-home interaction from a psychological perspective: Development and validation of a new questionnaire, the SWING. *Work and Stress, 19*(4), 319–339.

Greenhaus, J. H., & Beutell, N. J. (1985). Sources of conflict between work and family roles. *Academy of Management Review, 10*, 76–88.

Grzywacz, J. G., & Marks, N. F. (2000). Family, work, work-family spill-over and problem drinking during midlife. *Journal of Marriage and Family, 62*, 336–348.

Hãrenstam, A., & Bejerot, E. (2001). Combining professional work with family responsibilities—a burden or a blessing? *International Journal of Social Welfare, 10*, 202–214.

Hobfoll, S. E. (1989). Conservation of resources: A new attempt at conceptualizing stress. *American Psychologist, 44*, 513–524.

Hobfoll, S. E. (1998). *Stress, culture and community: The psychology and philosophy of stress*. New York: Plenum.

Lee, H., & Kuchroo, M. (n.d). *ANOVA: A Test of Analysis of Variance*. www.bbn-school.org/us/math/ap_stats/.../anova_kuchroo_lee.ppt Accessed 2 May 2013.

Lero, D. (1992). *Parental work and child care needs Catalogue, 259-529 E*. Ottawa: Statistics Canada.

Mokomane, Z. (2012). Social protection as a mechanism for family protection in sub-saharan Africa. *International Journal of Social Welfare*. doi:10.1111/j.1468-2397.2012.00893.x.

Ngo, H., & Lau, C. (1998). Interference between work and family among male and female executives in Hong Kong. *Research and Practice in Human Resources Management, 6*(1), 17–34.

Noor, N. M. (1995). Work and family roles in relation to women's well-being: a longitudinal study. *British Journal of Social Psychology, 34*, 87–116.

Okiy, R.B. (2002) Honour well deserved. *The Guardian*, 2002, December 12, No. 21.

Okonkwo, A.E. (2011).*Work-family conflict as predictor of burnout among mothers in human service profession*. Unpublished Ph.D Thesis, Department of Psychology, Enugu State University of Science and Technology, Enugu, Nigeria.

Oomens, S., Geurts, S., & Scheepers, P. (2007). Combining work and family in the Netherlands: Blessing or burden for one's mental health? *International Journal of Law and Psychiatry, 30*, 369–384.

Patton, M. Q. (1990). *Qualitative evaluation and research methods*. London: Sage Publication.

Pines, A., Aronson, E., & Kafry, D. (1981). *Burnout from tedium to personal growth*. New York: The Free Press.

Pleck, J. H. (1977). The work-family role system. *Social Problems, 24*, 417–442.

Repetti, R. L. (1989). Effects of daily workload on subsequent behaviour during marital interaction. The roles of social withdrawal and spouse support. *Journal of Personality and Social Psychology, 57*, 651–659.

Rothausen, T. J. (1999). Family in organizational research: a review and comparison of definitions and measures. *Journal of Organizational Behaviour, 20*, 817–836.

Rozario, P. A., Morrow-Howell, N., & Hinterlong, J. E. (2004). Role Enhancement or Role Strain: Examining the Impact of Multiple Roles on Family Caregivers. *Research On Aging, 26*(4), 413–428.

Small, S. A., & Riley, D. (1990). Towards a multidimensional assessment of work spill-over into family life. *Journal of Marriage and Family, 38*(1), 15–28.

Stryker, S. (1980). *Symbolic interactionism*. Benjamin/Cummings: A social structural view. Mento Park. CA.

Voyandoff, P. (1988). Work role characteristics, family structure demands, and work/family conflict. *Journal of Marriage and the Family, 50*, 749–761.

Weiss, R. S. (1990). Bringing work stress home. In J. Eckenrode & S. Gore (Eds.), *Stress Between Work and Family* (pp. 17–38). New York: Plenum Press.

Williams, K., & Alliger, G. (1994). Role stressors, mood spill-over and perceptions of work-family conflict in employed parents. *Academy of Management Journal, 37*(4), 837–868.

Zedeck, S., & Mosier, K. L. (1990). Work in the family and employing organization. *American Psychologist, 45*(2), 240–251.

Chapter 6
Sexual Harassment as a Contributory Factor in Work–Family Conflict: Implications for Policies in the Workplace

Francine Masson and Eleanor Ross

Introduction

The South African government is committed to promoting family life and strengthening families, as articulated in the Green Paper on Families (Republic of South Africa 2011). According to the Green Paper, the South African family is under threat due to the legacy of colonialism and apartheid; high levels of poverty, inequality and unemployment; teenage pregnancies; HIV and AIDS; illiteracy; gender inequality; absent fathers; domestic violence and high numbers of orphaned and vulnerable children. However, a factor that has been neglected in the country's family research literature is the impact of sexual harassment in the workplace and its deleterious effects on marital and family life of both the harasser and the harassed persons as well as significant others in the family.

Overall, while there is recognition of the adverse effects of sexual harassment on work productivity, staff morale, staff turnover and the legal costs for companies in terms of lawsuits and a negative public image (LaBand and Lentz 1998), minimal attention seems to have been paid to the personal costs arising from the emotional stress, guilt, jealousy, lack of trust and disrupted relationships which spill over from work-to-family and exacerbate work–family conflict.

While mindful that work is not the only place where sexual harassment occurs, that men as well as women can be subject to this phenomenon, and that sexual harassment can take place between same-sex persons as well as opposite sexes (Naylor 2010), the focus of this chapter is primarily on sexual harassment by males

F. Masson (✉)
Department of Social Work, University of the Witwatersrand, 1 Jan Smuts Avenue, Braamfontein, Johannesburg 2000, South Africa
e-mail: Francine.Masson@wits.ac.za

E. Ross
Centre for Social Development in Africa, University of Johannesburg, House No. 9, Research Village, Bunting Road Campus, Auckland Park, Johannesburg, Gauteng 2006, South Africa
e-mail: eross@uj.ac.za

Z. Mokomane (ed.), *Work–Family Interface in Sub-Saharan Africa*, International Perspectives on Social Policy, Administration, and Practice,
DOI: 10.1007/978-3-319-01237-7_6, © Springer International Publishing Switzerland 2014

on females in the workplace. This chapter discusses the definitions of sexual harassment in the workplace; the historical context; theoretical approaches; causes or antecedents; consequences and responses; policy and legislation; conclusions, and recommendations for addressing this form of gender discrimination and source of work–family conflict.

Sexual Harassment in the Workplace

There appears to be no universally accepted definition of sexual harassment as laws, customs and cultures differ from country to country. However, what is apparent is that definitions of sexual harassment have altered with time as various ideologies, discourses, and contexts have influenced understanding of the phenomenon. Scarduzio and Geist-Martin (2010) maintain that ideologies constrain and shape the sense that people make of sexual harassment in the workplace. Moreover, the decisions that victims, harassers and witnesses make regarding sexual harassment are all influenced by various discourses.

Definitions about sexual harassment have usually referred to sexually derogatory or demeaning actions from men towards women and were often defined according to type, purpose and severity of harassment (Chamberlain et al. 2008). Sexual harassment can affect women and men of all ages, disability, physical appearance, background, sexual orientation, or occupational status. Sexual harassment can occur in any work environment and alongside bullying and physical violence can be understood in terms of 'organisational violation', when the organisational culture allows individuals to be abused and treated without respect. Hunt et al. (2007) argue that whilst anyone can be sexually harassed, it is usually young, single or divorced women with relatively low levels of education that are most vulnerable to sexual harassment. They further identify ethnic minority groups; lesbians, gays and bisexuals; and disabled employees as being particularly vulnerable to being sexually harassed at work.

Women working in male-dominated professions and workplaces are also often subjected to sexual harassment as they are often required to depend upon men for training and mentoring. In essence, many occupational spheres are still largely constituted along gender lines, where patriarchal structures still exist and men's status is elevated over women's, placing women in an inferior and vulnerable position (Walby 1988). Overall, therefore, in order for a woman to obtain organisational authority she is often required to manage not only harassment from her co-workers or supervisor but also from her subordinates (Ramsaroop and Brijball Parumasur 2007). Particular kinds of work also invite sexualisation more than others and as a result certain workplaces tend to have high incidences of sexual harassment. Once sexual behaviour becomes accepted in a work environment, it becomes a natural aspect of the work milieu (Renzetti et al. 2001).

Research conducted by Icenogle et al. (2002 as cited by O'Leary et al. 2009) further found that blue collar workers were not as likely as white collar workers to label behaviours as sexually harassing. Almost a fifth of the blue collar workers in a manufacturing plant did not even perceive the promise of job rewards in return for sexual favours as sexual harassment. It is, therefore, imperative that sexual harassment is clearly defined in order to eliminate confusion and to create clear boundaries in the workplace.

One also needs to take into account that there are gender differences in the perception of sexual harassment, and that women are more likely than men to label certain behaviour as sexually harassing (Steenkamp 2010). Men are more likely to assume several ideological positions when explaining their understanding of sexual harassment, including the impact of hegemonic masculinity, the complicated process of consent, and the contrasting experiences of male and female victims (Scarduzio and Geist-Martin 2010). In a study conducted at a South African university involving 827 students, Mayekiso and Bhana (1997) found that men were less likely than women to classify the verbal forms of sexual harassment, such as derogatory remarks, jokes, or suggestive looks as sexual harassment. Their study also found that African students were less likely to acknowledge the prevalence of sexual harassment as opposed to other racial groups. These findings indicate gender and cultural differences in the understanding of sexual harassment.

Most of the research that has explored personality characteristics of harassers have only looked at the personality profiles of male harassers. Characteristics that have been identified include: A propensity to engage in sexual violence; a cognitive understanding that connects social dominance with sexuality; a preference for traditional male sex-role stereotypes; limited empathy; misogynistic attitudes and beliefs and power-driven personalities with low levels of honesty and humility (O'Leary-Kelly et al. 2009).

A brochure distributed by the South African Cape Peninsula University of Technology about Sexual Harassment (n.d.) (2012) identifies the different types of harassers into six categories:

- *Mr. Macho* or one of the boys: This category refers to groups of men who embarrass women with comments, jokes and/or show sexually graphic material. Whilst this behaviour may only be considered as verbal or visual harassment, it can contribute to creating a hostile work environment;
- *The Great Gallant*: This personality refers to the type of individual who is gallant and makes comments that are sexually inappropriate or embarrassing for the recipient. Whilst the harasser might think of himself as appealing and desirable, the recipient generally does not share these views.
- *The Opportunist*: This kind of harasser is usually promiscuous and will take any opportunity to take advantage of the situation. He may start his amorous behaviour in the presence of others and then try to continue in private. The opportunist if confronted will insist that the action is consensual and does not take responsibility for his inappropriate behaviour.

- *The Power Player*: This kind of harasser asks for sexual favours in exchange for benefits that he can offer the employee, such as promotion and so forth. This kind of harassment is also known as quid pro quo harassment and is an abuse of power and trust.
- *The Serial Harasser*: This category of harasser is psychologically disturbed and plans his advances and strikes in private, so that it is his word against his victims. He establishes an image so that people would not think this kind of behaviour is possible for him and would tend to not believe the victims should they speak out.
- *The Situational Harasser*: The behaviour of this kind of harasser usually results from a psychological trauma or situation that the harasser is experiencing. Examples would include divorce, illness of a spouse or substance abuse problems. If there is a change in the situation, the harassment often stops.

What is evident is that there are many different kinds of harassers who use different situations to sexually harass an individual. Today there is a much broader understanding of the concept than earlier definitions of sexual harassment which focused only upon legal and psychological perspectives. Furthermore, due to the greater acknowledgement of the problem at both national and international levels, the apparent increase in the incidence of sexual harassment could possibly be attributed to the fact that this behaviour is no longer tolerated; that is, as societies become more focused on promoting equality and prohibiting discrimination, the issue of sexual harassment has gained prominence (O'Leary-Kelly et al. 2009).

Particularly in the last decade, South Africa has made significant progress in acknowledging the range and extent of sexual harassment in the workplace. South Africa is one of the first countries in the world to have such extensive legislation concerning sexual harassment, namely the *Amended Code of Good Practice on the Handling of Sexual Harassment Cases in The Workplace* (Republic of South Africa 2005) in which sexual harassment in the workplace is viewed as a form of unfair discrimination and is prohibited on the grounds of sex and/or gender and/or sexual orientation, and is defined as:

> unwelcome conduct of a sexual nature that violates the rights of an employee and constitutes a barrier to equity in the workplace, taking into account all of the following factors:
>
> - whether the harassment is on the prohibited grounds of sex and/or gender and/or sexual orientation;
> - whether the sexual conduct was unwelcome;
> - the nature and extent of the sexual conduct; and
> - the impact of the sexual conduct on the employee.

Different kinds of sexual harassment are acknowledged by the amended code including unwanted physical, verbal, non-verbal, victimisation, quid pro quo harassment and sexual favouritism. These different types are elaborated upon as follows:

- *"Physical conduct* of a sexual nature includes all unwelcome physical contact, ranging from touching to sexual assault and rape, as well as strip searches by or in the presence of the opposite sex.
- *Verbal conduct* includes unwelcome innuendos, suggestions, hints, sexual advances, comments with sexual overtones, sex-related jokes or insults, graphic comments made about a person's body made in their presence or to them, inappropriate enquiries about a person's sex life, whistling of a sexual nature and the sending by electronic means or otherwise of sexually explicit texts;
- *Non-verbal conduct* includes unwelcome gestures, indecent exposure and the display or sending by electronic means or otherwise of sexually explicit pictures or objects;
- *Victimisation* occurs where an employee is victimised or intimidated for failing to submit to sexual advances;
- *Quid Pro quo harassment* occurs where a person such as an owner, employer, supervisor, member of the management, influences or attempts to influence an employee's employment circumstances (for example engagement, promotion, training, discipline, dismissal, salary increments or other benefits) by coercing or attempting to coerce an employee to surrender to sexual advances. This could include *sexual favouritism,* which occurs where a person in authority in the workplace rewards only those who respond to his or her sexual advances" Republic of South Africa (2005:27).

Whilst this understanding of sexual harassment is progressive and attempts to address some of the contentious concerns that are present when trying to determine whether sexual harassment has occurred, there are still aspects of the Code of Practice that can be debated. For example, the Code stipulates that there are numerous ways in which the employee may indicate that the harassment is unwelcome such as walking away or by not responding to the perpetrator. However, this type of behaviour may be difficult to prove and may be reduced to one person's word against another. The Code also mentions that the impact of the conduct on the employee needs to be considered when establishing whether sexual harassment occurred. It mentions that the conduct should constitute an impairment of the employee's dignity taking into account the circumstances of the employee as well as the respective positions of the employee and the perpetrator in the workplace. This perspective highlights the subjective nature of sexual harassment as an event or experience that might impair one employee's dignity while not necessarily impairing the dignity of another person.

Historical Understanding of Sexual Harassment

From a review of the literature it appears that the term 'sexual harassment' emerged in the 1970s in the United States of America as attention began to be placed upon the sexual harassment of women in the workplace (Hunt et al. 2007).

In 1979 MacKinnon, an American Law professor, published her seminal work on sexual harassment in the work environment, which laid the foundations for the introduction of policies and laws addressing sexual harassment. Initially, the American courts did not know where to place sexual harassment and it was dealt with as a form of sexual discrimination. Although the Civil Rights Act of 1964 prohibits employers from discriminating against individuals with respect to terms, conditions, or privileges of employment on the grounds of an individual's race, colour, religion, sex or national origin, it did not sufficiently address sexual harassment, and it became apparent that specific legislation needed to be promulgated to address this phenomenon. MacKinnon emphasised the discourse that sexual harassment is a form of discrimination and that it is often linked to the notion of power (Naylor 2010; Le Roux et al. 2002).

The understanding of sexual harassment as a human rights issue has continued to grow and gain momentum internationally. At the United Nations Women's Conference in Beijing in 1995, a programme was adopted to advance women's rights which included prohibiting sexual harassment at work, and in December 2000 the United Nations passed a new complaint procedure for female victims of discrimination. This procedure permitted women to submit sexual harassment complaints to the United Nations if the employer was unwilling to investigate such allegations (Lederer 2000 cited by Paludi and Paludi 2003).

By the same token, the European Commission passed a nonbinding council resolution for its Member States, which helped to initiate a formalised and standardised definition of sexual harassment, and in 2002 the European Union adopted a 'Code of Practice' which required all Member States to promote awareness of sexual harassment and introduce programmes to reduce its occurrence (International Trade Union Confederation 2008). The International Labour Organisation Convention 111 also deals with sexual harassment at work under the Discrimination in Employment section. However, while sexual harassment as a problem is becoming internationally acknowledged and some countries have developed laws to specifically address it, many countries still do not have specific laws against sexual harassment.

Historical Context and Development of South African Legislation on Sexual Harassment

In a country like South Africa with its history of discriminatory apartheid laws and practices, unequal power relations based upon race and gender, patriarchal cultures and belief systems, the potential for sexual harassment is rife. Apartheid promoted discriminatory practices that not only discriminated against people on the basis of their race and culture but also against their gender. Therefore, black women as the most exploited members of the working class were the most likely victims of sexual harassment (Naylor 2010).

During the apartheid era, sexual harassment in the workplace was barely acknowledged or even recognised. Whilst under common law all employees were afforded the right to privacy, dignity and humane treatment, this framework did little to curb sexual harassment. Employers were required to ensure that the work environment was safe, conducive to work and free from hostility and disrespect. However, employers tended to focus on ensuring the physical safety of the work environment, and placed little or no emphasis on the elimination of sexual harassment within the workplace (Naylor 2010). The concept of sexual harassment could be addressed under criminal law, which included acts such as rape as well as indecent assault. Sexual Harassment could also be addressed in terms of the Labour Relations Act of 1953 and the subsequent amendments to the Act in 1979, 1980 and 1988 under the concept of "unfair labour practice". Prior to the 1988 amendment the industrial court could not award damages to a victim of sexual harassment but could only instruct the employer to stop any unfair labour practice and restore the person to the position which existed prior to the introduction of the unfair labour practice (Sutherland 1992).

Critics of this Act such as Mowatt (1986) claimed that the relief provided for under the act was relatively ineffective. Cameron et al. (1989) also highlighted the fact that the Industrial Court only offered protection and relief for those already in employment so that applicants who were offered employment in exchange for sex were not protected. Furthermore, legislation did not cover all categories of workers. Domestic workers were excluded from this legislation and consequently were offered no protection against sexual harassment in the workplace. Sutherland (1992) also argued that what was needed in the "unfair labour code" was an exact definition of sexual harassment, in order to provide guidelines for employers on how to prevent this phenomenon in the workplace, as the current legislation left too many unanswered questions.

In 1987 a case of unfair labour practice was brought before the industrial court, where a married female employee and a married senior partner of a firm had had a consensual affair. When the affair ended the manager asked the female employee to resign as he found it stressful to continue to work with her and he wanted to assure his wife that the affair was over. When the employee refused to resign she was subsequently fired on the basis of numerous unsubstantiated allegations. She filed an unfair labour practice suit against the firm and was reinstated by the Industrial Court (G vs. K, 1987 as cited in Naylor 2010). What this ruling challenged was the presumption that had existed amongst many employers that when an employee has an affair with her employer, the employer can dismiss the employee when the affair is over in order to prevent embarrassment.

It was only in 1989 that the first officially reported case of sexual harassment was heard before the South African Industrial Court, in the case of J vs. M Ltd. This case involved a senior executive of an unknown company who was alleged to have sexually harassed a female employee against her will (De Kock 1989). Significantly in his ruling on this case, Judge De Kock drew upon international research on sexual harassment and found the defendant guilty of sexual harassment. Furthermore, Judge De Kock acknowledged that a wide spectrum of activities constituted sexual harassment and that sexual harassment could be physical or verbal in nature. He also recognised that a single act can constitute sexual harassment (Sutherland 1992). This case highlighted the concern that sexual harassment in South Africa had not received sufficient attention by either employers or the employees and that the effects of sexual harassment were underestimated and ignored.

In the same year as the infamous case of J vs. M, sexual harassment began to appear on the agendas of trade unions. The Transport and General Workers Union identified sexual harassment and sexually exploitative behaviour as a concern at the Congress of South African Trade Unions (COSATU). Whilst agreement about what constituted sexual harassment could not be reached, much debate and discussion about sexual harassment was generated and laid the foundations for further consciousness in this area to be developed and fought for by the trade unions (Sutherland 1992).

South African Policies and Legislation to Curb Sexual Harassment

As mentioned previously the ground breaking case of J vs. M was the first case to be brought before court in South Africa. Since then numerous policies and legislative acts have been promulgated that have acknowledged or addressed sexual harassment.

The Constitution of the Republic of South Africa

The South African Constitution, which was passed by parliament in 1996, is often referred to as one of the most progressive in the world. The Constitution of the Republic of South Africa upholds democratic values of equality, human dignity and freedom as well as security of the person. Section 10 (p. 1247) stipulates that, "everybody has inherent dignity and the right to have their dignity respected and protected". Section 12 states that "everyone has the right to bodily and psychological integrity, which includes (b) the right to security in and control over their body" (Republic of South Africa, 1996:1247). These rights can be specifically applied to protecting citizens against sexual harassment.

The Employment Equity Act No. 55 of 1998

The purpose of the Employment Equity Act (EEA) is to promote equal opportunity in the workplace by, 'promoting equal opportunity and fair treatment in employment through the elimination of unfair discrimination'. Chapter 2 of the act prohibits unfair discrimination and stipulates that "no person may unfairly discriminate, directly or indirectly, against an employee in any employment policy or practice, on one or more of grounds including race, *gender*, marital status, family responsibility, ethnic or social origin, colour, sexual orientation, age, disability, religion, HIV status, conscience, belief, political opinion, culture, language, and birth" (Republic of South Africa 1998). Section 60 of this Act addresses employer liability stipulating that it is the employer's responsibility to investigate any alleged misconduct or discrimination and failure to do so will be seen as contravention of this Act.

The Labour Relations Act no 66 of 1995 (Republic of South Africa 1995) did not make any provision for an employer to be held liable when an employee sexually harassed another employee. If the harassed person elected to resign due to the intolerable circumstances of her employment, the onus would be upon that employee to show that she had resigned due to the harassment and not for other reasons. This claim of constructive dismissal would in terms of the Labour Relations Act be deemed as unfair as the resignation occurred as a result of discrimination on the basis of sex and/or gender. However, in terms of the EEA an employer has a duty and obligation to investigate complaints and allegations of unfair discrimination and it is not sufficient for an employer to simply attempt to eliminate unfair discrimination in the workplace. As (Naylor 2010) points out, Section 60 (1) of the EEA is important as it increases the vicarious liability of the employer and incorporates alleged acts that occurred 'whilst at work' and not only in the course and scope of employment. An employer can therefore be found to be vicariously liable for acts of sexual harassment by employees where: An employment relationship exists; an act of sexual harassment as defined has occurred; the sexual harassment is brought to the attention of the employer; the employer fails to consult all parties and fails to take the necessary steps and act in a reasonable fashion.

One of the first cases of employer liability to be brought before the South African courts was Ntsabo vs. Real Security CC. Ntsabo a South African woman obtained a position as a security guard with Real Security in 1999. Her supervisor began sexually harassing her, and would threaten her with a poor performance review if she would not engage in a sexual relationship with him. Ntsabo informed the management of Real Security about the situation. After the supervisor had attempted to rape her, Ntsabo's family phoned the management and complained. However, the management did not address the issue and instead said that the supervisor had complained of Ntsabo's poor work performance. Ntsabo subsequently resigned and in June 2000 sued Real Security for damages under the EEA for failing to protect her. Acting Judge Pillay, taking into account section 60 of the EEA found the employer, Real Security, liable and ordered that the employer pay patrimonial and non-patrimonial damages to Ntsabo for future medical expenses, her pain and suffering and for impairment of her dignity (Naylor 2010).

The Code of Good Practice on the Handling of Sexual Harassment

The Code of Good Practice on the Handling of Sexual Harassment was initially published in 1998. The objective of the code was to eliminate sexual harassment in the workplace and establish workplaces where sexual harassment is not tolerated and where the individual's integrity, dignity, privacy and right to freedom are respected. This code provides the appropriate procedures when dealing with sexual harassment and explains how to prevent its recurrence (Naylor 2010). However, this code was amended in 2005 as it was felt that sexual harassment was not comprehensively defined. Section 60 of the amended code specifies that where sexual harassment is of a serious nature, the complainant should be encouraged to inform the employer. This code also allows friends, colleagues or human resource officials acting on the request of the complainant to report the incident of sexual harassment. The application of the code extends beyond employers and employees and includes clients, suppliers and anyone who has dealings with the business. A code of good practice could only be considered when interpreting or applying the Labour Relations Act. However, this has changed and now codes of good practice are taken into account when any law is interpreted or applied (Naylor 2010).

Women Empowerment and Gender Equity Bill

This Bill, which was passed in 2012, establishes a legislative framework for the empowerment of women; encourages gender mainstreaming; and provides for an offence for practices with adverse effects. Furthermore, the Bill recognises "that certain practices, including cultural, patriarchal, traditional, customary or religious practices may impair the dignity of women and undermine equality between men and women" (Republic of South Africa, 2012). This Bill speaks to the empowerment of women and attempts to reduce gender inequality that is still prevalent in South African workplaces today.

Theoretical Approaches to Sexual Harassment

There are numerous theoretical approaches for understanding harassment; however, only the most salient of these approaches are described.

Berdahl's (2007) Theory of Harassment

This theory locates sexual harassment within the broader harassment literature and advocates that underlying tenets of this harassment are goal-directed behaviour. Berdahl identifies three influencing variables: (i) the fact that the underlying motive of harassment is to protect the harasser's social status; (ii) the existence of a gender hierarchy; and (iii) that distinctions are made between sexes as well as within them. Berdahl understands the occurrence of sexual harassment to be influenced by both contextual and personal factors (cited in O'Leary-Kelly et al. 2009).

Accountability Theory

Accountability theory suggests that where there are insufficient accountable procedures in place in an organisation, harassers do not feel restricted in their actions. This situation would be common when there is fragmentation of responsibility, competing role expectations, and reluctance to impose standards on levels of behaviour (O'Leary-Kelly et al. 2009).

De Coster et al.'s (1999) Theory

This theory suggests that some individuals are more susceptible to being sexually harassed as the nature of their work is more likely to bring them into contact with predators. The process of harassment involves three aspects, namely, a motivated harasser; a suitable target and the absence of guardians or policies to prevent victimisation (O'Leary-Kelly et al. 2009).

The Multi-perspective Framework of Sexual Harassment

Bowes-Sperry and Tata (1999) acknowledge three different theoretical perspectives of sexual harassment. These different perspectives provide an expanded understanding of what constitutes sexual harassment, showing the complex nature of the phenomenon.

- Firstly, the *individual/subjective perspective* refers to any behaviour of a sexual nature that an individual subjectively considers to be offensive and involves behaviour that is not welcomed by the recipient;
- Secondly, the *conceptual/behavioural perspective* maintains that this behaviour consists of three primary dimensions, namely: *gender harassment*—harassing behaviours are exhibited and expressed towards the opposite sex, without

gaining sexual co-operation; *unwanted sexual attention*—sexual advances or behaviours are not wanted by the recipient and *sexual coercion*—with this kind of behaviour, sexual co-operation is implicitly or explicitly linked to job-related outcomes; and

- Thirdly, *the legal perspective*—this approach refers to sexual harassing behaviour that violates the laws of the country in which the incident took place.

Causes or Antecedents of Sexual Harassment

Patriarchal Cultures and Gender Socialisation

Chamberlain et al. (2008) maintain that organisations are located within the broader sociocultural environment, which is often characterised by patriarchal cultures and gender socialisation which promote sexist attitudes and tend to prime individuals for advancing and receiving sexual harassment in the workplace. However, although patriarchy and gender socialisation help to explain the cultural foundations underpinning sexual harassment, it is the organisational context that determines whether and how sexual harassment occurs in a particular work environment. The three main features of organisations that influence sexual harassment include worker power, workplace culture and gender composition.

Worker Power

Chamberlain et al. (2008) posit that three sources of power have been implicated in sexual harassment, namely, self-direction, formal grievance procedures and job security. Power differences arising from workers' relative importance in the labour force may provide protection for some employees while making others more vulnerable to sexual harassment. Self-direction can potentially reduce harassment because self-directed employees are usually more skilled and harder to replace than other sectors of the work environment. At the same time, women with high levels of organisational power may provoke resentment and consequently be subjected to sexual harassment. Workers may also derive a degree of power through protective policies and formal grievance procedures which signal an organisation's commitment to discourage sexual harassment. In addition, job insecurity tends to heighten vulnerability. For example, temporary workers who lack even minimal job security have an economic interest in remaining silent and not reporting sexual harassment.

Workplace Culture

Four aspects of workplace culture are relevant for sexual harassment, namely, co-worker solidarity, supervisor harmony, workplace anonymity, and physicality of the work (Chamberlain et al. 2008). De Coster et al. (1999) found that work group solidarity and a supportive work group culture limit the degree to which sexual harassment is regarded as a problem at work. They attributed these relationships to co-workers' commitment to one another's well-being, their willingness to intervene and stop harassment, and provide support for victims' actions in defending themselves through formal and informal procedures.

De Coster et al. (1999) also argue that harmonious relations with supervisors can reduce sexual harassment as supportive supervisors offer guardianship directly, by protecting workers from abuse, and indirectly, by encouraging employees to help themselves through following various grievance procedures.

Degree of anonymity can also influence the likelihood of sexual harassment. On the one hand, large organisations may provide a modicum of anonymity for perpetrators relative to smaller work settings. On the other hand, large organisations may have bureaucratic structures that can prevent the most severe forms of sexual harassment (Dobbin and Kelly 2007).

A further aspect of workplace culture is the physicality of work. Particularly in male-dominated workplaces, physically demanding work may increase sexual harassment due to the sexualized, masculine culture where women's presence may be perceived as a threat to workers' masculinity and physical safety. In such environments, sexual harassment could also be used to defend privileged job opportunities and wages against the incursion of lower paid female labour (Chamberlain et al. 2008). Moreover, according to Pellegrini (2001) men in groups tend to behave with more aggression and bravado than they would as individuals.

Gender Composition

Women in gender-mixed and mainly male settings are believed to be at the greatest risk for sexual harassment, whereas women employed in predominantly female work environments are at the least risk due to the reduced frequency of their contact with men. Women working in traditionally male settings tend to be targeted because of their high visibility and threat to male identity and male bonding. However, women who work in groups with high numbers of females but who have relatively low status such as maids and waitresses are at an increased risk for sexual harassment because of their low power and subordinate status (Chamberlain et al. 2008).

Other causes or antecedents of sexual harassment include lack of company policies around sexual harassment; lack of credibility of the victim versus the perpetrator; blaming the victim for provoking the harassment through her dress, lifestyle and private life and a moral culture where "one-night stands" are regarded as acceptable. In addition, O'Leary-Kelly et al. (2009) maintain that due to the high prevalence of marital stress and divorce in western society, some men and women come to work in a state of emotional distress which makes them vulnerable to sexual harassment.

Consequences of, and Responses to, Sexual Harassment

Over the last few decades significant attention has been paid to perceptions and attributions about sexual harassment but only recently has attention been given to the consequences of sexual harassment. Moreover, empirical research that has been conducted has focused more on the responses of the 'victim' as opposed to the effects on the family of both the alleged perpetrator and the victim or upon the organisation (Lee et al. 2004).

Consequences for the Victim

The victim may experience stress-related physical and mental illness. Physical effects may include frequent illnesses, ulcers, trouble sleeping or the need to sleep all the time, headaches, nightmares, fatigue and lack of energy. Psychological effects may include a loss of self-esteem and confidence, reduced motivation, suicidal thoughts, feelings of humiliation and the perception of intimidation. They may feel degraded, ashamed, embarrassed or angry (Naylor 2010; Cape Peninsula University of Technology, n.d.). As a result victims sometimes resort to abusing drugs and/or alcohol in order to cope. Furthermore, victims may not report the harassment for fear of stigma and labelling that may occur as well as more long-term effects such as limited promotion opportunities or dismissal. Some prefer to request a transfer or leave the job rather than confront the harassment. Rudman et al. (1995, as cited by Kariaga 2010) explain that women who resign because of sexual harassment issues often have difficulty in finding alternate employment, as they may struggle to obtain good references from the previous employer or they may be afraid to explain to potential employers the true reasons for leaving the previous employment for fear of being labelled or stigmatised in the potential new workplace.

Work–Family Overspill: Consequences for the Family of the Victim

The victim may also exhibit behavioural changes which include isolation, as well as a deterioration of work and family relationships, and may become preoccupied with the experience and focus all his or her energy on the experience to the detriment of the family. In the worst cases some victims have even resorted to suicide (International Trade Union Confederation 2008). The following case study illustrates how sexual harassment can be a source of work–family conflict:

Case Study A: The Case of M

M was a competent, goal-driven executive manager in a large organisation. She experienced unwanted sexual overtures from B, a fellow manager in the company. Initially, she tried to ignore his advances, but when he became increasingly persistent, she complained to the Chief Executive Officer (CEO) of the firm. Despite the existence of a company sexual harassment policy, the CEO appeared to trivialise the issue and tried to persuade M not to pursue the matter. M experienced the work environment as increasingly hostile and eventually resigned from her position.

After leaving the organisation, she decided to take legal action against the company and B. In the early stages she received support from her husband. However, as the case began to receive increasing media exposure, the husband began to feel more and more stressed. B had said that M had been receptive to his advances and he claimed that her flirtatious manner and style of dress had signalled to him that she was open to having an affair. Her husband wondered about M's role in the relationship and he began to mistrust her. He also felt increasingly uncomfortable with the snide comments made about M by his work colleagues.

The couple's two school-age children also felt ashamed, embarrassed and resentful when their classmates discussed their mother and made jokes about her. Tensions within the family increased and 6 months later the husband sued for divorce and sole custody of the children. M subsequently won her harassment case in the courts but her family and marital life were irrevocably damaged.

Effects on the Victim's Work Performance

A victim's work performance may also deteriorate due to impaired concentration and judgement, demotivation, compromised teamwork, and increased absenteeism. In addition, victims may feel isolated or alienated at work (sexual harassment, n.d.) and, as already discussed, may not report the harassment for fear of stigma and labelling that may occur as well as more long-term effects such as limited promotion opportunities or dismissal. Some victims would rather request a transfer or leave the job than confront the harassment. Adopting these kinds of options, however, may have adverse effects for the victim's career opportunities and indirectly, their family's well-being.

Consequences for the Alleged Harasser

An area that has clearly not received much research is the effect that sexual harassment allegations may have upon the alleged harasser. Once a formal complaint has been filed against the alleged harasser, many organisations choose to suspend the employee. This procedure can be professionally embarrassing and result in long-term consequences for the alleged harasser. The effects of these allegations can also be detrimental to the partner or spouse and the family of the alleged harasser, as they try to cope with the allegations surrounding the harassment. Sometimes opportunists can see the financial advantages of claiming harassment as the alleged harassers may prefer to reach a financial settlement rather than endure the humiliation and other consequences of a sexual harassment suit. The case study below illustrates this example.

Case Study B: The Case of X the Executive Director

X, a senior executive of a company was working alongside the firm's accountant Y in attempting to save the company from closure and retrenching 230 employees. This meant that X and Y spent many late nights trying to plan and strategize to save the company. The executive's wife complained that he was never home and that she had to care for their three young children on her own, despite also holding down a highly stressful job.

The pressure of trying to ensure that the company did not close continued to place undue stress upon the marriage as X felt that his wife was not supporting him sufficiently while his wife felt that he was neglecting her and their children. X started having an affair with Y. However, he made it clear to Y that he was not prepared to leave his wife for her, despite her demands that he terminate his marriage.

After a few months X decided to end the affair and work on his marriage. Y was angry and hurt as she had believed that there were long-term prospects for this relationship. She then decided to lodge a sexual harassment complaint with the board of the company, claiming that X had continually harassed her and that he had threatened to ruin her career if she did not comply with his demands. X was suspended and admitted to his wife that he had regrettably had an affair but insisted that he had not sexually harassed Y. He felt humiliated, angry and resentful as his wife requested that he move out of the marital home. Employees at work were horrified by the story that Y told of continual harassment and distanced themselves from X. The board of executives asked X to resign in order to save the company's image. Y became unemployed, with his marriage in tatters and his career ruined due to false sexual allegation claims.

Consequences for Co-workers

According to the International Trade Union Federation (2008), co-workers who observe or are aware of sexual harassment within the organisation may also experience detrimental effects which can impact on their attitudes to work. These deleterious effects can lead to co-workers experiencing decreased job satisfaction and psychosomatic problems. Sexual harassment investigations can also lead to serious divisions between the staff as some people feel compelled to choose the side of the alleged harasser while others choose the side of the alleged victim. O'Leary-Kelly et al. (2009) found that the interpersonal work dimension (relationships with co-workers and supervisors) was more adversely affected than the victim's sense of work satisfaction. In addition, their study established a negative relationship between the sexual harassment experience and the victim's sense of organisational commitment, thereby underscoring the deleterious effects of such experiences.

In 1997 Glomb and her colleagues expanded our understanding of the work environment by introducing the construct of '*ambient sexual harassment*' as a group-level phenomenon. This construct refers to the general level of sexual harassment in a work group which is reflected in individual level outcomes such as job satisfaction, health conditions, psychological conditions and work and job withdrawal. They argued that co-workers are often aware of colleagues' experiences of sexual harassment and this awareness contributes to a stressful work environment. Higher levels of ambient sexual harassment were found to be associated with higher levels of team cohesion and lower levels of team citizenship behaviours and ultimately affected the overall productivity and financial performance of the team (Glomb et al. 1997 as cited by Raver and Gelfand 2005).

Consequences for Employers

Human capital is an essential resource and sound interpersonal relations are a crucial ingredient for organisational effectiveness. Sexual harassment can, however, have a negative impact on an organisation's human capital by creating a hostile and intimidating work environment that infringes upon the rights of employees (Ramsaroop and Brijball Parumsar 2007). Organisations may also experience a loss of productivity due to impaired judgement, compromised teamwork, demotivation of staff and absenteeism. Another consequence may be that potential applicants may not apply for vacancies at particular workplaces if they are aware that sexual harassment is tolerated and not appropriately dealt with (International Trade Union Confederation (2008). Despite this, many authors such as Raver and Gelfand (2005) argue that researchers have not paid sufficient attention to the impact of sexual harassment beyond the individual level and that the effects for the organisation have been neglected. A call for more attention to these areas has been made by others such as Lee et al. (2004).

Conclusion and Recommendations

The prevalence and impact of sexual harassment are clearly an under-acknowledged problem, the consequences of which are far reaching, affecting not only the workplace but also the families of those involved. It is important that workplaces create environments that are free from discrimination and where principles such as equality and the right to privacy are encouraged. Moreover, in view of the fact that sexual harassment is mainly (but not always) perpetrated by men against women, we need to consider gender asymmetries from a broader perspective. Unless sexual harassment is addressed on a societal level, and efforts are made to change the status of women's subservient role in society, women will continue to experience inequality at work and have limited access to high status and well-paid jobs that have traditionally been occupied primarily by men. All these factors can potentially exacerbate work–family conflict.

Social Policy

In line with the Amended Code of Good Practice on Handling of Sexual Harassment Cases in the Workplace (Republic of South Africa 2005), it is recommended that all employers should adopt a sexual harassment policy. Kariaga (2010) in a study of three banking institutions in Zimbabwe found that the occurrence of sexual harassment was much higher in the bank that did not have a sexual harassment policy, and concluded that the absence of a sexual harassment policy contributes to the prevalence and acceptance of sexual harassment in organisations.

Sexual harassment policies should state that sexual harassment is a form of unfair discrimination on the basis of sex and/or gender and/or sexual orientation which violates the rights of the complainant and represents a barrier to equity in the workplace. Such policies should emphasise that sexual harassment in the workplace will not be permitted or condoned, and that complainants have the right to follow the procedures in the policy and appropriate action will be taken by the employer. Policies should further state that it is considered a disciplinary offence to victimise or retaliate against an employee who in good faith lodges a grievance of sexual harassment. Moreover, sexual harassment policies should clarify the procedures to be followed by the complainant and the employer in reporting sexual harassment, provision of advice and assistance, formal versus informal procedure options, disciplinary sanctions and the ensuring of confidentiality.

Measures to constantly measure and assess the workplace culture should be incorporated into the policy. Realistic appraisals can help to monitor any discriminatory practices and sexual harassment that are occurring. Reese and Lindenberg (2004 as cited by Ramsaroop and Brijball Parumasur 2007, p. 32) identify specific factors that need to be incorporated when trying to develop a suitable organisational culture, that is free of harassment. These factors include:

- Promoting a work climate of dignity and integrity;
- Adopting anti-discriminatory practices in order to promote gender equality; and
- Changing gender-role socialisation and gender-role stereotyping.

It is also imperative that the company has a policy on what is an acceptable dress code for work as an employee's appearance and dress code have been found to be influential factors in determining the prevalence of sexual harassment. Ensuring an acceptable dress code and a culture of mutual respect can help to promote a respectful and anti-discriminatory workplace (Ramsaroop and Brijball Parumasur 2007).

Training and Awareness Programmes

In the aforementioned study that Kariaga (2010) undertook which explored sexual harassment in Zimbabwean banks, she found that whilst some of the banks did have a sexual harassment policy, employees were not aware of the existence of this policy and did not know how to address the problem when incidents of harassment occurred. This finding emphasised that the existence of a sexual harassment policy is not sufficient and training and awareness about the sexual harassment policy needed to be conducted with all employees, and not only with management.

The contents of the policy should be communicated effectively to all employees through orientation, education and training programmes so that they cannot claim to be unaware of the policy. It is also crucial that both employers and employees are helped to become aware of what constitutes sexual harassment and the procedures to be followed by complainants and employers. However, in addition to implementing effective policies in the workplace, it is important for all stakeholders to understand how the organisational context, the characteristics of the harasser and the target, all interact in complex ways to shape sexual harassment. Ramsaroop and Brijball Parumasur (2007) suggest that the appointment of sexual harassment advisors, who are effectively trained in managing sexual harassment, can be an effective strategy for assisting with sexual harassment complaints.

Research

Monitoring and evaluation need to be conducted to assess the effectiveness of existing policies. Hunt et al. (2007) maintain that the evaluation and monitoring of sexual harassment programmes can potentially assist organisations to ensure that their programmes are relevant and effective. They identify numerous ways of monitoring and evaluation including: Conducting incident surveys of sexual harassment; assessing proxy indictors such as absenteeism rates, staff turnover, etc.; monitoring of formal and informal complaints; conducting qualitative research on the organisational climate and assessing what defines acceptable and unacceptable behaviour; regular meetings to discuss policy and procedures; obtaining feedback on training programmes and gathering information from exit interviews. Furthermore, a critical area that is often neglected and needs to be researched is the gap between policy and practice, which can guide the organisation on where to focus attention and how to introduce initiatives to address the gaps.

When conducting research in the area of sexual harassment, the researcher needs to be careful of the way in which questions are phrased and which research method would be most appropriate to employ, qualitative or quantitative. Whilst qualitative methods can help to gain in depth understanding of the experiences of either the alleged victim or alleged harasser, one needs to consider that due to the sensitivity of the issue many people may feel uncomfortable discussing the issue face to face with a researcher and would prefer to remain anonymous (Hunt et al. 2007).

Further research needs to be conducted into specific areas, including: research on the sexual harassment of male employees and the impact of such harassment on work–family conflict; research on sexual harassment by the same sex; empirical research exploring sexual harassment via electronic media and individuals' experiences of this phenomenon; the influence and impact of leadership styles of the managers on the incidence of sexual harassment; and most importantly research into how the sexual harassment claim affects both the alleged victim and alleged perpetrator's family.

References

Berdahl, J. L. (2007). Harassment based on sex: Protecting social status in the context of gender hierarchy. *Academy of Management Review, 32*, 641–658.

Bowes-Sperry, L., & Tat, J. (1999). A multi-perspective framework on sexual harassment: Reviewing two decades of research. In G. N. Powell (Ed.), *Handbook of gender and work* (pp. 263–280). Thousand Oaks, CA: Sage.

Cape Peninsula University of Technology (n.d.) *Sexual Harassment*. Retrieved December 23, 2012 from http://active.cput.ac.za/sc/web/Our%20services/docs/Sexual%20harassment%20 booklet.pdf.

Cameron, E., Cheadle, H., & Thompson, C. (1989). *The new labour relations act*. Pretoria: Juta.

Chamberlain, L. J., Crowley, M., Tope, D., & Hodson, R. (2008). Sexual harassment in organizational context. *Work and Occupations*, doi: 10.1177/0730888408322008.

De Coster, S., Eates, S. B., & Mueller, W. C. (1999). Routine activities and sexual harassment in the workplace. *Work and Occupations, 26*, 21–49.

De Kock, A. (1989). J v M Ltd, Industrial Court 22 February 1989, 16 March 1989. *Industrial Law Journal, 10*, 755–762.

Dobbin, F., & Kelly, E. L. (2007). How to stop harassment: Professional construction of legal compliance in organizations. *American Journal of Sociology, 112*, 1203–1243.

Hunt, C., Davidson, M., Fielden, S., & Hoel, H. (2007). *Sexual harassment in the workplace: A literature review*. Manchester: Equal Opportunities Commission.

International Trade Union Confederation. (2008). *Stopping Sexual Harassment at work*. Retrieved December, 22, 2012 from www.ituc-csi.org/IMG/pdf/Harcelement_ENG_12pgs_BR.pdf.

Kariaga, P. (2010). Women's views on the causes and consequences of sexual harassment: The case of three International Banks in Harare. Unpublished Masters Dissertation, University of the Witwatersrand.

LaBand, D. N., & Lentz, B. F. (1998). The effects of sexual harassment on job satisfaction, earnings, and turnover among female lawyers. *Industrial and Labor Relations Review, 51*, 594–607.

Lee, J., Heilmann, S., & Near, J. P. (2004). Blowing the whistle on sexual harassment: Test of a model of predictors and outcomes. *Human Relations, 57*(3), 297–322.

Le Roux, R., Orlwyn, T., Rycroft, A. (2002). Sexual harassment in the workplace: Law. In A. C. Levy & M. A. Paludi (Eds.), *Workplace Sexual Harassment*. New Jersey: Prentice Hall.

Mayekiso, T., & Bhana, K. (1997). Sexual harassment: Perceptions and experiences of students at the University of Transkei. *South African Journal of Psychology, 27*, 230–235.

Mowatt, J. G. (1986). Sexual harassment: New remedy for old wrong. *Industrial Law Journal, 7*, 637–652.

Naylor, N. (2010). *Sexual harassment and the amended code of good practice on the handling of sexual harassment in South Africa*. Cape Town: Women's Legal Centre.

O'Leary-Kelly, A. M., Bowes-Sperry, L., Bates, C. A., & Lean, E. R. (2009). Sexual harassment at work: A decade (plus) of progress. *Journal of Management, 35*, 503–536.

Paludi, M., & Paludi, C. (2003). *Academic and workplace sexual harassment: A handbook of social science, legal, cultural, and management perspectives*. Westport, CT: Praeger.

Pellegrini, A. (2001). Special issue on evolutionary developmental psychology. *Journal of Experimental Child Psychology, 85*(24), 257–278.

Ramsaroop, A., & Brijball Parumasur, S. (2007). The prevalence and nature of sexual harassment in the workplace: A model for early identification and effective management thereof. *SA Journal of Industrial Psychology, 33*(2), 25–33.

Raver, J. L., & Gelfand, M. J. (2005). Beyond the individual victim: Linking sexual harassment, team processes, and team performance. *Academy of Management Journal, 3*, 387–400.

Renzetti, C. M., Edelson, J. L., & Bergen, R. K. (2001). *Sourcebook on violence against women*. Thousand Oaks, CA: Sage Publications.

Republic of South Africa. (1995). *Labour Relations Act, Act 66 of 1995*. Pretoria: Government Printers.

Republic of South Africa. (1996). *The Constitution of the Republic of South Africa, Act 108 of 1996*. Pretoria: Government Printers.

Republic of South Africa. (1998). *Employment Equity Act, Act 55 of 1998*. Pretoria: Government Printers.

Republic of South Africa. (2005). *Amended Code of Good Practice on the Handling of Sexual Harassment*. (General Notice 1357 published in Government Gazette 27865, 4 August 2005). Pretoria: Government Printers

Republic of South Africa (2011). *Green Paper on Families: Promoting Family Life and Strengthening Families in South Africa*. (2011). Pretoria: Department of Social Development.

Republic of South Africa (2012). *Women Empowerment and Gender Equality Bill*. (Government Gazette No .35637, 29 August). Pretoria.

Scarduzio, J. A., & Geist-Martin, P. (2010). Accounting for victimisation: Male professors' ideological positioning in stories of sexual harassment. *Management Communication Quarterly, 24*, 419–445.

Steenkamp, F. R. (2010). *The prevalence of sexual harassment within a student sample of Stellenbosch University. Unpublished Master's Dissertation*. University of Stellenbosch.

Sutherland, C. (1992). *Paying for stolen kisses? Sexual harassment and the law in South Africa*. Retrieved December 22, 2012 from http://www.csvr.org.za/wits/papers/papsuth.htm.

Walby, S. (1988). *Gender Segregation at Work*. Philadelphia: Open University Press.

Part III
Impact on the Families

Chapter 7
The Social Impact of Job Transfer Policy on Dual Career Families in Botswana

Dolly Ntseane

Introduction

As a result of rapid industrialisation, global competition and the development of high technology, the transfer and relocation of employees have become common practice for many corporations and organisations worldwide (Ntseane 2004). In Botswana the implementation of job transfer policy in the public service dates back to the period when the country was still under the British colonial rule. As early as 1890, the British administration established a small public service which was predominantly made up of police officers and magistrates (Temane 1989). As the provision of social services continued to expand, a transfer policy was formulated in 1934 as part of the standing instructions for public officers. This policy made it clear that public servants were to be transferred anywhere in the country and that the exigencies of the service would always be the decisive factor. It further stated that marriage or family would not be treated as ground for exemption when officers get transferred (Bechuanaland Government 1934).

When Botswana attained independence in 1966, the main challenge of the new government was to educate and train local manpower to provide services to the nation. These public officers were expected to be relocated wherever the country needed them. On the 16th September 1982, a cabinet directive was issued making job transfers mandatory for everyone in the public service (Government of Botswana 1982). However, in 1995 the government made a radical policy shift to make some provisions for married couples. Key guidelines in the policy were: to give transferees at least 3 month notice to prepare for relocation; where possible to avoid separating couples; to assist transferees to secure accommodation and finally to transfer public officers during the months of December and January to allow children to complete the school calendar year uninterrupted (Government of Botswana 1995).

D. Ntseane (✉)
University of Botswana, Gaborone, Botswana
e-mail: ntseaned@mopipi.ub.bw

Z. Mokomane (ed.), *Work–Family Interface in Sub-Saharan Africa*, International Perspectives on Social Policy, Administration, and Practice,
DOI: 10.1007/978-3-319-01237-7_7, © Springer International Publishing Switzerland 2014

Despite this new dispensation, married couples in the public service continue to be separated from their families. This chapter presents results of a study undertaken in 1996 to document the experiences of transferred public service officers and their families. The findings are still relevant given that in Botswana (i) the job transfer policy transfer has essentially remained unchanged over the last 18 years, and (ii) no empirical study has been conducted on this subject.

The chapter begins by presenting a brief literature review on the subject. This is followed by the study methodology, and the findings. The chapter concludes by providing short-term and long-term policies and other recommendations that could be implemented by government to minimise the trauma of job transfers and resultant experiences of work-family conflict on dual career families.

Literature Review

Literature on the effects of job transfers on the family in sub-Saharan Africa is essentially non-existent. This review is therefore based on research conducted in North America and Europe. For the purpose of this chapter, job transfer is defined as "....a relatively permanent job reassignment that entails the movement of an employee within an organisation from one of its operating sites to another" (Pinder and Walters 1984, p. 188). For dual career families, job transfers may entail geographic relocation of one spouse. This section presents a brief review on the costs and benefits of geographic relocation on family well-being.

Although past research viewed job relocation as an opportunity for new job challenges and future career enhancement (Marshall and Cooper 1976; Brett 1982), studies show that most employees now view relocation as stressful, especially for couples with working spouses (Taylor and Lounsbury 1988; Friedman 1989; Pinder 1989; Croan et al. 1991; Munton 1993; Riemer 2000). In their investigation of the effects of job transfers on the family, Marshal and Cooper (1976) found that transfer separation is a crisis point in marriage. In their analysis of the attitudes of women towards the move, they found that women adopted a "self-sacrificing attitude towards moving, playing down their own needs in an attempt to ease the way for their husbands and children" (Marshal and Cooper 1976, p. 45).

Analysing the rewards and strains associated with the lifestyle of dual career couples, Gross (1980) found that there was a significant difference between younger "adjusting" and older "established" couples. For example, older couples, those married longer, those who had a working spouse, and those freed from childcare responsibilities found relocation less stressful than newlyweds. Similar findings were arrived at by Gerstel and Gross (1984). In their examination of the impact of relocation on couples who live apart, they confirmed that commuting was likely to be less stressful when: (i) couples had moderate to high incomes; (ii) spouses had intense motivation for career advancement; (iii) couples had been married longer and had older children and (iv) spouses could reunite regularly on weekends.

Using a more comprehensive methodology, Brett (1982) conducted a study to investigate the relationship between job transfer and the well-being of male employees, their wives and their children. Two aspects of mobility were investigated in this study: Frequent mobility, defined as numbers of transfers per years in the work force; and mobility versus stability defined as the number of years of residence in the community. Five hundred employees were selected randomly, 50 each from 10 United States companies. The results of this study revealed that employees and wives in the transfer sample were significantly more satisfied with marriage and family life than were men and women in the quality of life sample.

In 1988, Brett and Reily conducted a follow-up study to examine factors predicting job transfer decisions. This study made a substantial contribution to Brett's earlier (1982) findings. The results of the 1988 study revealed that the decision to accept or reject job transfer is associated with some key variables: demographic, attitudinal and career attributes. For example, they found that: (i) having many children at home lowered an employee's willingness to move; (ii) high job involvement and positive attitudes towards moving raised willingness to move and (iii) employees whose wives were working were less willing to move and actually turned down the transfers more frequently than did those whose wives were not employed. In conclusion, the authors recommend that managers should take note of specific demographic and career attributes such as age, tenure and family stage before they transfer someone. They also advocate strongly that companies should provide job-finding assistance for the relocating spouse.

In the same vein, Taylor and Lounsbury (1988) in their study of dual career couples and geographic transfers found that the ratings of geographic transfers were significantly affected by the couples' prior attitudes towards the move as well as the current presence of a commuter marriage. Using a sample of 151 executives, the authors found that the majority of the executives did not favour the idea of separating spouses because they feared that this would lower their productivity level. Other respondents feared that a commuter marriage would result in either a divorce or a decision to leave the company (Taylor and Lounsbury 1988).

Further, Friedman (1989) conducted an exploratory examination of the aftermath of job transfers among executives and their families at a multi-national high tech Fortune 500 firm. This study was the first of its kind to compare data from transferred executives, promoted executives and a control group of executives and their families who had not experienced either transition. The findings of the study revealed that for both employees and their spouses, the promotion group reported greater satisfaction with family life, followed by the control group. On the other hand, the transfer sample reported the least satisfaction with the quality of family life. Friedman argues that "promotions seem to correlate with increased quality of marital satisfaction whereas transfer events are more stressful and correlate diminished satisfaction" (Friedman 1989, p. 175). Friedman suggests that the history of mobility as opposed to the experience of a recent transfer event is a far superior predictor of job-related, health-related and family-related outcomes. He postulates that the long-term effects of multiple transfers are more significant and pronounced than ramifications of a recent transfer event (Friedman 1989, p. 234).

Supporting Friedman's findings, (Munton 1993) using a sample of employees throughout the United Kingdom, found that 75 % of the respondents rated relocation as a very stressful life event. Secondly, families moving over a considerable distance reported that they experienced more difficulties. The findings of the study confirmed Brett's (1982) observation that loss of social networks is a significant source of stress for those families that relocate.

Pinder (1989) conducted a longitudinal study to examine the financial, social and psychological effects of transfers on a sample of 800 managers and their spouses. Consistent with previous findings, Pinder found that transfers have tremendous effects on family life and family structure. Most people in his sample reported that their marriage suffered because of the transfer. Secondly, there was an overall consensus that transfers were disruptive to the extended family structure. Pinder posits that a combination of three factors seem to exacerbate the problem: (i) a sudden and unprecedented call to transfer late in one's career; (ii) a degree of existing marital discord before the transfer and (iii) a spouse's forced resignation from a desired job as a result of the employee's transfer (Pinder 1989, p. 55). Evidence from this study suggests that there are some areas where commuting couples report more costs than do dual career couples living together. These costs are primarily in the couples' relationships and in the families. For example, commuters in this study indicate that they are less satisfied with their relationship with their partner and less satisfied with their family life. Further, they report that they were less satisfied with life as a whole than were single-residence dual career respondents.

The notion that a commuting lifestyle can have both rewards and costs is also supported by Gerstel and Gross (1984). Their study suggests that the major costs of commuting include lack of regular deep and open communication; joint leisure activities; physical affection and unhurried regular sex. She points out that in missing such interactions, commuters experience some frustration and those who relocate for work often face forced self-reliance, a lack of family support and an increase in family demands. The study further confirmed that relocation costs money, takes time away from family, and is potentially damaging to the family structure (Reimer 2000, p. 211). Finally, a more recent study conducted in the Netherlands by Brummelhuis et al. (2010) showed that work and family demands increase time and energy deficits. The authors argue that energy deficits due to heavy demands result in feeling of distress among dual earner couples.

A number of studies selected from the military literature examine the impact of military induced separation on quality of family life. Orthner et al. (1980) examined the needs married and single parent families in 16 sites of the United States Air Force (AF). A sample of 657 subjects were used in this cross-sectional study. The results of the study revealed a more positive picture about Air Force life. For example, when respondents were asked about the major disappointments with Air Force life, more than one half (58 %) the AF husbands, 52 % of the AF wives and 57 % of civilian wives indicated that they were satisfied with moves in the AF; two-thirds of single parents (67 %) expressed satisfaction with the move (Orther et al. 1980, p. 81). Satisfaction with base assignment was related to high job morale among both AF married women and AF single parents. Although respondents expressed concerns regarding the effects of moving on children, there was an overall consensus that moves did not disrupt family relations.

On the contrary, Lavee et al. (1985) showed that relocation has a negative impact on the family. Using a sample of 288 families, Lavee and colleagues examined variables that buffer or moderate the impact of relocation strains on the adaptation of US army families to an overseas relocation. The authors identified four major life events which intensify the level of relocation stress: the birth of a child; financial problems; illness; and death of a family member. Drawing from the findings of this study, the authors recommended that concerted efforts needed to be made to strengthen families, improve communication channels and promote their level of social support.

Croan et al. (1991) study supports the findings advanced by Lavee et al. (1985). Their study explored the impact of relocation on US army members and families using a sample of 8,976 subjects. In general, the findings of Croan et al. study indicated that relocation is a cost to family life and that the people who are likely to experience more difficulties are couples with children, and those who are older. The results suggest that support services, like pre-move and post-move information, may significantly decrease the hardships that are associated with relocation.

Methods

This research is based on data collected during a study conducted to examine the effects of job transfers on the family well-being. The study was conducted among a sample of Batswana teachers who had experienced job transfer, and this study utilised exploratory and descriptive designs. Triangulation of quantitative and qualitative research approaches—namely a survey, documentary review, informal discussions, participant observations, conference presentations, focus groups—was used to address the research objectives. The qualitative component of the study provided insights into the experiences of dual career families and ascertained internal validity. Aware that qualitative research has a potential problem with reliability, a survey questionnaire and the resultant quantitative data were used to counteract this weakness.

Data Collection

A structured mailed questionnaire was administered among 361 transferred teachers nationwide. A list of teachers was obtained from the Ministry of Education. Using multi-stage probability sampling technique 361 out of 486 questionnaires were returned. For the qualitative phase, a sample of 20 married couples ($n = 40$) was interviewed through face-to-face technique in their homes. This sample was selected from the South Central region of the country through purposive sampling technique. The reason for selecting this region is that it has a high concentration of dual career couples. Throughout the data collection process ethical standards of anonymity, voluntary participation and confidentiality were adhered to.

Data Analysis

Data from the survey were analysed using the Statistical Package for the Social Sciences (SPSS). Univariate statistics were used to provide the general description of the sample. Frequency tables provided useful percent summaries of respondents in each variable category. Bivariate statistics was used to test for the existence of a relationship between each independent variable and dependent variable. HyperResearch—a computer programme that can be used by qualitative researchers for the analysis of qualitative data—was used in the analysis of qualitative interviews (Hesse-Bider et al. 1991). Open-ended questions from survey data were also analysed separately using this technique.

Results and Discussion

Sample Description

As stated earlier, a total of 361 secondary school teachers participated in the quantitative component of the study. Of these, a little over half (53 %) were male and the rest (47 %) were female. This sample is fairly representative of the transfer population. For example, most transfers are affected on promotion to higher level positions. There are also a higher proportion of men occupying higher level positions. Consequently, this explains why in this sample we have a higher percentage of men than women despite the fact that the teaching profession is dominated by women. From this sample, 20 respondents were selected for the qualitative interviews. Through contact with them, their spouses were identified and located. In total, therefore, a sample of 40 individuals were used for the qualitative component of the study.

With respect to age, most respondents in quantitative sample (53 %) fell under the 31–40 year age range. The mean age was 29 years. Two-thirds of the respondents (64 %) were married. One-third (31 %) were single; the rest fell into the following categories: Divorced (3 %), separated (1 %) and engaged (0.3 %). There seems to be a reasonable balance between younger and older couples. For example, a quarter of the respondents (26 %), had been married for between 3 and 6 years. A third of the sample (32 %) had been married for 7 years or more.

A small proportion (8 %) was newlyweds. Slightly more than half (53 %) had one or two children; a quarter (25 %) had three to four children, 7 % had five children or more; whilst 15 % had no children.

In terms of educational qualifications, two-thirds (66 %) of the respondents had completed 3 years of university or college education. A third (29 %) had completed degree programmes and the rest (5 %) were master's degree holders. In line with this, most respondents participating in this study (62 %) held fairly high positions in the teaching field. Seemingly, there was a corresponding trend in income. Majority of married transferees (71 %) lived in separate residences from their spouse. Information pertaining to distance between transferees and spouse reveals very interesting findings. Almost a third of transferees (30 %) lived further than 152 km apart. On average, these couples lived 300 km apart.

Out of the 40 couples selected for the qualitative component of the study, half the sample was males and the other half females. Their spouses came from different professional backgrounds including the teaching field. Concerning their educational background, two-thirds of the respondents had completed 3 years of university or college education and hence were teaching in either community junior secondary schools or senior schools. On average, couples in the qualitative component were also living 300 km apart.

Factors Affecting Willingness to Relocate

Once a transfer decision has been finalised by a government department, the potential transferee is notified in writing. Normally, the transfer letter does not specify the underlying reasons behind the transfer except to mention that the officer is transferred to "carry out the exigencies of the service". In this study, 72 % of participants reported that they did not know the underlying rationale behind their relocation. Surprisingly, over half of the sample (59 %) indicated that they were given at least 2 weeks to prepare for relocation. More than a third (39 %) said they were given 3–6 weeks to prepare and only 1 % said they were given 6 weeks or more to prepare for relocation.

Asked to indicate why they accepted a transfer that entailed separation from family, majority of respondents reported that they had no choice because a transfer decision is mandatory. Having secured their jobs, they cited career advancement as another important consideration. For most participants, a rejection of a transfer decision automatically jeopardises one's career path unless the teacher has an additional qualification from another professional field. For similar reasons, spouses of transferees also expressed concern that if they followed their trailing spouses, they too would forfeit chances to advance their career goals. One woman described her career goals with these words:

> I feel that my career should advance. The family should not be an excuse. Our culture makes us feel that we should and must take care of the family. Most women are not

> prepared to go anywhere because this will jeopardise their family life…they believe "mosadi ke mosalagae" [meaning a woman's role is in her house]…I used to feel that I'm the only one who can hold the family together…I felt that my career shouldn't advance at the expense of my family. I don't feel that anymore.

Another woman spoke in similar terms about the importance of her job:

> My job and family are equally important. However, in the final analysis, I wouldn't compromise my job for my marriage. I don't know what will happen to this marriage. I don't even understand the extent to which my husband is investing in this marriage…the marriage might break…so I need to concentrate on my job.

Besides career advancement, the need to become financially independent was also a factor that was frequently cited as a motivation for accepting a transfer. Majority of women in the study resisted the idea of resigning from their jobs to join their transferred husbands because they aspired to have a regular wage. In sum, these findings confirm earlier studies that career attributes are significant predictors of job transfer decision (Brett and Reily 1988; Friedman 1989; Lee and Johnson 1994; Deding and Filges 2010).

Acceptance of transfer, however, automatically alters family roles and responsibilities. Before transfer, all dual career families interviewed reported that their roles and responsibilities were less complex. Both husband and wife went to work in the same town or village and then reunited with the family either during lunch time or in the evening. Although women still carried a heavier load of childcare responsibilities, all couples reported that they made some effort to enhance the quality of family time through, for example, budgeting together; planning and making joint decisions; running errands and providing emotional support.

Experience of Work-Family Conflict and Dilemmas

Through probing, it emerged that most couples experienced a sense of collegiality and competence. With geographic transfers, however, these roles and responsibilities changed drastically. The couples started to face work-family conflict and dilemmas normally experienced by dual career families. These include: role overload, role cycling, identity and normative dilemmas (Rapoport and Rapoport 1976).

Role Overload Dilemma

Role overload dilemma occurs when dual career families attempt to balance two major roles: their jobs as well as family responsibilities. Normally, such physical exhaustion and strains are felt by wives since they take on the extra burden of domestic responsibilities (Sekaren 1986). Interestingly, in this study both men and women experienced role overload dilemmas since they both had to take care of domestic responsibilities. For men, this was even more burdensome because of lack of adequate socialisation in this area. One man remarked:

> The stress of taking care of the family is increased…the running of the household which used to be done by two adults is done by one, single-handedly. I really miss meals that my wife used to prepare.

Another man made this statement about his new role:

> When your wife is not there, there is a tendency for people to want to help you. This could cost you a lot. You then start comparing the services rendered. I mean for example, if the woman cooks better than your wife, this may shake you a little. Lady friends come genuinely to prepare lunches…before you know it, you have made a mistake of falling for her.

It is interesting to observe that unlike men, women did not receive any sympathy about their additional responsibilities. There was a cultural expectation that they could handle their respective roles. Women, in turn, internalised and perpetuated this culture and gender bias. For example, with respect to childcare, all women in the study felt that it was their responsibility to take care of children. When situations did not permit, some women felt frustrated that their husbands had to assume this role:

> Generally, separation is painful. I find it difficult to concentrate. I keep thinking about children and wondering if they are ok. I also worry about their protection. I feel that if I was around, I could do something to help.

Another woman expressed similar sentiments about helping her husband to deal with their teenage daughter:

> We have three children, the girl is a teenager. She has come to a stage where she needs me around. I am really worried about her because she has started to go through a lot in her life. Her father is good, but I believe he needs me to deal with this situation.

It follows from the sentiments presented above that despite the changing family structure, the societal norms and values about women's roles have not radically changed.

Role Cycling Dilemmas

In addition to role overload, dual career families in this study experienced role cycling dilemmas. According to Rapoport and Rapoport (1976), role cycling dilemmas occur when dual career couples are compelled to make decisions about various issues that arise at different stages of their cycles. Chief among these are decisions regarding career goals, the ideal time to start a family, the size of the family, and other pertinent areas of the family well-being. In addition, these couples have to make major decisions about the impact of separation on the well-being of the children such as who will take care of childcare responsibilities, choice of schools, children's academic performance, children's health, as well as relationships with friends and other family members. Throughout their career paths, these couples go through a continuous battle of sorting out trade-offs between work and family demands.

Identity Dilemmas

The third dilemma that the couples in the study experienced is the internal conflict of trying to establish who they are and what they are becoming. Historically, women were regarded as socially inferior to men, and within customary law were generally treated as minors (Schapera 1955). In recent years, Botswana has made significant progress towards gender equality. Enrolment statistics show that gender disparity in primary and secondary education has been eliminated (Government of Botswana/UNDP 2010). This being the case, more women are now opting to be full-time employees. By choosing a dual career lifestyle, women challenge the gender-based roles and traditional values they have internalised over a long period of time. Inevitably, tension and conflict often arise as they negotiate trade-offs between becoming self-actualised or assuming traditional familial roles. The decision to adopt a commuter lifestyle exacerbates the situation because, in addition to advancing careers, women are now called upon to become temporary heads of households.

Normative Dilemmas

Whereas identity dilemmas arise from internal pressures, normative dilemmas occur as a result of the discrepancies which exist between the lifestyles of dual career couples and the norms and values prescribed by the society (Rapoport and Rapoport 1976). From the qualitative interviews, it was evident that dual career couples experienced normative dilemmas. The findings reveal that their friends, workmates as well as some extended family members were opposed to the commuter lifestyle. Consequently, this created a feeling of shame and guilt as they were frequently asked questions such as "when are you going to join your spouse"?; "who is taking care of the children"?; "how often to you see each other" and so forth. Consistent with these findings, Reimer (2000) revealed from his study in the United States that being away from home was perceived negatively by friends and families. The study shows that family and friends often made long-distance demands that produce both guilt and strain for those who had relocated (Reimer 2000, p. 212).

Perceived Benefits of Living Apart

Despite the above-mentioned challenges and dilemmas, dual career families reported that living apart presented them with some rewards. The three most enriching experiences were: expressiveness and self-worth; collegiality and sense of competence.

Expressiveness and Self-Worth

The ability to pursue a career is a rewarding experience for most Batswana. Educational opportunities are hard to come by and hence everyone wants to make use of the limited opportunities. In addition, the current socio-economic climate requires an educated society. With the current unemployment rate of 17.8 % (Central Statistics Office 2011), coupled with a high rate of inflation, career development is a critical means to survival. Above all, for dual career families, career advancement provides an avenue for accomplishment and creativity. It also offers an avenue for self-actualisation. Batswana women in particular aspire to get their talents and skills recognised. They also want to make a meaningful contribution to nation building. Through enhancing their career goals, they experience enhanced self-esteem and self-worth and gain a greater sense of importance.

Collegiality

Dual career marriages also provide husbands and wives with stimulating academic environments where they can both discuss issues at the same level, thus enhancing and sharpening each other's skills. In this study over 60 % of the professionals in the sample were educators. This similarity in career interests demonstrates how these families desire to have marriages that will further enhance their career development.

Sense of Competence

Commuter lifestyle is very challenging. As noted earlier, the couples are constantly faced with the dilemma of how to balance work and family pressures. It was also evident that they long to live together with their spouses. However, in lieu of their current situations, they have accepted the fact that they have no choice. This ability to persevere and be hopeful provides these couples with greater energy and motivation to face even greater life challenges.

Other Benefits

More than half of the women interviewed valued the freedom that commuter lifestyle provided. For example, they shared how this lifestyle allowed them to have more flexible time schedules, how it motivated them to be autonomous and to have a greater sense of self-esteem and, finally, how they felt relieved from the pressure of taking care of household chores such as: maintaining high levels of cleanliness and cooking special meals for their husbands. These findings confirm related studies (for example Gerstel and Gross 1984; Jehn et al. 1997; Klis and Karsten 2009) that living apart can bring forth substantial enrichment for some couples.

Perceived Disadvantages of Living Apart

Notwithstanding the foregoing perceived benefits, it also emerged that for many, relocation and living apart have had negative impact on marriage relationships, intimacy, parenting, family finances and work.

Impact Marriage Relationships

Past research reveals that job transfer is a source of strain on marriage relationships Participants in this study reported that the level of marital relationship changed as a result of transfer. For example, whereas 77 % of married teachers were satisfied with marriage before transfer, this figure dropped to 47 % after transfer, showing significant decline in marital satisfaction. Hence, consistent with earlier findings, geographic transfers have a negative impact on marriage. Having established this fact, the factors that may contribute to the decline in marital satisfaction were examined. Using a Chi square test, it was found that two variables were statistically significant at $p < 0.000$: type of residence and distance between transferee and spouse. Results show that 90 % of transferees who lived in a single residence with their spouse were satisfied with marriage, whereas only a handful (10 %) were dissatisfied with marriage. For those transferees who lived apart, over two-thirds of them (71 %), were dissatisfied with marriage after transfer and only a third were satisfied.

Further, distance between transferee and spouse influenced the level of marital satisfaction after transfer. Transferees who lived closer to their spouse (50 or less km) seem to be more satisfied with marriage than their counterparts who live further away. These findings are consistent with earlier findings that geographic transfers are a source of strain for married couples (Marshall and Cooper 1976; Gross 1980; Brett 1982; Taylor and Loundsbury 1988; Friedman 1989; Munton 1993; Hendershott 1995).

Impact on Intimacy and Fidelity

Majority of respondents (65 %) reported that that living apart had a negative effect on their intimacy and sexual relationships. Respondents cited problems such as loneliness, lack of regular physical contact, and infidelity. A husband described his dying passion with these words:

> Transfer entailed separation with family and this had a negative effect on the relationship. My wife was moved four times and we have not had a chance to stay together. The relationship is not as close as it was before. There's a lot of mistrust and suspicions. Certainly, this separation has been costly to my relationship with my wife. It decreases the love I have for her. I'm maintaining the marriage because we need to keep the vows. There's no close and active relationship. We are kept close only by children and the property we've acquired together. The children keep us going, but the love is gone.

Another husband echoed the same concern:

> Living in separation creates a superficial bond between couples. We were from two different families. We had to learn, accept and accommodate things. We needed to sacrifice for each other. This becomes very difficult when we were apart. We do not have a proper base or foundation. This is not the best option for us. I don't believe that there are many positives when people live in separate residences.

A woman also expressed the same feelings:

> This is a hard time for us. We used to be very close friends, now we are slowly drifting apart. Separation puts marriage under enormous strain. This begins with the emotional gap. The only strength is that we love each other and we have the fear of the Lord. The common good is that we have children as well. Separation brings intense things to the marriage. I don't want this to ever happen to a family. I love my family; I find it difficult to stay separated. I cannot cope with this kind of experience. When I'm at work, I get absent-minded. Each time I come home and go the children cry. This makes me feel very bad. The difficulty is that my husband is my best friend. No one wants to part with a best friend.

There was, however, a variation across the sample with respect to the frequency of sexual contact. For example, whereas weekly commuters did not experience a major decline in their sexual contact, those who visited monthly or bi-monthly reported that they experienced a radical decline in the quantity of sexual interaction. However, for some geographic separation rekindled their love relationship. Below are typical comments illustrating how distance made the heart grow fonder:

> The fact that we don't stay together increases the longing for one another, when we meet, it is always romantic.

> Our relationship gets renewed each time my husband gets home. When he is away, I miss him, but when he comes, our relationship gets rekindled.

Concerning infidelity or extramarital relations, an overwhelming majority of respondents (80 %) stated that job transfers contributed significantly to this problem. Commenting on factors contributing to extramarital affairs, two male respondents made these remarks:

> If you are far, you can't see the family regularly...we have constraints, transport, money. You then find yourself a girlfriend and there's a tendency to neglect your home.

> We are human, we can't discount that we cannot be involved in adulterous relationships...there are many temptations when you are alone. Women approach you with genuine feelings of wanting to be helpful...this tends to result in a relationship growing.

One man shared how and why he had to literally stay away from his lonely house:

> I have fears that I will fall into temptations, as a result, I don't spend a lot of time in the house: I make sure that I'm always with friends and family...my wife was told that I was engaged in an affair, this traumatised our relationship.

Another man said he tried not to focus on this issue:

> Temptations will usually come and I fear that I will be unfaithful to my wife. I try as much as possible to resist. I try to have the will power to stand by my vows. But this is difficult. If I were staying with my wife, I will not be thinking this way, but now with separation, a lot of thoughts come through your mind. Separation breeds insecurities...the best way to survive is not to think negatively about the other person...pretend as though everything is ok. If you vow not to get tempted, expect that your partner does the same thing.

Another man expressed similar sentiments:

> I've conditioned myself psychologically. I've created room for disappointments. If I hear that she has committed adultery, I will be hurt, but I will forgive her. If you over-trust, you create problems for yourself. My attitude is that my wife is not an angel; she's capable of making mistakes.

Older couples seemed to be more confident about their relationship than younger couples. Overall, they were less anxious about possibilities of extramarital affairs and more trusting of their mates. One woman expressed her feelings this way:

> I've come to a stage where I trust my husband. I do not have fears that he has a relationship. We are mature. If being apart is too costly, we will make a radical decision to stay together. My long term goal is to stay in this relationship.

Another woman made the same kinds of remarks about her feelings of security:

> We have not reached a stage where we are saturated. I don't have fears that my husband is cheating. I'm very comfortable because I communicate with him a lot. I know that he is taking this marriage very seriously.

Impact on Children

Past research confirm that a job transfer decision negatively impacts on the well-being of children (Gross 1980; Lavee et al. 1985; Wood et al. 1993). Consistent with these findings, respondents were of the view that living apart was a source of strain for children. In addition parents feel helpless and guilty that they are not there at all times to take care of their children. Stroh and Brett (1990) established that relocation is particularly stressful for adolescents. Mothers in this study had this to say about this situation:

> The children miss their father a lot; they feel his absence. But obviously, they're closer to me than their dad. There is a distance between them and him. Sometimes they make remarks like *'Wa ba a tsile'* meaning 'he has come to bother us.' When he is home, he is considered an outsider by the children.

Another woman expressed how her son misses his father:

> My four year old is very sad that my husband is not around all the time. He complains and cries every day. He doesn't understand why his father is away for too long. I think this is really affecting him. Sometimes he asks 'please get me another daddy because my daddy is not coming back.' This really makes me feel overwhelmed.

The second challenging area for mothers was handling their teenage children:

> It's very hard to bring up kids single-handedly. His nephew is a real problem. I don't think he wants to stay with me. He refuses to obey and I'm finding it difficult to handle him. If my husband was here, it would be much better.

Another mother expressed similar concerns:

> I don't think my children understood why I had to move to another place. The two teenagers have been very difficult especially my 17 year old son. His school work has dropped so much that I'm very doubtful whether he will make it in his final Form 5 examinations [final year of high school].

In response, fathers too were concerned about the impact of their absence on the children. The following statement summarises some of the fathers' feelings about parenting at a distance:

> I must admit that it's hard to stay away from the children. I miss them a lot, we used to do a lot of things together, every single day, now I don't have that luxury.
>
> I don't have personal contact with my three children. My children are going to blame me for not being a good father. Now I'm forced to divide my time between work and taking care of them. Before, I was always home, we could play every time. Children depend on us for comfort, love and security. If we are not there for them, children lose out. I really value my children; I have a close bond with them.

Impact on Family Income

Prior to relocation, government provides transferees with assistance to cover relocation costs. This assistance comes in the form of a transfer allowance, transportation, subsidised housing and, where applicable, a remote area service allowance. The latter is a type of incentive provided to all transferees who work in remote areas of the country. Despite these incentives, over 90 % of the couples interviewed complained that maintaining two separate households drained family financial resources. The following costs were frequently cited as burdensome: travel expenses; telephone bills; rent; utilities; food; household goods and services.

Interestingly, those transferred on promotion concurred that despite getting an increase in their salary, living apart was not cost effective. One headmaster made these remarks about family finances: *Although this was a promotion, the money I get doesn't help. The net expenditure ends up being higher.* His wife echoed the same sentiments:

> My husband was transferred on promotion. However, we don't really feel the difference in the salary because we spend a lot of money taking care of two homes.

Further, majority of respondents reported that financial hardships in turn strained the quality of the marriage relationship. Articulating some of the stresses in the family, a husband said:

> Before the transfer, we had enough money. We therefore didn't care about how it was used. After separating, we started to account for every little expense…justifying for small items made us argue a lot. Lack of trust in each other became a problem. I started to think that my wife was not capable of managing our finances.

Another husband spoke in similar terms about the effects of financial strains:

> Maintaining two households is not a joke. Every time we buy two of everything. This strains us badly and sometimes this puts strain in our relationship.

In sum, these results confirm earlier findings that living apart also affects the economic well-being of the family (Gerstel and Gross 1984; Shaklee 1989; Pinder 1989; Hendeshott 1995). Because couples are forced to maintain two separate households, resources are duplicated which makes it difficult for them to have adequate savings. What further compounds this situation is the fact that these couples do not have the luxury to jointly plan and organise their budgets on a regular and consistent manner.

Impact on Work

Most transferred teachers participating in the study reported that they were satisfied with work after transfer. However, a close examination of the married group revealed interesting results. The length of marriage, distance between transferees and their spouse, and the type of residence had a significant effect on the level of work satisfaction. For example, transferees who were married longer (11 years and over) were more dissatisfied with work after transfer than their counterparts who were married for relatively shorter periods. However, all respondents unanimously agreed that living apart was a significant barrier to their work. Commenting on her output level, one teacher remarked:

> When you're not happy, output at work is affected. We're both employed by government and we see that the government does not care about our welfare. Half of the time, we talk about frustrations instead of doing work. You spend half a day worrying about your family. Sometimes you're worried about the security in the house. These are bad times, we have burglars at night. This too affects productivity. Generally not being together does not enhance the quality of output. When you go to work, you're not yourself; this threatens productivity.

Another teacher made a similar remark about lack of motivation:

> On a scale of 0–100 my productivity level is 30. I don't enjoy my work; I don't derive any pleasure from it. I'm working to earn a living. I have adopted a negative attitude towards my job. Separation from family affects your productivity because you're always thinking about them. My son is asthmatic. Whenever my wife writes to say he's sick, I get worried and lose interest in the job. I only recover when I receive another letter saying he's now fine. It is natural to get affected when your children are not doing well.

Some teachers talked about how long distance travel affected their work as well:

> I am always late to work due to the fact that I travel long distance. This affects my work. I am not able to help the sport department during the weekends because I have to visit my husband. Even catching up with students' work has to wait until I came back from home. My heart is completely not on the job because I worry about the condition of my family. I have a divided mind.

Another teacher agreed:

> You can't be creative and show initiative when your mind is far away. Work gets affected and your professional development gets disturbed. Government loses money because we don't work full hours. On Mondays people come late and leave early on Fridays. Time is also lost on phone calls, which could be avoided if people lived together. Service is also affected because people don't give their best.

Further analysis showed that age and type of residence appear to be the strongest predictors of whether an individual will be dissatisfied with work or not. In essence, older transferees seemed to be more dissatisfied with work than other age groups. Seemingly, transferees who were separated from their spouse were also more likely to be dissatisfied with work than their counterparts who lived in the same location with their family members. In addition, these employees experienced more conflict between work and family.

Policy Implications and Recommendations

It is evident from the findings discussed in this chapter that, as in other parts of the world, geographic transfers have a negative impact on the well-being of dual career families who live apart in Botswana. While not all transferees are dissatisfied with the current transfer system, the findings suggest that it is imperative for the government of Botswana to devise plans to accommodate the needs of public officers who are affected and often inconvenienced by transfers and make the transfer system a rewarding developmental experience for all officers and their families. To this end, two sets of policy recommendations—short-term and long-term—are worthy of consideration.

Short-Term Policy Recommendations

In the short term, the following policy options seem feasible:

- Potential transferees should be given at least 3 months to prepare for relocation. Where possible, couples should be separated only as a last resort. If there is a need to separate couples, the transferring agencies should, to the extent possible, ensure that couples are located within a radius of not more than 80 km.
- To the extent possible, transferring agencies should aim at transferring couples to the same location.
- Where possible, public officer who are older (50–55 years) should be transferred closer to their home towns or villages.
- To enhance productivity, transferees should be kept in remote areas for a maximum of 2 years.
- Transparency should prevail in the transfer decision making process. Dialogue between various government departments and transferees should be promoted to facilitate effective transition for all parties involved.
- Government should assess the possibility of providing more financial incentives for transferees who work in remote areas.
- Given the fact that not all transferees are reluctant to accept a transfer decision, the current transfer system should be made voluntary. Public officers have a free choice of where they want to work.
- Transfer policy guidelines should be documented outlining succinctly, the objectives of the policy and the implementation machinery.

Long-Term Policy Recommendations:

The findings from this study suggest that transferees and their families need to be provided with other assistance beyond transfer allowance, transportation and subsidised housing. This study revealed that transfer policy is a source of strain on marriage and family relations. To this end, the following may be viable intervention strategies:

An Employee Assistance Programme

Private sector companies in many countries are utilising Employee Assistance Programmes (EAPs) as a way of providing support for families who are relocated. Within the Botswana public service EAP could fulfil the following specific functions:

Preparation and Orientation

- Provision of pre- and post-transfer interviews to determine the needs of the family;
- Counselling and professional support services;

- Transfer stress management;
- Dissemination of resource literature.

Special Assistance for Special Needs

- Connecting the family to a network of resources in a new area such as medical services, schools, social services and other community agencies;
- Identifying job opportunities for the spouse;
- Notifying providers ahead of time about special needs of family members;
- Addressing financial and emotional needs of extended family members.

Public Relations

Findings from this study have revealed that transferees who live apart often experience difficulties adjusting in new communities. The role of EAP in this area would therefore be to: (i) improve public receptivity of relocating families and to enhance their positive image as community contributors and developers, and (ii) develop a database of transferred employees which could be made accessible to other user departments and other transferring agencies.

Resource Implications

Implementation of an EAP has implications for additional resources. Government ministries will need to employ professionals, such as social workers, who are adequately trained to deal with family dynamics. Professionals with social work background will be best suited to implement such an EAP within the Department of Placement and Procurement.

Inter- and Intra-departmental Collaboration

All government departments could join hands in creating a family-oriented work system. Private as well as parastatal organisations would also be encouraged to embrace this philosophy in their workplaces.

Research and Training

Research is needed to guide policy development in the area of work and family in Botswana. To date, no study has been undertaken to address this issue. Social science and business management/administration curricula at universities and other tertiary institutions in Botswana should be reviewed to sensitize students on issues of work-family interface.

Employment Creation in the Rural Areas

Government has come up with a number of policies to accelerate rural development. Effective implementation of these policies is a key for the diversification of the economy as well as creation of employment opportunities for dual career couples. Currently, most jobs are concentrated in the eastern part of the country. In addition, this is where the best schools, health facilities, telecommunication services and other essential services are located. The reality is that dual career couples want the best for their children. It goes without saying that the long-term solution to minimise the trauma of transfers will be to make rural areas more attractive by providing essential services and improving infrastructural development. Once this goal is reached, employees will not hesitate to relocate with their families.

References

Bechuanaland Protectorate. (1934). *Standing Instructions.* Mafikeng. p. 86: Section 153.

Brett, J. M., & Reily, A. H. (1988). On the road again: Predicting job transfer decision. *Journal of Applied Psychology, 73*(4), 614–620.

Brett, J. N. (1982). Job transfer and the family well-being. *Journal of Applied Psychology, 67*, 450–463.

Brummelhuis, L. L., Haar, J. M., & Lippe, T. (2010). Crossover of distress to work and family demands in dual earner couples: A dyadic analysis. *Work and Stress, 24*(4), 324–341.

Central Statistics Office. (2011). *Preliminary results of Botswana core welfare indicators poverty survey 2009/10.* Central Statistics Office: Gaborone.

Croan, G. M., Levine, C. T., & Blankinship, D. A. (1991). *Family adjustment to relocation (Technical Report).* Alexandria: U.S. Army Research Institute for Behavioral and Social Sciences.

Deding, M., & Filges, T. (2010). Geographic mobility of Danish dual-earner couples: The relationship between change of job and change of residence. *Journal of Regional Science., 50*(2), 615–634.

Friedman, H. B. (1989). *Psychological assessment of the effects of job transfers on executives and their families.* Unpublished dissertation, University of Michigan.

Gerstel, N. & Gross, H. (1984). Commuter marriage: couples who live apart. In: B. N. & Campbell, J. (Ed.), *Framing The Family Contemporary Portraits.* Illinois: Waveland Press, Inc.

Government of Botswana. (1982). *Personnel Directive #8 of 1982*, p. 2.

Government of Botswana. (1995). *Circular Savingram DP 19/72 of August 1995.*

Government of Botswana/UNDP. (2010). *Millennium development goals status report Botswana.* Gaborone: Government Printer.

Gross, H. (1980). Dual career couples who live apart: two types. *Journal of Marriage and Family, 50*, 567–576.

Hendershott, A. (1995). *Moving for work: The sociology of relocating in the 1990s*. New York: University Press of America, Inc.

Hesse-Biber, S., Dupuis, P., & Kinder, S. (1991). HyperResearch: A computer program for the analysis of qualitative data. *Qualitative Sociology, 14*(4), 289–306.

Jehn, K. A., Stroh, L. K., & Von Glinow, M. A. (1997). The commuting couple: Oxymoron or career freedom? In Y. Altunex (Ed.), *Careers in the new millennium* (pp. 163–178). Brussels: Academic Cooperative.

Klis, M., & Karsten, L. (2009). The commuter family as a geographic strategy for the work-family balance. *Community, Work and Family, 12*(3), 339–354.

Lavee, Y., McCubbin, H. I., & Patterson, J. M. (1985). The double ABCX model of family stress and adaptation: An empirical test by analysis of structural equations with latent variables. *Journal of Marriage and Family, 47*, 811–825.

Lee, W. W., & Johnson, D. R. (1994). Reactions to job transfer by job type and career stage. *Journal of Business and Psychology, 8*(3), 377–390.

Marshall, J., & Cooper, C. (1976). The mobile manager and his wife. *Management Decision, 14*(4), 179–220.

Munton, A. G. (1993). Job relocation, stress and the family. *Journal of Organisational Behaviour, 11*, 401–406.

Ntseane, D. M. (2004). Personnel transfers: Experiences of Batswana teachers, Pula: Botswana. *Journal of African Studies, 18*(1), 65–76.

Orthner, D. K., Bowen, C. L., Orthner, B. F., & Mancini, J. A. (1980). *Families in Blue*. Greensboro: Family Research and Analysis, Inc.

Pinder, C. C. (1989). The dark side of executive relocation. *Organisational Dynamics, 17*(4), 48–58.

Pinder, C. C., & Walter, G. A. (1984). Personnel transfers and employee development. *Research in Personnel and Human Resources Management, 2*, 187–218.

Rapoport, R., & Rapoport, R. N. (1976). *Dual Career Families*. Hammonsworth: Penguin.

Riemer, J. (2000). Job relocation, sources of stress, and sense of home. *Community Work and Family, 3*(2), 205–217.

Schapera, I. (1955). *The Tswana Law and Custom*. Great Britain: International African Institute.

Sekaren, U. (1986). *Dual Career Families*. San Francisco: Jossey-Bass.

Shaklee, H. (1989). Geographic mobility and the two earner couple: Expected costs of a family move. *Journal of Applied Social Psychology, 19*(9), 728–743.

Stroh, L. K., & Brett, J. M. (1990). Corporate mobility: After the move, what do children think? *Children's Environment Quarterly, 7*(3), 7–14.

Taylor, A. S., & Loundsbury, J. W. (1988). Dual career couples and geographic transfers: executive reaction to commuter marriage and attitudes towards the move. *Human Relations, 41*, 407–424.

Temane, B.K. (1989). *The Evolution and Development of the Public Service in Botswana (1890–1990)* Unpublished Report. Gaborone.

Wood, D., Halfon, N., Scarlata, D., Newacheck, P., & Nessim, S. (1993). Impact of family relocation on children's growth, development, school function and behavior. *Journal of the American Medical Associations, 270*(11), 1223–1225.

Chapter 8
Workplace Changes and Its Implications for Work–Family Conflict and Gender Asymmetries in South Africa

Zitha Mokomane, Francine Masson and Eleanor Ross

Introduction

From an ecological perspective, the family and work are two key social systems that coalesce and converge, and are crucial for individual well-being (Werbel and Walter 2002). Despite momentous demographic, social and economic changes occurring around the world, the family continues to fulfil important functions in terms of physical maintenance, adaptation and change; procreation, socialisation and communication; education and protection of children; control of social and sexual behaviour; social support and maintenance of its members' morale; and motivation of members to perform roles inside and outside the family (Sherriff et al. 2010; United Nations 2012). Work, on the other hand, matters in a market-based economy because it allows individuals to sell their capacity to labour as a means of survival while providing opportunities for self-esteem, self-actualisation, dignity and respect. Despite family and work being fundamental requirements for fulfilment of our sense of humanity, the intersections between family and work can also be sites of conflict, collision and contestation (Bolton and Houlihan 2009). This has been the case since the second half of the twentieth century due to the significant increase in women entering the labour market, an increase in dual-earner families, and an erosion of the male breadwinner model whereby men work

Z. Mokomane (✉)
Population Health, Health Systems and Innovation, Human Sciences Research Council of SouthAfrica, 134 Pretorius Street, Pretoria, South Africa
e-mail: zmokomane@hsrc.ac.za

F. Masson
Department of Social Work, University of the Witwatersrand, 1 Jan Smuts Avenue, Braamfontein, Johannesburg, South Africa
e-mail: Francine.Masson@wits.ac.za

E. Ross
Centre for Social Development in Africa, University of Johannesburg, Auckland Park, Johannesburg, South Africa
e-mail: eross@uj.ac.za

Z. Mokomane (ed.), *Work–Family Interface in Sub-Saharan Africa*,
International Perspectives on Social Policy, Administration, and Practice,
DOI: 10.1007/978-3-319-01237-7_8, © Springer International Publishing Switzerland 2014

outside the home to earn a wage and provide for their families while wives stay at home to do domestic work and care for family members (Pascall and Lewis 2004). All in all people's time and energy have been diverted away from their families as employment has become increasingly demanding. This has led to increased awareness of the challenges workers face in their attempts to combine domestic and family tasks with their work responsibilities. In developing countries these problems are amplified due to poverty and high unemployment rates (Paddey and Rousseau 2011).

While there is a plethora of literature on the impact of a changing workplace on the family, minimal attention would appear to have been focussed on gender asymmetries, contradictions and ambiguities in the form of employed women versus unemployed male partners; females occupying high status and high income positions relative to their males partners holding lower status and lower income jobs; as well as the impact of such asymmetries and inequitable power relationships on men—particularly in traditionally patriarchal societies. With a particular focus on South Africa, this chapter endeavours to address these issues by interrogating traditional notions of work and its multiple meanings; the changing contemporary workplace, gender roles and gender segregation; and the impact of these changes on the family.

The Meaning of Work

Work occupies a central role in people's lives touching upon economic, social and psychological aspects of their existence. As Ardichvili and Kuchinke (2009:155) explain, "work is central to human existence, it provides the necessities for life, sources of identity, opportunities for achievement and determines standing within the larger community". These authors maintain that from a constructivist frame of reference, the meanings and experiences that one attributes to work define one's choice of career, educational path, job satisfaction, work motivation and work performance. It is therefore important to briefly explore the significance and importance of work in one's life.

Almost 60 years ago Friedmann and Havighurst (1954) researched the different meanings of work for people in different occupations, and found that these included the ability to maintain a minimum level of existence; having something to do; being a source of self-respect, status and recognition; providing relationships with peers, subordinates and superiors; providing a purpose to life; an opportunity for service to others; and providing a platform for creative expression. Despite this research being almost 60 years old, it still has relevance today for understanding the role and meaning of work in a person's life. In essence what Friedmann and Havighurst showed is that work not only provides an income, but it also gives the worker identification, some status, and association. It also helps to provide structure, a way of expending time and energy, and a source of meaning in one's life. This is consistent with Karl Marx's notion that work is a primary human activity that has the potential to either fulfil people's potential or to destroy and distort not only their nature but also their relationship with others. Marx believed that if people were unable to find satisfaction or fulfilment in their labour or the products of their labour, they would become alienated and become strangers to themselves. To this end, work can be viewed as an avenue for people to not only fulfil their basic needs but also to ensure their humanity (Haralambos and Heald 1985).

Work is also one of the most important means to build one's self-concept and self-identity, both of which are developed through the influence of a complex interplay of internal and external factors, such as local customs, cultural norms of an ethnic group, religious beliefs and organisational cultures. These factors contribute to a positive or negative self-image and help to shape what is considered acceptable work and what work should be avoided (Ardichvili and Kuchinke 2009). The personal values of the worker are other variables that have been shown to be significant in the meaning of work. Whilst traditionally financial reimbursement and promotional opportunities were the strongest influences on job choice decisions, other work values such as achievement and concern for others have been found to have great influence (Cox 2004). For example, the Trobriand Islanders found in the Western Pacific have a cashless economy, and the social obligation to the community is the only key reason that these islanders engage in work activities (Malinowski 1984, cited in Grint 2005). The implication is that the meaning of work is subject to change as people's values may change over time and so might the kind of work that they find meaningful.

Notwithstanding the foregoing, the most important aspect of research on the meaning and value of work is possibly the fact that it draws attention to the phenomenon of unemployment when individuals deprived of the regular activity afforded by employment plus all the material and psychological benefits of work are at risk of suffering severe psychological and financial distress. Indeed, "unemployed people have consistently been found to experience higher levels of depression, anxiety and general distress, together with lower self-esteem and confidence" (Fielden and Davidson 1999:86).

The research also draws attention to the issue of work–family conflict which "arises when demands and pressures from the work impede employees' participation in their family role" and can, as discussed elsewhere in this book, negatively affect the well-being of workers and their families, and exert a negative impact on the workplace and society in general (International Labour Organisation 2007; Ilies et al. 2012). To this end it is important to acknowledge that work not only brings benefits and positive experiences but can also be a source of stress. In the words of Bolton and Houlihan (2009:2):

> work matters because it is rarely only that; it is about esteem and disrespect, status and subordination, opportunity and cost, commitment and alienation…work and workplaces are fields of struggle where interests can both coincide and clash, and personhood is both attacked and maintained.

Changes in Contemporary Workplaces

Changes in Women's Work Roles

As stated earlier, in the traditional male breadwinner model, a woman's work focused upon the home and on rearing children. However, the industrial revolution brought about a marked shift in women's employment as many women went to work outside of the home, particularly in factories. In fact factory workers would often prefer to employ women and children as they could pay them less than they would pay men (Walby 1986). The employment of women outside the home became particularly widespread during the Second World War due to labour shortages which arose when men went off to fight in the war and women became an invaluable and available pool of labour needed to boost economies. This trend has persisted over the years and according to the International Labour Organisation (2007), despite regional variations, women's participation in income-earning activities outside the home has been increasing conspicuously and significantly in almost all countries and "there have never before been so many economically active women (International Labour Organisation 2007:2).

Furthermore, unlike in the past when women often relinquished their careers and become the 'trailing spouse' in order to accommodate their husband's career moves, there has in recent years been a significant change from the historical view of men as the main breadwinners. Gordon and Whelan-Berry (2005), for example, conducted an exploratory qualitative study among dual-career couples in the United States with the aim to discover whose career took precedence. Most (58 %) of the women in the study felt that both careers held equal precedence, 22 % felt that their husband's career took precedence, whilst only 19 % felt that their careers had precedence—something they attributed predominantly to financial factors.

Despite the shift in the view that men are the primary breadwinners, and the increased engagement of women in paid work outside the home, women continue to fulfil the roles of homemakers, wives and mothers. In consequence, women worldwide generally work longer hours than men, when one considers all work, paid and unpaid, that women still do. In South Africa data from the 2000 Time Use Survey Africa (the only such study to have been done in the country) showed that each day women in the country spend more than double the time men spend on household maintenance and care of persons, but much less time than men on learning, social and cultural activities, and mass media use (Fig. 8.1). Although the Figure does not refer specifically to employed men and women, Valodia and Devey (2005) showed that the pattern is similar among the employed population.

Analysis of data from the 2000 Time Use Survey data also revealed that where both members of the household are employed in the formal sector, men on average spend 18 units of time in paid work compared to women's 15 (Table 8.1). The table also shows that when a female member of the household is employed in the informal economy, unpaid household work increases to 12.2 time units while time

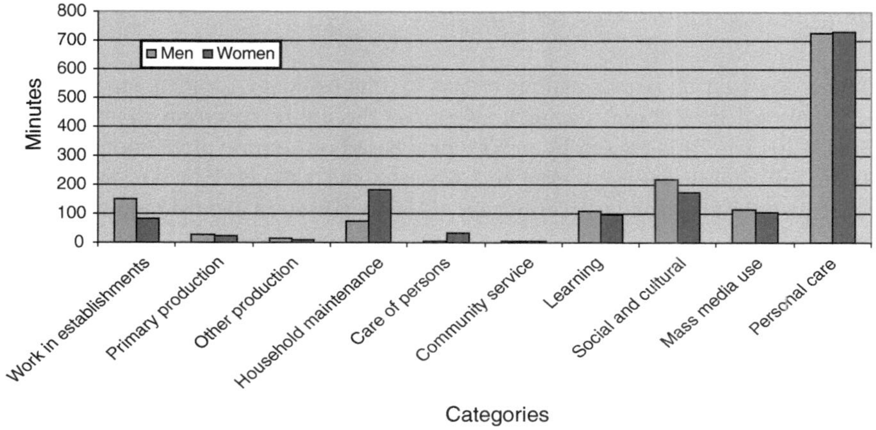

Fig. 8.1 Mean number of min per day spent on activities by type of activity and gender, *Source* Budlender et al. (2001)

Table 8.1 Time use patterns by gender and employment (30 min time units), South Africa 2000

Employment combination	Paid work		Unpaid work		Leisure and personal	
Male: Female	Male	Female	Male	Female	Male	Female
Formal : Formal	18.0	15.3	2.4	7.9	34.3	32.9
Formal : Informal	17.3	8.8	2.3	12.2	34.2	34.5
Informal : Formal	16.8	14.0	2.9	7.2	34.8	32.8
Informal : Informal	10.8	9.1	2.9	12.5	40.0	34.2

Source Adapted from Valodia and Devey (2005)

spent on paid work falls. This combination contrasts sharply with the opposite work combination where the male member is in informal work and the female member in formal work. In the last combination, where both the male and female household members are employed in the informal economy female members spend significantly higher proportions of time on unpaid work while their male counterparts, on average, spend more time on leisure and personal activities (Valodia and Devey 2005).

Among other things, the females' time use patterns can result in what Budig and England (2001) describe as 'the wage penalty of motherhood', that is, mothers (and indeed other women with caring responsibilities) are likely to earn less than what they could actually earn because they spend more time at home attending to their caring responsibilities, and interrupting their job experience or, at least, interrupting fulltime employment (Budig and England 2001). To the extent that experience and seniority have positive returns because they involve on-the-job training that makes workers more productive (Becker 1964), the time use patterns of working women in South Africa imply that the women will continue to earn less (see Muller 2008) because they spend more time in attending to domestic tasks, and less time on productive activities.

Gender Segregation in Occupations

Gender segregation in occupations relates to "the tendency for men and women to be employed in different occupations across the entire spectrum of jobs" (EU-OSHA 2013:1). It is caused by gender bias based on stereotypical, biological and social differences between men and women, and as such can be viewed as a consequence of men and women's patterns of socialisation and the identification of tasks traditionally seen as 'women's work' or 'men's work'.

Occupational gender segregation has two specific dimensions: horizontal and vertical. Horizontal segregation is where the workforce of a specific industry or sector is mostly made up of one particular gender. Examples include construction, engineering and medical fields where men are more dominant, and the administration, nursing, teaching and social work fields which are dominated by women (EU-OSHA 2013). Vertical segregation on the other hand is where opportunities for career progression within a company or sector for a particular gender are narrowed such as where more senior or managerial positions tend to be occupied by men while lower, more junior positions are generally occupied by women (Glover and Kirton 2006; EU-OSHA 2013).

Gender segregation in occupations can sometime arise when women consciously choose "mother friendly" jobs that are easier to combine with parenting and care work, the most common of these being part-time work (Budig and England 2001). These jobs, however, often have negative consequences for women in terms of pay and promotional opportunities. For example, women working part-time have been found to typically earn significantly less than men in terms of both average hourly and monthly wages as well as much less than their counterparts who work full-time (see Muller 2008). The literature has also shown that working women may also earn lower wages because their caring responsibilities leave them exhausted or distracted at work, making them less productive (Budig and England 2001). As a result, these women may be penalised because the image persists that they are not committed to their jobs and careers. For these same reasons, managers may also hesitate to hire women for certain types of jobs, often those with better career prospects, and/or to invest on their training (International Labour Organisation 2004; Heymann et al. 2007).

Recent studies (for example, Muller 2008; Mutedi 2003) suggest that this might already be happening in South Africa. Muller (2008) for example, posits that more than 20 % of South African women's increase in wage employment between 1995 and 2006 can be attributed to the growth in part-time wage employment. Table 8.2 below also shows that the proportion of those employed part-time who are women increased notably from 51.4 % in 1995 to 65.4 % in 2006. Conversely, men's employment in part-time work accounted for only about six percent of the total increase in male employment over the period.

Although this pattern of part-time work cannot be assumed to be directly related to work–family conflict, analysis of various national surveys shows that female part-time workers in South Africa are more likely to live in households under

Table 8.2 Part-time wage employment (000s) by gender, South Africa 1995–2006

	1995	1999	2001	2006
Women				
Total wage employment	2,829	3,632	3,795	4,323
Part-time wage employment	279	552	573	583
Proportion of part-time wage employed who are women	51.5	58.1	60.1	65.4
Proportion of employed women who work part-time	9.9	15.2	15.1	13.6
Men				
Total wage employment	5,325	4,986	5,310	6,016
Part-time wage employment	263	397	380	309
Proportion who work part-time	4.9	8.0	7.2	5.2

Sources Muller (2008:21)

Table 8.3 Conditions of employment, part-time and full-time workers by gender, South Africa, 2001–2006

Proportion of all wage employed	Part-time				Full-time			
	2001		2006		2001		2006	
	Men	Women	Men	Women	Men	Women	Men	Women
Written contract	0.35	0.31	0.45	0.43	0.58	0.49	0.74	0.71*
Temporary or casual work	0.49	0.51	0.55	0.51	0.14	0.16	0.20	0.21
Pension fund contribution	0.32	0.20*	0.22	0.15	0.56	0.47*	0.55	0.50*
Medical insurance	0.16	0.12*	0.11	0.07*	0.32	0.28*	0.26	0.25
Paid leave	0.33	0.29	0.25	0.29	0.63	0.59*	0.63	0.61
UIF contribution	0.37	0.30*	0.99	0.99	0.62	0.54*	0.99	0.99
Trade union member	0.25	0.13	0.13	0.07*	0.39	0.31*	0.33	0.29*

Sources Muller (2008:22)

which children (those aged 0–14 years) also live (Muller 2008), thus suggesting that work–family conflict may be a major factor.

From the perspective of equity, it is evident that women doing part-time-work face inferior conditions in comparison to men and women working fulltime (Table 8.3). For example, in 2006, only seven percent of women working part-time reported that they were receiving medical aid contributions from their employer, compared to 11 % of their male counterparts. Women working part-time were also less likely to have pension fund contributions and paid leave than women working full-time.

Conclusion and Recommendations

As in other parts of the world, South Africa has undergone various changes in the workplace that have, in a way, increased the burden of care faced by working women as they try to balance the demands of their work and domestic roles. In response to these changes, many working families have had, over the years, to reallocate and redistribute family responsibilities in order to address the needs of their children. Possibly the most significant adaptation that has taken place is the increased role that fathers now have in looking after their children (Gottfried and Gottfried 2008 as cited by Paddey and Rousseau 2011). With the emergence of these so-called 'new' or 'modern' fathers, many fathers are "no longer mere breadwinners … but are increasingly aware of, and concerned about what they do as fathers and how they do it" (Richter et al. 2011:65). Swartz and Bhana (2009), for example, found that despite the myriad of challenges they face as they attempt to be involved in their children's lives, many young fathers in South Africa "do want to make the effort to remain involved as loving and present parents" (Swartz and Bhana 2009:18). Even in traditional patriarchal societies, the increasing role of the father and his involvement in child rearing activities has become common as noted in a study of husbands' perceptions of their changing roles in the dual-earner economy among South African white Afrikaans males (Smit 2000). The study found that there were significant shifts towards equality in the marriage as well as pronounced changes in Afrikaans men's involvement with rearing their children.

For the most part however, many South African men, particularly from the Black African racial group, are not actively involved in their children's upbringing. According to the South African Institute of Race Relations (Holborn and Eddy 2011), the proportion of fathers in South Africa who are "absent and living" increased from 42 % in 1996 to 48 % in 2009. Conversely, the proportion of those fathers who are present decreased from 49 % to 36 % in the same time period. When the data are disaggregated by race "African children under 15 years had the lowest proportion of present fathers in 2009 at 30 %, compared to 53 % for coloured children, and 85 % for Indians and 83 % for Whites" (Holborn and Eddy 2011:4). Drawing from other previous research on the subject, Holborn and Eddy argue that this "absent father' phenomenon can largely be attributed to poverty and high rates of unemployment in South Africa as a large number of fathers are financially unable to take responsibility for their children … The burden of failure as primary providers becomes particularly "intolerable for those who lack the capacity to generate enough income as uneducated and unskilled labourers" (Holborn and Eddy 2011:5). Regardless of the reasons, this situation means that a large number of mothers in South Africa are the sole careers and economic providers for their children.

The overall conclusion, therefore, is that work–family conflict is an aspect of the South Africa social and economic landscape that needs to be considered and addressed by both employees and employers. Given the fact that gainful employment is regarded as the single most important factor in combating poverty, policies designed to support parental employment and facilitate work–family balance play a key role in development. Moreover, since poverty rates have been found to be lower in dual-earner households, policies responsive to the realities of dual-earner families are needed to reduce poverty and make it easier for both parents to reconcile their work and family responsibilities (United Nations 2012). "Lack of attention to work–family reconciliation strategies negatively affects not only the job quality, health and productivity of workers, but also their families and children" (United Nations 2012:17). It is therefore imperative to acknowledge the critical need for care in South Africa and to put in place to mechanisms to reduce gender asymmetries and help employees balance their roles as parents and employees. As Dancaster (2008) pointed out:

> We need to recognise the role of employees as caregivers through legislative provisions encompassing a range of leave circumstances, with the right to request flexible working arrangements. These measures are a means of valuing women as the main providers of this vital societal function and are necessary considerations if there is to be true equality of opportunity in the workplace

Although the rights of employees in South Africa are significantly acknowledged and advocated for with the Basic Conditions of Employment Act and the Labour Relations Act of 1997, work–family–work spill-over or conflict is not adequately addressed in current South African legislation. Paternity leave is not legislated and fathers are entitled to only three days family responsibility leave upon the birth of their child. Documents such as the Green Paper on Families (Department of Social Development 2011) are starting to acknowledge the critical role that families have in the development and mentoring of future employees and citizens. Nonetheless, the need for accessible, supportive and flexible work environments for employees with family commitments remains critical in ensuring the development of an equitable and just South African society for future generations.

Flexible leave provisions are based on the recognition that "the direct, short-term cost of granting leave to working parents is outweighed by economic and social gains in employment retention and human capital development" (United Nations 2012:7). In order to increase the chances of such policies being successful, Paddey and Rousseau (2011) emphasise the need to develop, implement, monitor and evaluate work–family policies based on a process of collaboration and consultation with employees about their individual needs regarding the balance between their work and family lives. The post-Fordism model of 'negotiated flexibility' which allows for active union participation, flexibility to meet employee needs and a wider worker involvement is worthy of consideration in this regard. Adopted by countries such as Holland and Sweden, this model allows for far greater incorporation of employee and family needs. This is in contrast to the post-Fordism model of 'capital orientated flexibility' which is market-driven, promotes privatisation, and in which unions have limited power and there is increased financial inequality between rich and poor and insecure employment Koch (as cited in Smith 2006).

Other recommendations include time management to allow employees to deal with work demands in a better and more timely manner; job crafting which involves changing the boundaries of the job to better fit the needs of the job incumbent (Ilies et al. 2012) and telecommuting (United Nations 2012). Barling (1990:236) also emphasises the value of adequate maternity and parental leave, child allowances, care for sick children and family members and assistance with transportation and housing. In order to address family-work conflict and the impact of gender asymmetries, there is a need for alternative work schedules with the three kinds of flexibility advocated by Schneider and Waite (2005), namely: flexibility in scheduling, flexibility in the amount of time that individuals spend in working, and career flexibility with effective entry and exit points including leave, sabbaticals, and time out.

In closing, we hope that this chapter will stimulate further research on the role of gender asymmetries in work–family conflict and help advance the literature on this topic. Fox et al. (2011:716) describe work and family as 'greedy institutions', where changing demands, gender roles and identities require sufficient time and energy and accommodating workplaces. We have probably asked more questions about gender asymmetries than provided answers but hopefully through creating greater understanding of these challenges practical insights will evolve for assisting men and women to cope more effectively with gender demands and stresses that interfere with their family lives. Equal career precedence should be more strongly advocated for, whilst acknowledging that this scenario may require tradeoffs and sacrifices from both partners and even assess their commitment not only to their careers but also to their families. Whilst precedence may be predominantly economically driven, the influencing factors such as logistics, early socialisation, or personal ego needs cannot be underestimated (Gordon and Whelan-Berry 2005). Finally, we wish to highlight the importance of introducing policies that reduce the negative impact of patriarchal beliefs and practices and provide support for more egalitarian, gender congruent work and family roles for men and women.

References

Ardichvili, A., & Kuchinke, K. P. (2009). International perspectives on the meaning of work and working: current research and theory. *Advances in Human Development, 11*, 115–167.

Barling, J. (1990). *Employment, stress and family functioning*. UK: John Wiley Sons Ltd.

Becker, S. B. (1964). *Human capital: A theoretical and empirical analysis, with special reference to education*. Chicago: University of Chicago Press.

Bolton, S. C., & Houlihan, M. (Eds.). (2009). *Work matters: Critical reflections on contemporary work*. Hampshire: Palgrave Macmillan.

Budig, M. J., & England, P. (2001). The wage penalty of motherhood. *American Sociological Review, 66*(2), 204–225.

Budlender, D., Chobokoane, N., & Mpetsheni, Y. (2001). *Time use in South Africa: Finding out how South Africans spend time*. South Africa: Statistics Pretoria.

Cox, P. L. (2004). The meaning of work: studs Terkel's working as a teaching tool. *Journal of Management Education, 28*, 757–769.

Dancaster, L. (2008). *Mom at work.* Available at http://mg.co.za/article/2008-09-18-mom-at-work. Accessed 10 October 2012.

Department of Social Development. (2011). *Green paper on families: Promoting family life and strengthening families in South Africa*. Pretoria, Department of Social Development, Republic of South Africa.

EU-OSHA [European Agency for Safety and Health at Work]. (2013). What does 'gender segregation in occupations' mean? Retrieved April 17, 2013 from https://osha.europa.eu/en/faq/women-and-health/what-does-2018gender-segregation-in-occupations2019-mean.

Fielden, S. L., & Davidson, M. J. (1999). Stress and unemployment: A comparative review and research model of female and male managers. *British Journal of Management, 10*, 63–93.

Fox, M. F., Foneca, C., & Bao, J. (2011). Work and family conflict in academic science: Patterns and predictors among women and men in research universities. *Social Studies of Science, 41*(5), 716–734.

Friedmann, E. E., & Havighurst, R. J. (1954). *The meaning of work and retirement*. Chicago: University of Chicago Press.

Glover, J., & Kirton, G. (2006). *Women, employment and organisations*. London: Routledge.

Gordon, J. R., & Whelan-Berry, K. S. (2005). Contributions to family and household activities by the husbands of midlife professional woman. *Journal of Family Issues, 26*, 899–923.

Grint, K. (2005). *The sociology of work*. Cambridge: Polity Press.

Gottfried, A. E. & Gottfried, A. W. (2008). The upside of maternal and dual-earner employment: A focus on positive family adaptations, home environments, and child development in the Fullerton longitudinal study. In A. Marcus-Newhall, D. F. Halpern, & S. J. Tan (Eds.), *The changing realities of work and family* (pp. 25-42). United Kingdom: Wiley-Blackwell.

Haralambos, M., & Heald, R. M. (1985). *Sociology: Themes and perspectives*. London: Unwin Hyman Limited.

Heymann, J., Earle, E., Rajaraman, D., Miller, C., & Bogen, K. (2007). Extended family caring for children orphaned by AIDS: balancing essential work and caregiving in a high prevalence nation. *AIDS Care, 19*(3), 337–345.

Holborn, L., & Eddy, G. (2011). *First steps to healing the South African family*. Johannesburg: South African Institute of Race Relations.

Ilies, R., De Pater, I. E., Lim, S., & Binnewies, C. (2012). Attributed causes for work-family conflict: Emotional and behavioural outcomes. *Organizational Psychology Review, 2*(4), 293–310.

International Labour Organisation. (2004). *Work and family responsibilities: What are the problems?* (Information Sheet No. WF-1). Geneva: International Labour Organisation.

International Labour Organisation. (2007). *Global employment trends for women: Brief March 2007*. Geneva: International Labour Organisation.

Malinowski, B. (1984). The Primitive Economics of the Trobriand Islanders. In C. R. Littler (Ed.), *The Experience of Work* (pp. 15-22). London: Heinemann.

Muller, C. (2008). *Trends in the gender wage gap and gender discrimination among part-time and fulltime workers in post-apartheid South Africa*. Development Policy Research Unit, School of Economics, University of Cape Town.

Mutedi, A. M. (2003). *Marital status and the South African labour market. Occasional paper 2002/02*. South Africa: Statistics.

Paddey, M., & Rousseau, G. G. (2011). The effects of the global recession on the work structuring levels of managers in the South African automotive industry. *South African Journal of Economic & Management Sciences, 3*, 346–360.

Pascall, G., & Lewis, J. (2004). Emerging Gender Regimes and Policies for Gender Equality in a Wider Europe. *Journal of Social Policy, 33*(3), 373–394.

Richter, L., Chikovore, J., Makusha, T., Bhana, A., Mokomane, Z., Swartz, S. & Makiwane, M. (2011). Fatherhood and Families. In (United Nations Economic & Social affairs (Ed.), *Men in families and family policy in a changing world* (pp. 47–84). New York: United Nations.

Schneider, B., & Waite, L. J. (Eds.). (2005). *Being together, working apart: dual-career families and the work life balance*. Cambridge: Cambridge University Press.

Sherriff, B., Seedat, M., & Suffla, S. (2010). A critical overview of family functioning indices. *African Safety Promotion Journal, 8*(2), 20–38.

Smit, R. (2000). The husband's perception of his changing role in the dual-earner family: The South African experience of the white Afrikaner. In C. Harvey (Ed.), *Walking a tightrope: Meeting the challenges of work and family*. Hampshire: Ashgate Publishing Limited.

Smith, A. (2006). Living with unemployment. *Sociology, 40*, 949–955.
Swartz, S., & Bhana, A. (2009). *Teenage tata: Voices of young fathers in South Africa: Summary for policy makers and practitioners*. Cape Town: HSRC Press.
United Nations. (2012). *Report of the secretary-general on preparations for and observance of the twentieth anniversary of the international year of the family in 2014*. Geneva: General Assembly Economic and Social Council.
Valodia, I. & Devey, R. (2005). *Gender, employment and time use: Some issues in South Africa*. Paper prepared for the Conference on Unpaid work, Poverty and the Millennium Development Goals, Bard College, October 1–3.
Walby, S. (1986). *Patriarchy at work*. Great Britain: University of Minnesota Press.
Werbel, J., & Walter, M. H. (2002). Changing views of work and family roles: A symbiotic perspective. *Human Resource Management Review, 12*(3), 293–298.

Part IV
Coping Strategies

Chapter 9
The Role of House Helps in Work–Family Balance of Women Employed in the Formal Sector in Kenya

Gladys Muasya

Introduction

As in many other sub-Saharan African countries, transition to modern industrial economy has been slow in Kenya. About 67.7 % of the country's 38.6 million people (Kenya National Bureau of Statistics 2009) live in rural areas. Of the 32.3 % Kenyans that live in towns and cities, more than a quarter live in the country's capital, Nairobi (Kenya National Bureau of Statistics 2009). Although much of the population is still rural, recent decades have witnessed an increasing trend toward rural–urban migration due to declining land productivity and shrinking incomes from agriculture. Women make a significant proportion of this rural–urban migration stream, a trend that can be partly attributed to the increasing levels of education among females in the country.

As women increasingly move to cities, the majority of them end up taking employment in the informal sector because of prevalent unemployment in Kenya. According to Atieno (2010), Kenyan women constitute only 29 % of formal employment sector, where about 70 % are employed in low income jobs. By the same token, the informal sector absorbs most of the women who take jobs as casual laborers often in traditional female occupations.

To add on, poverty and the growing necessity for women to earn incomes are other factors pushing women into the labour market (Atieno 2010). For example, as in many other African countries, the increasing number of female-headed households in Kenya suggests that many women carry the sole responsibility as economic providers and caregivers for their children (Mokomane 2012). There is also anecdotal evidence that some men want spouses who participate in some income-generating activity to increase family incomes. This marks a departure from earlier decades when men preferred to marry women who simply stayed at home to take care of household chores.

G. Muasya (✉)
Arizona State University, Tempe, AZ, United Sates of America
e-mail: gmuasya@asu.edu

Z. Mokomane (ed.), *Work–Family Interface in Sub-Saharan Africa*,
International Perspectives on Social Policy, Administration, and Practice,
DOI: 10.1007/978-3-319-01237-7_9,

Thus, unlike 20 years ago, Kenyan women working in both formal and informal sectors now have to grapple with work and family demands, and face several challenges in trying to reconcile them. Indeed, a number of Kenyan scholars have identified work–family conflict as a major factor that inhibits women's potential in many areas of their life including ascendancy to positions of leadership in business and politics. Suda (2002), for example, examined gender disparities in the Kenyan market with the aim of identifying causes of poverty and ways to reduce this poverty. The study identified heavy domestic work load along with low education, lack of access to resources, limited skills, as well as cultural factors and perceptions as some of the factors that cause gender disparities in the Kenyan market.

In the same vein, an examination of social and cultural barriers that hinder Kenyan women's aspiration to leadership positions by Kiamba (2008) identified family and work–family conflict, coupled with culture and cultural expectations as major factors. Mangatu (2010) similarly ranked work–family conflict as the major factor out of nine reasons that affect women in leadership positions in Kenyan banks. Mangatu noted that although the banking industry had fairly equal number of male and female employees, only two women were chief executive officers in 45 commercial banks in Kenya. Mangatu attributed this partly to the "glass ceiling[1]" effect in their career advancement. A study on women's participation in educational leadership undertaken among female primary school teachers in Nairobi and Thika municipalities (Ombati 2003) found that while women constitute 59 % of teachers in municipal schools they were under-represented in school leadership: 42 % were deputy teachers and 45 % were head teachers. The failure to adequately reconcile the demands of work and family was cited as one of the reasons that affected women advancement to leadership positions in the education sector.

An important coping strategy for workers facing work–family conflict has, for a long time, been the extended family whereby the wide range of relatives is called upon to assist with childcare and other household responsibilities. For example, working women who cannot afford to employ a house help or to enroll their children in private daycare centers often take the children to stay with grandparents in rural areas. Furthermore, the widespread practice of co-residing with younger siblings and other relatives who often come to urban areas to seek higher education and/or employment opportunities provides working women with a source of social support for care and households responsibilities. However, with the ever increasing cost of living in urban areas, many families are no longer able to accommodate extended family members for long periods. Co-residence with relatives is thus becoming more or less a temporary measure.

Against this background the employment of domestic workers or "house helps" has emerged as an important coping strategy. It is estimated, for example, that half

---

[1] This has been described as "the unseen, yet unbreachable barrier that keeps minorities and women from rising to the upper rungs of the corporate ladder, regardless of their qualifications or achievements" (United States Department of Labor 1995, 4).

of households in Nairobi employ house helps (Family Health International 2009). While this is also the case in other parts of sub-Saharan Africa (see, for example, Chap. 3 in this book for Zimbabwe), the few sub-Saharan Africa studies on these domestic workers have tended to be one-sided, looking at the *labor* implications of employing young girls, and the maltreatment of these workers by their employers. Thus, to contribute to the closure of this research gap, this chapter explores the benefits and limitations of using house helps, and proposes plausible solutions that could alleviate the limitations and/or enhance the benefits of these types of assistance.

Why Families Seek External Help in Housework and Childcare

The inflexible work schedules that are characteristic of the urban formal sector in Kenya and, indeed in much of sub-Saharan Africa, forces many workers to employ house helps as a strategy to balance work and family demands. In this section, I use my own experiences as a working wife and mother, as well as my observations to discuss some of the benefits and limitations of this strategy.

Benefits

As discussed earlier, the majority of working women in Kenya are engaged in the informal sector. Not withstanding the poor productivity, poor economic security, high levels of poverty, and poor access to social security among workers in this sector, (Mokomane 2009), its relatively flexible hours means that the women working in it do not have major challenges in relation to combining work and family roles. Indeed, research from other African countries such as Angola (Ceita 1999 cited by González and Grinspun 2001), Zambia (JUDAI and Associates 2005), and Zimbabwe (Marcucci 2001) found that it is because of the flexible hours that women working in the countries' informal sector are able to efficiently fulfill their household and childcare responsibilities.

Work–family conflict, therefore, tends to be higher in the urban formal sector where working hours typically start from 08:00 to 17:00, Monday to Friday (weekends and public holidays are normally "off-days"). Many jobs in this sector are also shift-based with a typical shift lasting between six and eight hours in duration. Therefore, while many women prefer jobs in the formal sector because of the better working conditions and remuneration, they often find it difficult to organize work around their free time because of the fixed working hours. In essence, one is either at work the full day or for a great part of the day or night.

In Kenya, the demands posed by work and family domains also tend to differ depending on whether one works in a small town, in a peri-urban area, or a big city. For instance, my first job in the country was as a teacher in a high school in a peri-urban area, in the outskirts of a small town. The school had 14 staff members; 7 women, and 7 men. Mostly, the seven women had at least one child under the age of three. The women generally preferred a house help to other forms of arrangement such as childcare or daycare services because the child could be raised within the home environment. Thus, most of the women were adamant that the domestic worker should not be a total stranger but be a close relative or, at the very least, someone from the same ethnic group. Therefore, given that the school was located in an area populated by a different ethnic group from that of most teachers, many of them sought domestic workers from their villages. Overall, the teachers with young children only took them to daycare and other childcare arrangements as an ad-hoc measure while they looked for a house help or her replacement (if she left suddenly, without giving notice—which was a common). Although I had no children and did not need a house help per se, I also stayed with my sister who helped me with housework chores.

My second job was at a private university in Zimbabwe. At this time, I had a young baby, and the Zimbabwean breastfeeding policy allowed women to break early from work daily, to breastfeed until the baby was 6 months old. Additionally, the timetable at the university was fairly flexible especially in the mornings and evenings. I, nonetheless, preferred a house help who came in 6 days a weeks to help with childcare. This was also the case among the several international staff employed by the university. Like the natives, they also depended a lot on house helps—either as "day workers" (who came in for a few days a week) or as "stay-in" house helps—for childcare and other domestic chores.

Later, when I went back home to Kenya—by then having two young children—I got a job with yet another private university in Nairobi. The dynamics of the city are such that many workers leave very early for work and return home late at night as traffic jams are a daily phenomenon. Because of the transport challenges in Nairobi, it was very hard for me to be able to prepare my young children in the morning for the school bus that picked them up at 07:30 am. In addition, someone had to meet the children when the bus dropped them off at 16:40 pm. To this end, I preferred a house help to daycare services. House helps also often supervise children as they do their homework since parents arrive late from work. They also act as security agents during the day to protect their employers' houses and properties.

Limitations

The foregoing section illustrates how house helps are a sheer necessity in many of Africa's big cities and towns. However, relying significantly on these workers has its own limitations. To the extent that they are tasked with some of the most sensitive responsibilities in any household (such as looking after very young children and household goods), and that many of them are in fact strangers to their employers, if the employment relationship sours they can—as anecdotal evidence suggests—harm the children or collude with criminals to rob the employers of their valuable belongings. Furthermore, to the extent that mothers are seen as the best sources of high quality childcare (Duncan et al. 2004), over-reliance on house helps and daycare is often blamed for delegating the role of parents to others; for decreasing interaction between children and their parents; and for delinquency among children.

Another limitation of hiring house helps is that the tasks of the working mother are assigned to another (often relatively poorer) woman. This has been shown to reinforce the gender, racial, and class lines (Williams 2000). In the United States, for example, most of the people who work as house helps or nannies are poor women, mostly women of color, who work for predominantly white privileged women of the upper middle and upper classes. Williams blames this pattern for causing conflict between the working class and the middle class as women who cannot afford nannies or daycare centers end up staying at home to take care of their children while those who can afford manage to pursue careers and other income-generating activities. In sub-Saharan Africa, this system can, in the same vein, reinforce existing gender and class lines because it is the upper class middle income families employing those from low income brackets.

The work of house helps is also generally undervalued (Tracy 2008) and attracts low wages. Most of the pay and work conditions depend largely on the relationship between the employer and the house help. Indeed, it is common for house helps to simply quit a job without any notice, whatsoever, when they become unhappy about their work arrangement. In fact, many house helps use the quit strategy to manage their work and/or to negotiate better conditions or pay. This leaves the employer insecure and vulnerable because they never know when the house help may be leaving them (Tracy 2008).

It is also noteworthy that most sub-Saharan countries, including Kenya, are signatories of International Labour Organization and hence are mandated to enforce minimum wage legislation. However, if such legislation is fully enforced, it will make the use of domestic workers possible a preserve of the well-off. It may also worsen unemployment among domestic workers as many people may not be able to afford them (Kariuki 2011). Indeed, a new government legislation passed in 2011 to enforce minimum wages for domestic workers in Kenya was met with mixed reactions from the Kenyan population (Muiruri 2011); many families that currently employ domestic workers wondered whether they would be able to afford them in the first place, with many facing litigations over unpaid statutory fees (Karambu 2011). Others speculated that new housework and childcare arrangements may now emerge to fill the gap once provided by the house helps, and that some women may have to remain at home with their children until they attain school age (Juma 2011).

Plausible Solutions

In discussion, there are several options that can be explored to either reduce over-reliance of house helps or improve their utilization so as to enhance work–family balance among working women in Kenya. These include community-initiated solutions; employer-initiated solutions; family-initiated solutions; as well as the improvement of communication between employers and house helps.

Community-Initiated Solutions

Community-initiated solutions are childcare arrangements in the form of daycare centers similar to those set up by women in Senegal, Ghana, and Ethiopia in the 1990s (Mehra et al. 1992). In Senegal, the rural daycare centers were seasonal and used mostly during the rice planting season. In Ethiopia, the women started the "Melka Oba" which was a cooperative society that catered for children aged between 45 days and 6 years. In the Ghanaian capital of Accra, women in retail business set up the "Accra Market Women's Association" to care for their young children (Mehra et al. 1992). While these community programmes eventually required additional financial assistance from other sources to be sustainable, they proved to be very reliable, in that they were near where the mothers worked or lived, and operated throughout the day to match the mothers' work schedules. Although these specific centers provided for only a few children, it is possible to replicate the concept in other regions and countries in sub-Saharan Africa. Furthermore, given that childcare has traditionally been viewed as a collective role in African households, these community models can be particularly useful for women working in the informal sector with minimum assistance from the government and donor agencies.

Employer-Initiated Solutions

Employer-initiated models are arrangements where organizations have family-friendly policies designed specifically to minimize the conflict between work and family or home demands. The employer may allow flexible work schedules and/or built day care centers within or close to the place of work. In Western countries, such as the United States, Canada, and Australia, the adoption of family-friendly policies is left entirely to individual organizations to implement. In other countries like the United Kingdom it is enforced by employment legislation that enables caregivers of young children, disabled persons, and elderly parents to have flexible work hours. In Japan, the legislation mandates parental leave, shorter weekly working hours and flexible work schedules as a way to increase women's participation in the formal sector (Beauregard and Henry 2009).

The utilization of these policies, however, tends to depend on direct supervisors who are in a position to make a decision on the use of the policies, and to determine the fit between the employee needs and organization needs (Beauregard and Henry 2009). Studies in the United States, for example, have shown that managers who have directly benefitted from family-friendly policies are more likely to endorse them in their own organizations than those who have not benefitted from such policies. For instance, executives who have had stay-at-home wives were less likely to endorse family-friendly policies than those who have had working wives (Tracy and Rivera 2010). Nonetheless, employer-initiated solutions are worthy of consideration in sub-Saharan Africa where they are yet to be developed.

Family-Initiated Solutions

Family-initiated solutions include arrangements where couples scale back on work commitments at different times to provide for the family and children, and for each other's career progression (Becker and Moen 1999). A study of middle income couples in upstate New York showed that some couples came with their own work–family balance arrangements, while some employed scaling-back strategies. The latter entail one spouse having a "job" and the other a "career", and both accepting the resulting limitations and tradeoffs (Becker and Moen 1999). This is often the case when the couples have young children: one spouse would do a part-time job and the other engages in a career that requires more time.

The strategy could also entail putting limits on the type of jobs, couples would take for the sake of the family. For example, one spouse or partner would turn down jobs or promotions that required relocation or a lot of traveling so as to create time for the family. Sometimes, when one partner or spouse had established himself or herself in their career, they would then spend more time with the family, and the other would put in more hours at work to catch up (Becker and Moen 1999). By doing this, both partners managed to have time for their families and career.

While this idea could also be applied also in sub-Saharan Africa there are several potential limitations. For example, as discussed earlier most formal jobs in the sub-continent typically have fixed reporting and departure time, and most lack any type of flexibility. Workers, who are able to work flexible time, are to a large extent, those in self-employment or in the informal sector. However, while any partner who is self-employed is in a position to invest more time for the family, women are more likely than men to scale their hours or to do the informal jobs and create time for the family. This is largely due to cultural stereotypes that dictate that housework and childcare are the responsibilities of the woman.

Improved Communication Between House Helps and Their Employers

Given the generally poor implementation of labour laws in many sub-Saharan African countries, if an employer is unhappy with a house help, they can dismiss the helper immediately without notice. Similarly, if the house help is unhappy with the terms of work, they may leave their jobs with literally no notice to the employer. Thus, one of the keys to successful relationships between house helps and their employers is the nature of communication between the two. Scholarship from the field of organizational communication suggests that effective communication between the employee and the employer is necessary in order to develop a productive working relationship. The way employers and their families communicate and treating domestic workers are very critical. A lack of good communication often leads to misunderstandings and conflict. This is largely, why some employers rarely retain the same domestic worker or house help for more than six months, while others manage to retain the same house help for more than three years.

There are several useful theoretical frameworks for understanding the important communication process in negotiating employer—house help relationships. One is Martin Buber's concept of 'I-Thou' dialog (Buber and Smith 2000); through which Buber encouraged human communication to be centered on "I-Thou" relationship rather than "I-It" relationship. The latter treats the other person as an object of manipulation while "I-Thou" looks at the whole person who is unique and should be accepted unconditionally. Buber also emphasized the concept of the interpersonal dialogue. It has also been argued that the interpersonal communication between two parties could be enhanced if the parties are willing to listen and enter into meaningful relationships that are genuine, respectful, and with empathic understanding (Broome 2009). Applying these notions, employer and domestic worker need to both treat each other with dignity and be willing to cultivate a meaningful working relationship.

Another useful framework is provided by Shell (2006), who encourages both parties to see the world from the other person's point of view and also consider how the interests and goals of the other party would further one's own goals. Similarly Fisher et al. (2011), encourage negotiating parties in an employment deal not to negotiate from their positions of power but rather to identify the interests and concerns of the other party. Since the employer is in a position of power, vis-à-vis the employee, then they have to identify the genuine interests of their workers, especially their pay package.

Summary and Recommendations

Using Kenya as a case study, this chapter explored some of the key challenges faced by working women who have childcare responsibilities in sub-Saharan Africa. The need for domestic workers or house helps, as well as the benefits and limitations of this coping strategy were also explored. The chapter further discussed the potential solutions—including improved communication between house helps and their employers—that can assist women to efficiently reconcile their family and family demands.

Based on the overall discussion, the key conclusion is that there is a need to address the challenges of work–family conflict as a topical policy issue in the same way as, say, climate change or HIV/AIDS is tackled in order to create awareness and sensitize people in sub-Saharan Africa. As Tracy (2008) asserts, work–family issues need to be addressed as societal or national issue, and not as a "women's issue".

It is imperative, however, that policies to enhance work-life balance in sub Saharan Africa are congruent with African culture and are not wholesale adoption of policies from the West. Thus, to the extent that much of the literature that informs such policies is located in the West, there is a need to undertake African-based research to inform the development of context-specific policies in the continent. Among the key research questions that are worthy of study are the following:

- Understanding—against the background of rapid urbanization, rising levels of female literacy and women participation in the formal employment sector—the emerging work–family challenges in sub-Saharan Africa by comparing contemporary issues with those of prior decades, as well as those in developed countries.
- Establishing the extent to which the high proportion of women in the informal sector can be explained by the challenges they face in combining work and domestic roles and exploring ways to reverse this trajectory.
- Establishing the attitudes of executives who are the gatekeepers of organizational policies including work–family policies and determining if they are aware of, or need to be sensitized on, the importance of these and other related policies.
- Investigating the effects of family-friendly policies (or the lack thereof) on the wellbeing of women and workers in general, and the productivity of institutions and organizations in sub Saharan Africa.
- Understanding how sub-Saharan Africa is responding to pressure from international institutions and organizations to formalize domestic workers remuneration arrangements. Will domestic workers be abandoned with consequent collapse of informal house help arrangements, in preference of more formal alternative professional childcare arrangements?
- Establishing the reasons why, despite Sub-Saharan Africa being a collectivistic society, very few community-initiated childcare arrangements have been established.
- Determine if there are differences in work performance and communication between house helps who have their own children and those who do not have any children.

- Comparing work–family balance challenges of (i) wage-employed versus self-employed females and (ii) women working in rural and in urban areas.

Acknowledgments I am sincerely grateful to Dr. Judith Martin of Hugh Downs School of Human Communication, Arizona State University, for her helpful comments in this book chapter.

References

Atieno, R. (2010). *Explaining female labor force participation: The case of Kenya informal sector and the effects of the economic crisis*. Paper presented to the 2010 Annual IAFFE conference, Buenos Aires,Argentina.

Beauregard, T. A., & Henry, L. C. (2009). Making the link between work life balance practices and organization performance. *Human Resource Management Review, 19*, 9–22.

Becker, P., & Moen, P. (1999). Scaling back: Dual-earner couples' work–family strategies. *Journal of Marriage and the Family, 61*, 995–1007.

Broome, B. J. (2009). Dialogue Theories. In Steven Littlejohn & Karen Foss (Eds.), *Encyclopedia of communication theory*. Thousand Oaks, CA: Sage.

Buber, M., & Smith, R. G. (2000). *I and Thou*. New York: Simon and Schuster.

Duncan, S., Edward, R., & Alldred, P. (2004). Mothers and child care: policies, values and theories. *Children and Society, 18*, 254–265.

Family Health International (2009). Project empowers Kenya's house girls.Retrieved September 21,2010 from www.fhi360.org/en/countryprofiles/kenya/res_house_girls.htm

Fisher, R., Ury, W., & Patton, B. (2011). *Getting to yes: Negotiating agreement without giving in*. New York: Penguin Books.

González de la Rocha, M.,& Grinspun, A. (2001). Private adjustments: Households, crisis and work. In A. Grinspun (Ed.), *Choices for the poor: Lessons from national poverty strategies* (pp. 55–87). New York: United Nations Development Programme.

JUDAI and Associates. 2005. *Work and family conflict in Zambia*. Unpublished Working Paper. Geneva: Conditions of Work and Employment Programme, International Labour Organisation.

Juma, V. (2011). *Kenya new laws lift cost of domestic workers beyond many homes*.Retrieved October 10,2012 from http://allafrica.com/stories/201106241058.html

Karambu, I. (2011). *Kenyan families face fines over unpaid maids' NHIF Pay. Daily Nation*, December 8.Retrieved October 10,2012 from http://nation.co.ke

Kenya National Bureau of Statistics. (2009). *Kenya census*. Retrieved March 21,2011 from www.knbs.or.ke/Census%20Results/KNBS%20Brochure.pdf

Kiamba, J. C. (2008). Women and leadership position: Social and cultural barriers to success. *Wagadu, 6*, 7–26.

Kariuki, J. (2011). *House girl' wages shoot up. The* Standard, September 22.Retrieved March 21,2011 from www.standardmedia.co.ke/

Mangatu, N. M. (2010). *Beyond the glass ceiling: A phenomenological study of women managers in the Kenyan banking industry*. Unpublished Dissertation, University of Phoenix.

Marcucci, P. N. (2001). *Jobs, gender and small enterprises in Africa and Asia: Lessons drawn from Bangladesh, the Philippines, Tunisia and Zimbabwe* In Focus Programme on Boosting Employment WEDGE, No. 58, Geneva: International Labour Organisation.

Mehra,R.,Kurz,K., & Paolisso, M. (1992). *Child care options for working mothers in developing countries*. Women and infant nutrition field support project (WINS) International center for research and women. Washington, DC.Retrieved June 4,2012 from *pdf.usaid.gov/pdf_docs/PNABT180.pdf*

Mokomane, Z. (2009). *Work family conflict and gender equality in South Africa*. Paper presented at the 26th International Population Conference, Marrakech, Morocco, 28th September–2nd October 2009.

Mokomane, Z. (2012). Social protection as a mechanism for family protection in sub-Saharan Africa. *International Journal of Social Welfare,*. doi:10.1111/j.1468-2397.2012.00893.x.

Muiruri, J. (2011). *Kenya: Storm over the house girls' new law*. July: Daily Nation. 5.

Ombati, O. F. V. (2003). *Women's participation in educational leadership in Kenya: The case of Nairobi and Thika municipal primary schools*. State University of New York at Buffalo: Unpublished Dissertation.

Shell, G. R. (2006). *Bargaining for advantage: Negotiation strategies for reasonable people*. New York: Penguins.

Suda, C. (2002). Gender disparities in the Kenyan labor market: Implications for poverty reduction. *Nordic Journal of African Studies, 11*, 301–321.

Tracy, S. J. (2008). Care as a common good. *Women Studies in Communication, 31*, 166–174.

Tracy, S. J., & Rivera K. D. (2010), Endorsing equity and applauding stay-at-home moms: How male voices on work-life reveal aversive sexism and flickers of transformation. *Management Communication Quarterly, 24* (1), 3–43.

United States Department of Labor (1995). *Solid investments: Making full use of the Nation's human Capital*. Washington, D.C.: U.S. Department of Labor,Retreived April 29,2013 from www.dol.gov/oasam/programs/history/reich/reports/ceiling2.pdf

Williams, J. (2000). *Unbending gender: Why family and work conflict and what to do about it*. New York: Oxford University Press.

Chapter 10
The Quest for a Family Policy in Zambia

Ndangwa Noyoo

Introduction

Over the past 2 decades, major United Nations and other world conferences and summits have called attention to issues affecting families, including family roles and responsibilities, gender equality and men's greater participation in family life. Notably, the 1995 Copenhagen World Summit for Social Development acknowledged the importance of providing help to families so as to enable them to perform their supporting, educating and nurturing roles. This would entail, among other things, enacting social policies and programmes designed to meet the needs of families and their individual members (United Nations Department of Economic and Social Affairs 2011:1). Despite these calls, families in many sub-Saharan African countries have not been adequately targeted by social policy. Typically families only inadvertently derive benefits from the outcomes of social policy and other social programmes, and not from mechanisms that directly targeted them. Instead, policies and programmes have been focused on individuals who comprise the family such as children, mothers, the young and older persons—whose interests and needs are related, but not identical to those of the family (Zeitlin and Megawanji. 1995). Moreover, such policies and programmes have in many instances not been comprehensive enough or well-thought out.

Due to the foregoing, this chapter uses the case of Zambia to illustrate the need for family policies in sub-Saharan Africa as it is evident that current social policies in many of the sub-continent's countries have not effectively responded to the institution of the family for decades. In addition, there is a dearth of evidence-based policymaking forays in the public sphere, coupled with a lukewarm culture of policy analysis. Lastly, in some countries such as Zambia, there seems to be no strong political will that can drive a forward-looking agenda of strengthening families in the country (Noyoo forthcoming 2013). Before proceeding, it is

N. Noyoo (✉)
National Department of Social Development, Pretoria, South Africa
e-mail: NdangwaN@dsd.gov.za

Z. Mokomane (ed.), *Work–Family Interface in Sub-Saharan Africa*,
International Perspectives on Social Policy, Administration, and Practice,
DOI: 10.1007/978-3-319-01237-7_10,

imperative to shed some light on the conceptual and theoretical underpinnings of this chapter, in order to lend clarity to some of the issues it raises.

Conceptual and Theoretical Considerations

According to the United Nations (2009), as the basic, natural and fundamental unit of society, the family is entitled to protection by society and the state. Mattessich and Hill (1987) assert that families are social groups that display four systematic features, namely: Intimate interdependence; selective boundary maintenance; ability to adapt to change and maintain their identity over time and performance of tasks. The tasks performed by the family include physical maintenance; socialisation and education; control of social and sexual behaviour; maintenance of family morale and motivation to perform roles inside and outside the family; the acquisition of mature family members through procreation; and the launching of young people from the family when mature (Mattessich and Hill 1987).

Defining the Family

Although the aforementioned definitions will guide this chapter's point of departure, a word of caution is necessary. Despite agreement about the pervasiveness and continuity of some form of familial relationships throughout human history, there is—in the current context—no single uniform agreed definition of what a family is. Conceptualisations about the form, function and utility of families change over time as a result of a unique interplay of historical, political, economic and social forces (Trask 2004). Overall, existing definitions of family can be categorised in two ways: (i) *structural definitions* that specify family membership according to certain traits such as blood relationship, legal ties or residence; and (ii) *functional definitions* that specify behaviours of family members such as sharing economic resources and caring for the young, elderly, sick and those with disabilities (Trask 2004).

Family Policy

Discussions about the family cannot be divorced from the policy constructs relating to the family. In most cases family policies are couched in welfare paradigms, the character of which will give expression to a unique set of policies related to the family. For example, whilst following the typology of Esping-Andersen (1990), Neyer (2003) explains that welfare-state research has shown that European countries can be grouped into distinct welfare-state regimes according to the intentions of their social policies and the principles on which they are based.

Consequently, universalistic welfare states are characterised by welfare-state policies that are targeted at individual independence and social equality between individuals (not families). Public policies aim at covering social and employment-related risks and at upholding high living standards for everyone. Social benefits are granted on the basis of individual social citizenship rights. Extended social services contribute to the defamilialisation of welfare, that is, a reduction of the family's contribution to welfare. In addition:

> Conservative welfare states direct their welfare-state policies towards status maintenance and the preservation of traditional family forms. Social benefits correspond to work performance measured through the level and duration of contributions to social-security systems, or they depend on marriage. Conservative welfare states rely heavily on familialism that is on the family as a provider of welfare. Liberal welfare states encourage market-based individualism through minimal social benefits and through subsidising private and marketised welfare schemes. Social benefits are usually means-tested and poverty-related. Social welfare depends on market provisions and on familialism. The Southern European welfare states are often considered part of the conservative welfare-state regimes; but their stronger familialism merits that they are viewed as a separate welfare-state regime (Neyer 2003:11).

Crucially, in the making of policy certain assumptions must be made about families and family roles. Family policy can be explicit or implicit; manifest or latent; direct or indirect; intended or unintended in terms of its family effects and consequences. What is useful about these terms is that they alert the observer to the different dimensions in which the family aspects of different policies and programmes can be analysed and examined (Zimmerman 1995). For instance, explicit family policies include those policies and programmes deliberately designed to achieve specific objectives regarding the family unit or individuals in their family roles. These may cover such major family functions as: family creation (for example, to marry or divorce, bear or adopt children, provide foster care); economic support (for example, to provide for family members' basic needs); child-rearing (for example, to socialise the next generation), and family caregiving (for example, to provide assistance for the family members who are ill, frail, with disabilities, or older and in need of assistance or care (United Nations 2009). Explicit family policies may also include population policies (pro or anti-natalist); income security policies designed to combat poverty and assure families with children in a certain standard of living; employment-related benefits for working parents; maternal and child health policies; child care policies, maternity and paternity leave; domestic violence and family planning. In this context, family policy may assume a diversity and multiplicity of policies rather than a single monolithic, comprehensive legislative act (United Nations 2009).

Gauthier (1996) cited in Millar (2003:157) identifies four main approaches to family policy. The first refers to the *pro-family/pro-natalist* where policies to help mothers reconcile work and family life, so that employment does not act as a barrier to child-bearing. The second approach is *pro-traditional* where preservation of 'the family' is the main concern. Governments take responsibility for supporting families here, but the most important sources of support are seen as families themselves, the communities they live in, and voluntary and charitable organisations including churches. These policies support women to stay at home rather than going out to work. The third slant is *pro-egalitarian,* where the promotion of gender equality is the main concern; here men and women are treated as equal breadwinners and equal carers and the policy aims to support dual parent/worker roles. The *pro-family but non-interventionist approach* is the fourth one which mainly is concerned with families in need. The families are viewed as basically self-sufficient and able to meet their own needs through the private market, with only limited help from the state.

For the purpose of this chapter family policy refers to the principles governing actions directed towards achieving specified ends, through the provision of welfare, minimum standards of income and some measure of progressive redistribution in command over resources, in such a way as to shape the development of families. In other words, the family policy identifies families as the deliberate target of specific actions, and the measures initiated are designed to have direct impact on family resources and ultimately on family structure (Harris 2004).

Social Policy

Social policy generally refers to the activity of policymaking to promote well-being by the state. It also refers to the academic study of such actions. It is an interdisciplinary field, drawing on and developing links with other cognate disciplines (Alcock 2003). Critically:

> In any society, social policy fulfils three main functions: social, political and an economic. The social function lies in reducing the life cycle risks through social insurance and alleviating poverty through social assistance. The political function of social policy lies in stabilising effects. Social justice and greater equality are vital factors for building trust and social cohesion and to contribute to political stability. The economic factor lies, among others, in widening the productive capacities of society through the inclusion of marginalised areas and social groups in the growth process, and through investments in improved health and education of the population (Economic and Social Commission for Western Asia 2009:1).

Since this chapter is examining the terrain of a developing country which is located in a mostly impoverished and deprived continent—Africa—the following definition will guide its perspectives in relation to social policy:

> Social policy is collective interventions in the economy to influence the access and the incidence of adequate and secure livelihoods and income. As such, social policy has always played redistributive, protective and transformative or developmental roles. Although these different roles always work in tandem and synergistically, the weight given to each of these elements of social policies has varied widely across countries and, within countries, over time. In the context of development, there can be no doubt that the transformative role of social policy needs to receive greater attention than it is usually accorded in the developed countries and much more than it does in the current focus of "safety nets" (Mkandawire 2004:1).

The Need for Family Policy in Zambia

Situated in south-central Africa, Zambia is a multi-ethnic country comprised of 73 different ethnic groups with unique cultures and linguistics. Although agriculture, and lately tourism have also experienced marginal increases, thus adding to the country's Gross Domestic Product (GDP) growth, copper is Zambia's major export and, as at April 2012, it accounted for 82.3 % of all major exports of the country.

Zambia's population stands over 13 million with 49.3 % being males and 50.7 % being females (Central Statistical Office 2011). The majority (60.5 %) of Zambians reside in rural areas whilst the remaining 39.5 % are found in urban areas. Zambia has a high population growth rate as suggested by the average annual growth rate of 2.8 % noted during the inter-censal period, 2000–2010. In addition, the country has a very young population with 45.4 % of its citizens below the age of 15 years. In rural areas 48.6 % of the population is below the age of 15 years compared to 40.5 % residing in urban areas. The population aged 15–24 makes up 20.8 % of the total population, of which 19.3 % are in the rural areas and 23.2 % are in urban areas (Central Statistical Office 2011). The implications of these youth statistics for social policy, in particular, and public policy in general, are that Zambia shoulders a huge dependency ratio. More resources are therefore needed to nurture and grow this young population for future productive endeavours.

From 1964 (when it gained independence from Britain) to 1991, Zambia was ruled by the United National Independence Party (UNIP) and its leader Kenneth Kaunda. For all the 27 years of this rule, Zambia was a socialist country and all policies were imbued with a socialist ethos, which entailed the State taking the lead role in economic activities. Thus, the Zambian economy was characterised by highly controlled markets and as a result of the rapid implementation of import substitution industrialisation strategies, a number of processing industries were established, and state involvement in business activities were intensified. Trade policy was inward-looking, with import and foreign exchange controls used extensively to influence imports and trading activities (OECD 2011:13). Despite this, evidence shows that between 1964 and the early 1970s, the country registered gains in economic growth and social welfare largely due to the good price of copper on the world market.

On the other hand, the post-1974 period tells a different story as Zambia exhibited a declining economic performance and most social indicators deteriorated. The situation worsened to such an extent that in 1985, the World Bank re-classified Zambia from a middle income to a low-income country. By the early 1990s, Zambia had reached a level where the United Nations General Assembly included it on the list of least developed countries (Saasa and Carlsson 2002:1).

In 1991, Kaunda and UNIP lost elections and were dislodged from power after a popular revolt against their one-party state system. The Movement for Multi-party Democracy (MMD) was voted into power and the late Frederick Chiluba became Zambia's second president. The MMD immediately embarked upon institutional reforms which saw the country implementing free-market policies and putting in place a comprehensive privatisation programme. However, Chiluba and his government were also seen by many Zambians as incompetent, corrupt and generally detrimental to the country's progress. When the late Levy Mwanawasa took over office from Chiluba in 2001, he waged a relentless campaign against corruption and also made the fight against poverty his number one priority through prudent macro-economic management and the stabilisation of the markets. He instituted pro-poor policies to not only reduce poverty, but also to help resuscitate families and the country's middle-class.

Mwanawasa, also ratcheted up Foreign Direct Investment (FDI) inflows through the resuscitation of mining (particularly copper) industries. Agriculture and tourism were also boosted during this period; and hence from 2004 economic growth rose to 5.5 % and the annual inflation rate dropped to 18 % from 30 % and slightly more in the previous decades. By 2010 the country's GDP growth rate had increased to 7.2 % and the annual inflation rate had dramatically decreased to 7.1 % in 2010 (Government of the Republic of Zambia 2011).

After Mwanawasa's death in 2008 the new president Rupiah Banda continued from where his predecessor had left off. However, this was only until 2011 when he lost elections to the Patriotic Front (PF) headed by Michael Sata. Despite its many promises during the campaigns in the run up to the 2011 elections, the new government has not, to date, been able to proffer any sound policy proposals in respect to elevating social and human development in the country. It remains silent on social policy matters and has not provided concrete proposals on how the country's vulnerable populations are going to be protected against adversities and how they are going to be empowered by the state (Noyoo 2013).

Thus, despite Zambia's encouraging economic performance between 2004 and 2012 (OECD 2011; Africa Economic Outlook 2012), the quality of life of the citizenry remains appallingly low. This is because the economy continues to be inequitable and devoid of in-built mechanisms crucial for the redistribution of the generated wealth. Further, state led anti-poverty measures as well as those of civil society have been palliative and not comprehensive enough. They remain adjuncts of economic policy which is more tailored towards a trickle down approach as opposed to the redistribution of wealth. It is due to this anomaly that many Zambian families continue to miss out on the reported economic growth. Consequently, families have also not meaningfully and effectively contributed to the country's development process. Indeed, this deficit is clearly reflected in the country's low human development levels. For example, in 2011 the country's Human Development Index (HDI) was 164 out of 187 countries (United Nations Development Programme 2011a). In the same vein, for three decades, Zambian families have consistently come under pressure from HIV and AIDS with 17.1 % of adults in Zambia reported to be living with HIV in 2008. Closely linked, half of the country's mortalities are attributable to the pandemic.

The country is also grappling with high levels of child and maternal mortality, the causes of which are preventable with low cost and effective interventions. Child protection services have also not been able to reverse the negative circumstances facing children in the country:

> Evidence of how the HIV and AIDS pandemic has hit hard on a population already highly vulnerable are the 1.2 million classified as orphaned and vulnerable children (OVC). As the parent generation has succumbed to HIV and AIDS children have often been left to the care of elderly grandmothers. To date, the response to these vulnerable children has struggled to keep up with the growing need for intervention. Deprivation is a characteristic of the lives of many of the country's children, living in homes where relentless poverty is the norm, often in communities far from any services, denied education and in situations where the concept of rights and protection from exploitation is little known or understood (United Nations Children's Fund 2008:1).

The circumstances facing women are equally precarious. With so many women working in the informal sector and continuing to face huge challenges in meeting their needs and those of their families, the family in Zambia remains extremely vulnerable. Since women are the cornerstones of the family, their continued marginalisation from the economic sphere has been translated into poor outcomes for families. Indeed, the Gender Inequality Index (GII) which reflects gender-based inequalities in three dimensions: reproductive health, empowerment and economic activity paint a gloomy picture. Zambia has a GII value of 0.627, ranking it 131 out of 146 countries in the 2011 index. Furthermore, unemployment is still very high in Zambia despite the country's improved economic growth. In 2005 unemployment hovered around 15.5 % with 70 % of the unemployed residing in urban areas and 30 % in rural areas (Central Statistical Office 2006). Again, women are at a disadvantage when it comes to employment opportunities available in the country, particularly in the formal sector. For example, male employment is around 71 %, compared to 29 % for females (United Nations Development Programme 2011, b). In 2005, women constituted 34 % of wage employment with the majority concentrated in the informal sector where they earned two-fifths of men's incomes (Central Statistical Office 2006). Furthermore, average earnings in the agricultural informal sector, where women are most prominent, were only slightly above half of those of the informal sector as a whole (United Nations Development Programme/ Government Republic of Zambia 2011).

In the rural areas, 82 % of people depend on the informal sector, and 90 % of them are women (Central Statistical Office 2006). In addition, many of the informal activities in the urban settings are survivalist in nature and do not offer meaningful income returns. Most of the work is highly labour-intensive and physical without corresponding financial rewards. Other activities entail the sale of agricultural produce on the sidewalks in cities and towns, and petty trading in all sorts of merchandise and wares. In this light, the informal sector also precludes women from balancing their work with family life, and thus they end up going with their children to the various hazardous locations where they ply their trade. The current situation where informality is the main source of income for many families is perilous and not sustainable for the country.

The growth of the economy has also been accompanied by high incidences of poverty and income inequality. The most recent statistics on poverty are from 2006, and they show that:

> There is a huge difference in the incidence of extreme poverty between urban and rural areas and that it varies widely from province to province. Extreme poverty is also strongly associated with a number of household characteristics, including gender, age and the educational level of the person heading the household. In 2006, extreme poverty stood at 57 % in female-headed households compared to 49 % for male-headed households. Households with older people were also more likely to be poor. Thus, 66 % of households headed by people above 60 years lived in extreme poverty compared to 50 % for households headed by those aged 30–59 years. Additionally, extreme poverty was influenced by education. It was highest in households with heads without education (77 %) (United Nations Development Programme/Government of the Republic of Zambia 2011:11).

Concomitantly, inequality in Zambia is very high. The Gini index, which measures income inequality, shows that while there was progress between 1991 and 1996, little changed between then and 2006. The index in fact shows that inequality deteriorated in urban areas, whereas it improved slightly in rural areas from 2004 to 2006 (United Nations Development Programme/Government of the Republic of Zambia 2011).

Development of Social Policy in Zambia

During the colonial period, Zambia's welfare regime was discriminatory, exclusionary and race-based in regard to access to life chances. As a result, colonial social policy was largely determined by the colonial mission; it took a residualist approach (Aina 2004; Mhone 2004; Noyoo 2010) and was also restrictive both socially and spatially. In many cases, as in various countries across Africa, social services were located only in urban areas or neighbourhoods where the colonisers were found in large numbers (Aina 2004).

By the same token, social policy in Zambia has not mirrored a transformative agenda in the decades following independence. For the most part, it has only been palliative and it was only in the decades of the 1960s and 1970s when it had come closer to being a transformative one (Noyoo 2013). During these past decades, social policy was also determined by collective interventions in the economy in order to influence the access to, and the incidence of, adequate and secure livelihoods and income (Mkandawire 2004). To this end, social policy in the country aimed at extending social service provision to those who had been neglected by colonialism. Consequently, there was heavy investment in education, health; in the promotion of social equity and narrowing the gap between the rich and the poor. The guiding principle for social policy formulation and implementation, as stated above, was the ideology of *Humanism* (Masiye et al. 1998), which recognised that production of the means of existence was the basis of human life and it was also connected with how the production was equitably distributed to the populace (Kandeke 1977).

In this regard, social policy in Zambia extended to subsidies in food; transport; price controls—especially of essential commodities; agriculture inputs like fertiliser, pesticides and seeds; and infrastructure development, such as the building of clinics, schools, colleges and hospitals. Employment was also guaranteed for the vast majority of Zambians through a localisation process known as *Zambianisation*. This ambitious post-independence programme of social reconstruction and development was made possible by finances from the sale of the country's main export, copper (United Nations Development Programme 2003; Mhone 2004; Noyoo 2010). However, nationalisation and import substitution strategies proved very costly for the country as Zambia failed to diversify the economy from copper mining. Import substitution industries also turned out to be inefficient and uncompetitive due to high input costs, high monopoly prices, reliance on government subsidies, and lack of technological dynamism.

More tellingly, Anderson et al. (2000) opine that the transition from one of the richest countries in Africa to one of the poorest took less than a generation. After 1991, the country's economy was extensively liberalised with all its facets deregulated. One such example was the comprehensive privatisation programme which led to the sale, unbundling or even closure of parastatal organisations, many of which were loss making entities. This resulted in the shedding of hundreds of thousands of jobs, with many Zambians suddenly finding no forms of livelihood. In the said period, the state was also compelled to reform the public sector which led to further shedding of jobs through retrenchments and downsizing. At this juncture, the economy was in rapid decline and people had to find ways of sustaining themselves. In order to survive many gradually gravitated towards the informal sector and self-employment ventures. The collapse of formal sector employment also saw the demise of employment-related benefits such as pensions, allowances, medical insurance, among others. There was also a rise in unpredictability in people's lives as many did not have incomes on a regular basis.

Hence, since 1991 Zambia's social policy has been reactive to the country's economic policy which is mainly neo-liberal in content. When Zambians rejected socialism in 1991 the government began to strictly adhere to the economic austerity measures of the World Bank and the International Monetary Fund (IMF) referred to as the Structural Adjustment Programme (SAP). However, SAP's economic prescriptions had serious and negative ramifications for family life in Zambia. Due to this, a multiplicity of challenges emerged in the country primarily from the breakdown of families. For example, the divorce rates rose during the 1990s as job losses and chronic poverty severely undermined family life and severely strained families. The hardest hit was the middle-class which simply imploded with the economic meltdown and the SAP antidotes. This was due to the fact that many middle-class families had breadwinners who were employed by the public sector and the various parastatal organisations which became redundant after 1991.

Evolution of the Family in Zambia

In the pre-colonial period families in Zambia varied as the manner in which lineage was reckoned determined their roles and responsibilities. Where family ties were matrilineal (where emphasis is the mother's lineage as opposed to the father's), women had more say in family matters. A patrilineal family, on the other hand, drew its essence from the father's lineage and was actually patriarchal. Those that were bilateral could either tilt towards matrilineal or patrilineal lineages depending on the prevailing circumstances. This was how families were defined in pre-colonial Zambia in the different ethnic polities (Noyoo 2000).

Regardless of whether it was patrilineal, matrilineal, or bilateral, the idealised family by Zambian politicians in the post-colonial era was the extended family as it was seen as the "African" way of existence. In this family system children could be looked after by uncles, aunts, grandparents or relatives if they were orphaned. However, the realities of urbanisation and the changing family patterns, engendered by the urban setting, militated against this notion of the family. In most cases, due to the economic realities, a good number of families began to gravitate towards the Western nuclear form. By the mid-1980s, with the economic stagnation setting in, and few Zambians managing to make ends meet, many families could not afford to take on extra mouths to feed. This scenario is corroborated by studies whose findings have shown that poverty decreases the altruistic allocation of resources, or the ability and willingness of the family to satisfy the needs and preferences of its members (Zeitlin and Megawanji 1995). In this sense, the extended family system was beginning to be seen by ordinary Zambians as a burden that threatened the well-being of the immediate nuclear family.

The latter part of the 1980s and the onset of the 1990s were witnesses to a new phenomenon of child-headed families, primarily due to the onset of the HIV and AIDS pandemic and its devastating effects on the social fabric. Equally, there was an exponential increase in the numbers of street children in Zambia, a problem which has been compounded since then by HIV and AIDS and an inequitable economic system. Previously, these children were *on* the streets—whereby they would come and beg on the streets, but later return to some kind of family set-up. Gradually, the children would not return to any family at all and have now become *of* the streets and as such, are a permanent feature of the Zambian urban landscape. Thus, just as industrialisation shaped and moulded the family in Europe in the nineteenth century, colonial penetration and urbanisation equally impacted on the Zambian family set-up in the early and mid-twentieth century. In contemporary times new forces such as, globalisation, migrations, interethnic or interracial marriages, among others, have emerged and equally left their imprints on the family.

Despite the many challenges brought about by these new forces, the family in Zambia has in most cases benefited from policies that have been implemented in other areas and which have had unintended outcomes or impacts for families. Moreover, in the post-colonial era, social policy was driven from the premise that the extended family was the pillar of family life. After independence, this understanding was cemented albeit unintentionally, as the extended family was idealised to the point of policy obfuscation. The post-colonial government had firmly believed that family life should be predicated on the traditional value system and then anchored in the extended family. This meant that the extended family took precedence over state provision in many family related matters. State policy seems to have been *pro-traditional*. For instance, the homes for the aged which were inherited from the colonial authorities were almost discontinued after independence because they were deemed as "European" or "Western" aberrations. The post-colonial government thought that it would gradually phase them out. For example, the ruling party's ideology of *Humanism* had discouraged institutional care and advocated for family and community care despite the prevailing material conditions which did not support this policy position. The country's Department of Social Welfare concedes:

> Although the department discourages institutional care of the aged persons in preference to family and community care, in line with the party and government policy, in practice it has been realised that due to factors such as urbanisation, childlessness and certain cultural taboos connected with aging, there will always be some aged persons for whom the only mode of care will be an institution (Department of Social Welfare 1979:6).

Interestingly, this was also the case during colonial rule as the British authorities had always believed that the extended family was the safety-net which was crucial to those Africans who were in need (Lewis 2000).

Policy Proposals and Future Prospects

Given the above-mentioned, this chapter calls for the development of a family policy in Zambia, the rationale for which stems from the gap of not having any policy in the country that directly focuses on the family—since Zambia's independence in 1964. In addition it is apparent that high numbers of Zambians, notably women and even children, are facing monumental social and economic challenges. Such a situation also poses serious threats to the quality of life of many citizens. The chapter's bone of contention is that Zambia's current formulation of social policy is inadvertently inimical to family life as it does not put forth programmes that embolden this institution, but seemingly allows its continued erosion through piece-meal actions.

In essence, current initiatives are not profound enough to dramatically reduce poverty and inequality in the country. This is because family life is rarely regarded as a development imperative by both politicians and policymakers. Indeed, people's ability to earn an income is a very important yardstick of human well-being and it also lends to a predictable measure of choice in regard to one's ability to purchase goods and services. Furthermore, the Sixth National Development Plan (SNDP) which was drafted by the MMD government only focuses on social protection in its palliative and residual form, and does not stem from a developmental and transformative social policy perspective.

Another way in which the family's standing is jeopardised in Zambia is through the outcomes and impacts of the inequitable economic system which is skewed in the favour of a small elite class. As Zambia continues to adhere to the neo-liberal tenets which gained currency in the 1990s, after the demise of socialism in the said period, the country's social policy is also cast in the same neo-liberal mould. Therefore, a progressive family policy which would duly consider labour-market variables and other economic factors in efforts to raise the living standards of Zambian families may be helpful.

Also given trends discussed in this chapter it is evident that Zambia needs a family perspective in policymaking. If better outcomes and impacts are to be attained in social and human development pursuits, families must be strengthened through a progressive and forward-looking family policy. Such a stance would acknowledge the important role that the family can play in a broad range of policy issues. Indeed, a family perspective in policymaking analyses the consequences of any policy or programme, regardless of whether it is explicitly aimed at families, for its impact on family well-being such as family stability, family relationships and the ability of the family to carry out its responsibilities (Bogenschneider 2006). This would require an integrated, holistic approach to family policy hinging on a better co-ordination and collaboration among all stakeholders, including the state, civil society organisations, and the private sector. In addition, families would need to have a stake in this process and empowered to participate actively in formulating and assessing family policy. Therefore, the country's family policy would have to be embedded in human dignity and uphold the rights of every individual in the family; be gender-sensitive, and observe the rights of children, older persons and persons with disabilities (United Nations 2009).

The first thrust of a family policy in Zambia would therefore have to be firmly placed on the base of mass employment for family strengthening. This is the surest way of redistributing the country's wealth to Zambians as well as enabling the state to mop up valuable tax revenues which could then be used for further social investments, for example, universal and high quality education and healthcare; high quality Early Childhood Development (ECD) services; and benefits for working mothers such as child allowances and a comprehensive maternity leave package. The following could be some of the pillars of such a policy:

- *Employment creation.* It is important for the state to generate employment opportunities in the country so that families can effectively meet their needs. Women must deliberately be targeted in such endeavours. But the jobs that are created must also be decent in the manner in which they enable Zambians to access benefits and other services, which then translate into viable, functional and economically stable families.
- *Improvement of informal sector conditions.* Since the evidence shows that the largest number of people who participate in the agricultural sector, on an informal basis are women, specific targeting of this group through: financial or

micro lending schemes, agricultural extension services and skills training could be prioritised by the government.

- *Tax rebates for Corporate Social Responsibility initiatives.* Tax breaks for mining conglomerates that are churning out enormous profits in the country could be made available by the government or to any other private firms in the manufacturing or tourism sectors, which are willing to engage in Corporate Social Responsibility (CSR) to improve the social and economic situation of some of the most vulnerable members of society and families.
- *Addressing harmful traditional practices.* An example of such a practice that undermines families is what may be termed as misplaced traditionalism whereby widows from certain ethnic groups fall victim to unscrupulous relatives of the deceased who come to "claim" their property even before burial. This phenomenon known as "property grabbing" continues despite legislation that was promulgated to safeguard widows in the 1990s and, in most cases, leaves families destitute after the head has passed on. There are also other traditions which undermine families that the family policy, in conjunction with other pieces of legislation, could counteract by, for instance, overhauling existing legislation which does not reflect twenty-first century realities or is not at par with international standards.

All the foregoing would need to be interwoven with a family strengthening framework which is a comprehensive approach that aims to improve health, social, educational and economic outcomes for entire families and not just individuals. It also takes place in organisations that are grounded in a specific neighbourhood and often employ people who live in the community. Sometimes called family support, family strengthening practice is committed to developing the integrity of families within the context of their beliefs, values, customs and culture. Reciprocity is encouraged to create bonds between the organisation and families through the process of giving and receiving (California Family Resource Association 2007).

The strengthening of families is based on *family economic success* which focuses on helping individuals improve self-sufficiency through expanded opportunities to work, earn a living wage that provides for the basic needs of the family and build assets that grow the family over time, such as home ownership and retirement accounts; *family support systems* which stress on building appropriate and adequate systems of support for healthy family development that encompasses: health care, child care, education, and other essential components of strong families (National Human Services Assembly 2004). Lastly family strengthening is predicated on: *thriving and nurturing communities* and emphasises on building a nurturing and supportive environment in which healthy families pursue long-term goals crucial for sustainable family development. Essential components for family success also include access to affordable housing, strong neighbourhood institutions, safe streets, supportive social networks, and an environment that promotes communities and strengthens bonds between families (National Human Services Assembly 2004).

References

Africa Economic Outlook. (2012). Zambia. www.africaneconomicoutlook.org/en/countries/southern-africa/zambia/. Accessed 12 October 2012.

Aina, A. (2004). Introduction. In A. Aina, C. S. L. Chachage, & E. Anna-Yao (Eds.), *Globalization and social policy in Africa* (pp. 1–20). Dakar: Council for the Development of Social Science Research in Africa (CODESRIA).

Alcock, P. (2003). The subject of social policy. In P. Alcock, A. Erskine, & M. May (Eds.), *The student's companion to social policy* (pp. 3–10). Malden: Blackwell Publishing.

Andersson, P. -E., Bigsten, A., & Persson, H. (2000). *Foreign aid, debt and growth in Zambia. Research Report No. 112*. Uppsala: Nordiska Afrikainstitutet.

Bogenschneider, K. (2006). *Family policy matters: How policymaking affects families and what professionals can do*. Mahwah: Lawrence Erlbaum Associates, Inc.

California Family Resource Association. (2007). *Strong families. Strong Communities.* http://californiafamilyresource.org/assets/docs/fes_brief/CFRA_FES_BRIEF.pdf. Accessed 5 December 2012.

Central Statistical Office. (2006). *Living conditions monitoring survey*. Lusaka: Central Statistical Office.

Central Statistical Office. (2011). *2010 Census of population and housing–Preliminary population figures*. Lusaka: Central Statistical Office.

Department of Social Welfare. (1979). *Annual report*. Lusaka: Department of Social Welfare.

Economic and Social Commission for Western Asia (2009). *Social policy and social protection.* www.escwa.un.org/information/publications/edit/upload/sdd-09-TP10.pdf. Accessed 27 July 2011.

Esping-Andersen, G. (1990). *The three worlds of welfare capitalism.* Cambridge: Polity Press.

Government of the Republic of Zambia. (2011). *International Monetary Fund World economic outlook dataset, April 2011*. Lusaka: Ministry of Finance and National Planning.

Gauthier, A. N. (1996). *The state and the family: a comparative analysis of family policies in industrialized countries*. Oxford: Oxford University Press.

Harris, L. (2004). *Family policy matters: Responding to family change in Europe*. Bristol: The Policy Press.

Kandeke, T. K. (1977). *Fundamentals of Zambian humanism.* Lusaka: National Educational Company of Zambia (NECZAM).

Lewis, J. (2000). *Empire state building: War and welfare in Kenya 1925–52*. Columbus: Ohio State University Press.

Masiye, G. P. C., Tembo, R., Chisanga, B., & Mwanza, A. (1998). Social policy and research environment in Zambia. *Journal of Social Development in Africa, 13*(2), 34–43.

Mattessich, P., & Hill, R. (1987). Life cycle and family development. In M. B. Sussman & S. K. Stenmetz (Eds.), *Handbook of marriage and the family* (pp. 437–469). New York: Plenum Press.

Mhone, G. (2004). Historical trajectories of social policy in post-colonial Africa: The case of Zambia. In T. Mkandawire (Ed.), *Social policy in a development context* (pp. 308–337). Geneva: United Nations Institute for Social Development (UNRISD).

Mkandawire, T. (2004). Social policy in a development context: Introduction. In T. Mkandawire (Ed.), *Social policy in a development context* (pp. 1–33). Houndsmills: Palgrave Macmillan.

Millar, J. (2003). Social policy and family policy. In P. Alcock, A. Erskine, & M. May (Eds.), *Social policy* (pp. 153–159). Oxford: Blackwell Publishing Ltd.

National Human Services Assembly. (2004). *Introduction to family strengthening.* www.nassembly.org/fspc/practice/documents/Briefs1.pdf. Accessed 7 December 2012.

Neyer, G. (2003). Family policies and low fertility in Western Europe. *MPIDR Working Paper WP 2003-021, July 2003*. Rostock: Max-Planck-Institut für demografische Forschung.

Noyoo, N. (2000). *Social welfare in Zambia*. Lusaka: Multimedia Publications.

Noyoo, N. (2010). *Social policy and human development in Zambia*. London: Adonis and Abbey.

Noyoo, N. (2013). *Social welfare in Zambia: The search for a transformative agenda*. London: Adonis and Abbey.

OECD. (2011). *OECD investment policy review of Zambia: Advancing investment policy reform*. Paris: Organisation for Economic Co-operation & Development (OECD).

Saasa, O., & Carlsson, J. (2002). *Aid and poverty reduction in Zambia: Mission unaccomplished*. Uppsala: Nordiska Afrikainstitutet.

Trask, B. S. (2004). *Globalisation and families: Accelerated systematic social change*. London: Springer.

United Nations. (2009). *Report of the expert group meeting on "family policy in a changing world: Promoting social protection and intergenerational solidarity"*. Doha, Qatar.

United Nations Children's Fund (2008). *The state of Zambia's children*. www.unicef.org/zambia/children.html. Accessed 2 October 2012.

United Nations Department of Economic and Social Affairs. (2011). *Men in families and family policy in a changing world*. New York: United Nations Department of Economic and Social Affairs.

United Nations Development Programme. (2003). *Zambia Human Development Report*. Lusaka: UNDP.

United Nations Development Programme. (2011a). *Human Development Report*. New York: UNDP.

United Nations Development Programme. (2011b). *Zambia Human Development Report*. Lusaka: UNDP.

United Nations Development Programme (UNDP)/Government Republic of Zambia (GRZ). (2011). *Zambia: Millennium Development Goals Progress Report*. Lusaka: UNDP/GRZ.

Zeitlin, M. F., & Megawanji, R. (1995). Economic perspective on the family. In M. F. Zeitlin, R. Megawanji, E. M. Kramer, N. D. Colletta, E. D. Babatunde, & D. Garman (Eds.), *Strengthening the family: Implications for international development* (pp. 38–49). Tokyo: United Nations University Press.

Zimmerman, S. L. (1995). *Understanding family policy: Theories and applications*. Thousand Oaks: SAGE Publications.

Chapter 11
State Measures Towards Work–Care Integration in South Africa

Lisa Dancaster

Introduction

The combination of work and care has remained largely absent from the government's policy agenda in South Africa. This is surprising given the crisis of care that exists. Not only has the demand for care risen sharply in the last few years, largely as a result of HIV and AIDS, but the foundation providers of this care, namely women, families and institutions, are precariously positioned to handle it. In particular, the fragmented nature of South African family structures, and the notable absence of fathers in families and in the provision of care has been well documented (Richter and Morrell 2006; Eddy and Holborn 2011). Allied to this care crisis is the fact that women, the primary providers of care in South Africa, have been entering the labour force in greater numbers and hence face an inevitable 'time squeeze' in their efforts to combine employment with the need to provide care.

Government ministers have, only very recently, started to articulate the need for the state to become more involved in work–care integration in South Africa. For example, in her address at the launch of the Green Paper on Families (Department of Social Development 2011) on the 15 May 2012, the Deputy Minister of Social Development, Mrs. Naria Bongi Ntuli noted that there was a "need to establish comprehensive legal and policy frameworks for balancing work and family life that allow for shared care responsibility between men and women, other family members, the State, the private sector and society as a whole".

This Chapter takes this call for legal frameworks in the area of work–care integration in South Africa a step further by outlining specific recommendations for legislative reform in this area. The discussion critically examines the adequacy of current legislative measures for work–care integration in South Africa and provides recommendations for change within a framework of comprehensive legislative measures to address work–care integration.

L. Dancaster (✉)
Honorary Research Associate, University of Cape Town, Cape Town, South Africa
e-mail: Lisa.dancaster@gmail.com

Z. Mokomane (ed.), *Work–Family Interface in Sub-Saharan Africa*,
International Perspectives on Social Policy, Administration, and Practice,
DOI: 10.1007/978-3-319-01237-7_11,

Legislating for Work–Care Integration in South Africa

Dancaster and Baird (2008), Cohen and Dancaster (2009a, b) and Dancaster and Cohen (2010) critically examine legislative measures for the combination of work and care in South Africa and argue that they are inadequate. The discussion in this section draws on the findings and recommendations for legislative reform from this existing research and expands on it through suggestions for additional legislative reform particularly in the areas of adoption, paternity and maternity leave.

Lewis (2006:111) notes that the following three provisions are crucial in securing genuine choice for carers to engage in paid and/or unpaid work, namely: (i) time: working time and time to care; (ii) money: cash to buy care, cash for carers; and (iii) services: for children, the sick and the elderly. The focus in this chapter is primarily on the first of these, namely time off to provide care. Considerations for legislative reform are discussed in relation to two main entitlements in this area, namely leave for caregivers and flexible working arrangements as longer term measures to accommodate employees who provide ongoing care.

This is illustrated in the framework in Fig. 11.1, which provides a comprehensive package of legislative measures regulating work and care and guides the recommendations for legislative reform discussed in this chapter. This framework recognises that leave is necessary for different reasons and at different stages to accommodate working carers and those they care for. For example, in some cases the leave is necessary for maternal wellbeing (maternity leave), at others it is necessary for infant wellbeing (maternity leave/emergency care leave) including early childhood development (parental leave) and at times it is necessary to encourage the participation of men in the provision of care (paternity and parental leave). Leave provisions that are ‘muddied’ such as those that permit employees to use personal sick leave to attend to ill family members, or those that incorporate maternity and/or paternity leave into parental leave, fail to recognise the different purposes of each of the leave categories identified in this framework.

Furthermore, the division of leave provisions in this framework recognises that at times there are socially desirable outcomes that may differ with each of the different leave categories. The separation of categories permits better articulation of these objectives and options for attaining these outcomes. For instance, involving fathers in infant care is achieved through a separate paternity leave and ‘fathers only’ parental leave provision (see discussion below) rather than a blanket inclusion under family responsibility leave or a general parental leave provision.

Finally, the comprehensive bundle of legislative provisions in this framework provides employees with choices. Not all employees will use all the leave options offered and in many cases affordability may limit use of arrangements when the arrangement results in loss of income. Nevertheless, the provision of maximum choice permits employees to tailor the solution to work–care integration to their individual needs, and recognises that there is not a one-size-fits-all solution to individual problems of work–care integration.

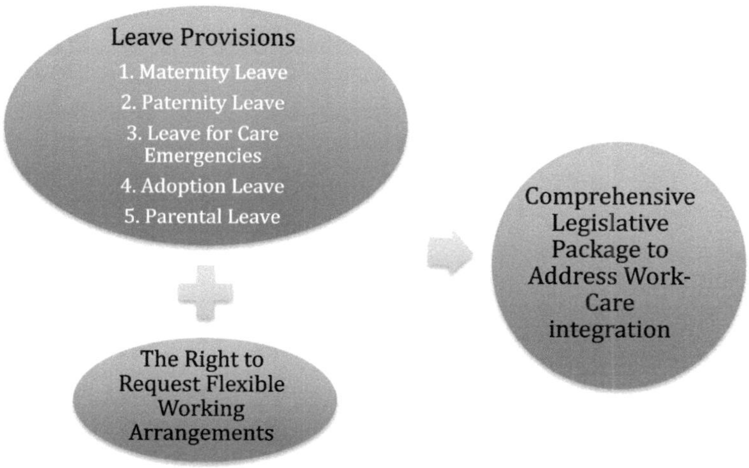

Fig. 11.1 Comprehensive legislative package to address work–care integration

Leave Provisions for Work–Care Integration

Leave Available at the Time of the Birth of a Child

Leave at the time of birth include maternity leave, adoption leave and paternity leave and each will be discussed in turn below.

Maternity and Adoption Leave

Maternity leave duration

The debate over the 'ideal' period of maternity leave embraces a range of arguments related to health protection for working mothers, equal employment opportunities for women, access to adequate antenatal and birthing care, maternal recovery, optimal nutrition for infants and gender equality within families.

The provision of 4 months maternity leave in South Africa in the Basic Conditions of Employment Act[1] (BCEA) is as good as the majority of countries in the world. A 2012 International Labour Organisation (ILO) review the duration of maternity leave by countries in its database (167 Member States) found that globally, 51 % of countries offer maternity leave of at least 14 weeks, which is the standard established by the ILO Convention 183. South Africa's 4 month duration of maternity leave is, however, not as long as that recommended in ILO recommendation 191 (18 weeks). About 20 % of the countries in the ILO database met, or

[1] 75 of 1997.

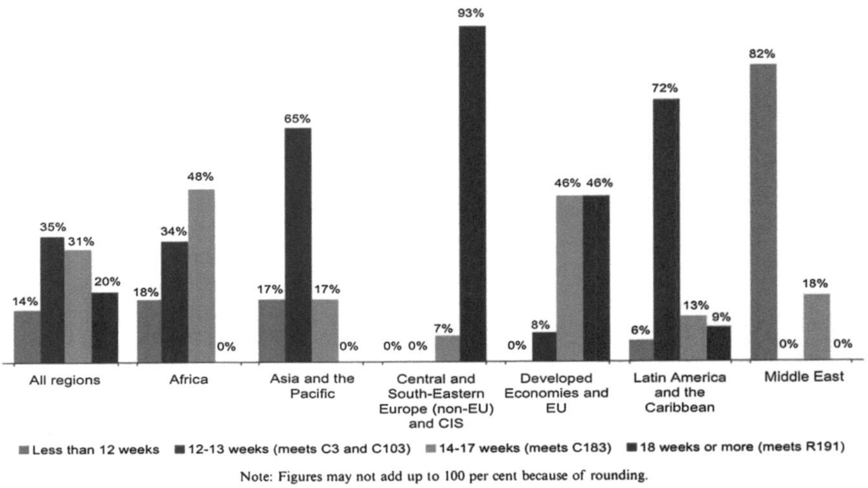

Fig. 11.2 Length of Statutory Maternity Leave, by Region, 2009 (167 countries). *Source* ILO Database of Conditions of Work and Employment Laws on maternity Protection (2009) cited by International Labour Organisation (2012)

exceeded the 18 weeks of leave suggested in Recommendation 191 (International Labour Organisation 2012). It is noteworthy that the World Health Organisation recommendation is 16 weeks, based on 4 months needed to establish breastfeeding.

The regional differences in length of maternity leave are illustrated in Fig. 11.2. It is evident from the figure that Africa lags developed economies and European Union (EU) countries as well as countries in Central and South Eastern Europe. It appears, however, to fare marginally better than countries in Asia and the Pacific and considerably better than countries in the Middle East.

Adoption leave

According to ILO Recommendation No. 191, maternity leave provisions should be available for adoptive parents to permit them to adapt to the arrival of the child. Surprisingly, there is no provision for adoption leave in the BCEA in South Africa. It is not covered in the section on maternity leave nor is leave granted for adoptive parents in terms of family responsibility leave. Nevertheless, adoptive parents who adopt a child under the age of 2 years are able to claim unemployment insurance benefits in terms of the Unemployment Insurance Act[2] (UIA) for time off during this period.

It is recommended that leave for the purposes of adoption should be included in the BCEA. This would correct the anomaly between the provision of adoption payments in the UIA and the absence of adoption leave in the BCEA. It would also correct the imbalance that exists between granting employee's time off on the

[2] 63 of 2001.

death of an adoptive parent (under family responsibility leave), but not providing the adoptive parent with time off when they adopt a child.

Combining adoption leave with maternity leave is not uncommon in legislation in a number of countries and the period of adoption leave will either correspond to that of maternity leave, or the leave entitlement for adoptive parents will be shorter than for biological parents because the prenatal leave often available for natural mothers is eliminated (International Labour Organisation 2012:56). It is recommended, however, that adoption leave should be separated from maternity leave in order to distinguish the purposes of the different types of leave and to ensure that men also have access to adoption leave in order to encourage male participation in parenting. ILO Recommendation No. 191 provides that adoption leave should be available for both parents. Maternity leave is a leave that is obviously only available to mothers and hence including adoption leave in it excludes fathers from utilising this leave.

This could be overcome if paternity leave was extended to fathers in the case of adoption, and if mothers could access maternity leave in the case of adoption. However, given the absence of a separate statutory entitlement to paternity leave in South African law (see discussion below), it is recommended that a separate provision regulating adoption leave is included in the BCEA. Not only does it overcome the difficulties mentioned above where adoption leave is included in maternity leave, but it also allows the purpose of adoption leave to be distinguished from other work–care leave provisions. The purpose of maternity leave is to contribute to the health and wellbeing of mothers and their babies (International Labour Organisation 2012:1). Adoption leave may be concerned with the well-being of babies provided that the child being adopted is very young, but the concerns for maternal health and wellbeing are of less significance for adoptive mothers.

The EU Directive on parental leave provides for an individual right for men and women workers to parental leave and adoption leave for at least 3 months. In some cases the adoption leave is an independent non-transferable right (e.g. Iceland) and in other cases the period of adoption leave can be taken by one parent or split between them. It is recommended that, in an effort to encourage men to become more involved in the care of their children, an independent non-transferable right to adoption leave should be considered for employees in South Africa.

The current provisions regarding access to unemployment insurance stipulate that the adopted child should be less than 2 years of age. In some countries the duration of the leave varies according to the age of the child with shorter periods being available when the adopted child is older.

The recommendations above are summarised as follows:

1. The gap in the South African law regarding the right to take adoption leave needs to be addressed. It is recommended that a separate and new provision on adoption leave be introduced into the BCEA. For the reasons provided above, it is recommended that it should not be combined with the current maternity leave provision;

2. It is recommended that this leave be drafted in a manner that encourages fathers to use the provision by making it available to both parents as an individual, non-transferable right and
3. Consideration should be given to not limiting adoption leave to instances where the child adopted is under the age of 2 and that differing durations of adoption leave should be considered according to the age of the adopted child.

Maternity payments

Debates over payment during maternity leave include who finances it, for how long and at what rate. Essentially it falls to three potential bodies to finance maternity payments either individually or in combination with one another, namely employers, taxpayers or employees. Employers, particularly small employers, argue that forcing them to finance paid maternity leave will act as a disincentive to hire young women and will erode narrow profit margins. In terms of the burden falling on the state, there are those taxpayers who argue that the decision to have children is an individual one that should not require others to shoulder the financial burden. Arguments against requiring individual employees to shoulder the burden point to the social desirability of providing state support to assist carers at the time of birth with tradeoffs for society as a whole.

ILO Conventions No. 3 and No. 103 state that employers should not be individually liable for paying maternity benefits and that benefits should be provided through social insurance and other funds. Research indicates that over the period 1994–2009 there has been a shift towards mixed systems in which employers and social security systems share responsibility for benefits and the number of countries in which employers are fully responsible for paying maternity benefits has declined slightly over this period (International Labour Organisation 2012:32).

Over half of the countries in the ILO database (53 % of 167 countries) provide cash benefits through national social security schemes. In 26 % of the countries, maternity benefits are paid solely by the employer (International Labour Organisation 2012). Figure 11.3 indicates who pays for maternity benefits in the different regions. There are marked differences between developed countries and countries in the EU who predominantly pay maternity benefits through social security schemes and countries in Africa, Asia and the Middle East which rely more heavily on employer liability.

Although South Africa would comply with ILO requirements in terms of the duration of maternity leave and the fact that maternity pay is financed through social security obtained from contributions by both employers and employees, it falls short of ILO standards in terms of the amount of maternity pay that employees receive (Olivier et al. 2011). In order to comply with Convention No. 183, the cash benefit paid during maternity leave should be at least two-thirds of a woman's previous earnings. UIF in South Africa range from 31 to 59 % depending on income but even at the top end, the payment falls short of the two-thirds required in the ILO Convention.

Article 7 of Convention No. 183 provides for countries with 'insufficiently developed' economies and social security systems and recommends that they

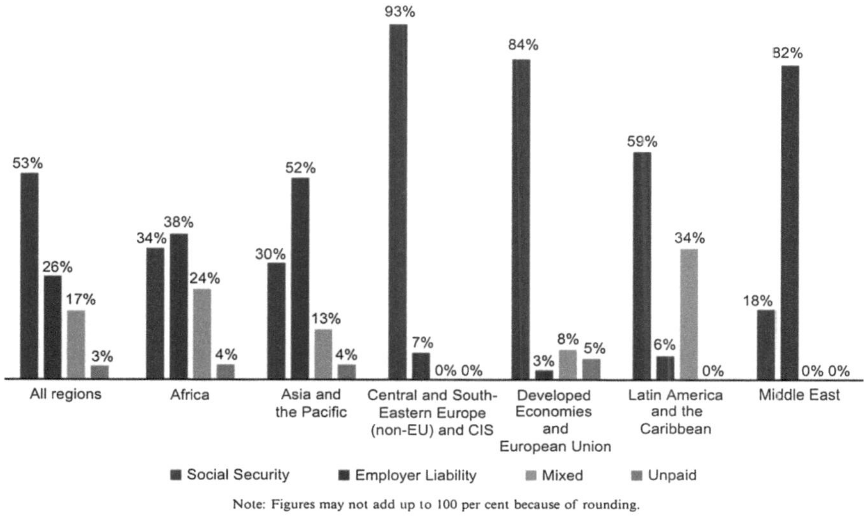

Fig. 11.3 Who Pays for Maternity Leave, by Region. *Source* ILO Database of Work and Employment Laws on Maternity Protection, ILO 2009 cited by International Labour Organisation (2012)

should pay cash benefits at a rate no lower than the rate payable for sickness or temporary disability in national laws and regulations. It is debatable whether or not South Africa, a middle-income country[3] with a fairly comprehensive social security system, would fall under the Article 7 'exceptions'. Nevertheless, the BCEA provides for fully paid sick leave for a period equal to the number of days an employee works in a 6-week period over a 36-month cycle. Accordingly, it is argued that Article 7 would provide no foundation for arguing that South Africa could comply with this Convention as it stands.

Furthermore, employees in South Africa who have not contributed to the UIF for a sufficiently long period of time, would not be entitled to receive the full period of maternity leave as paid (albeit partially) leave. This is because benefits from the fund accrue at 1 day's benefit per 6 days worked and accordingly to access the full entitlement of 17.32 weeks (121 days) an employee would need to have built up benefits by working for approximately 2 years.

In addition the benefits accumulated for payout will be reduced if an employee has claimed unemployment insurance benefits for another reason (e.g. illness or unemployment).[4] Accordingly, the right to the full entitlement of maternity pay in South Africa is conditional on having sufficient benefits built up through payments into the unemployment insurance fund, and not having reduced these benefits

[3] South Africa is classified by the World Bank as an upper middle-income country.

[4] The only instance in which the benefits are not reduced is where they have been paid out for maternity leave.

through the use of unemployment insurance payments for one of the benefit categories recognised in the UIA.

In 2004, the ILO Committee of Experts noted that in many countries the provision of cash maternity benefits is subject to a minimum qualifying period or coverage by the insurance system. The Committee accepted these restrictions, provided that the qualifying periods are set at a reasonable level and that women who do not meet the condition are provided (subject to certain means related conditions) with benefits financed through social assistance funds (International Labour Organisation 2012). It is doubtful as to whether 2 years is a reasonable qualifying period in order to access the full period of maternity pay. Furthermore, in South Africa there is no alternative benefit financed through social assistance to fund mothers who have not accumulated sufficient funds in UIF to provide them with payment during maternity leave. It is acknowledged that there are social grants for child support[5] but these are means-tested and not intended as a substitute for the lack of maternity pay, but rather as a measure for poverty alleviation. Consideration should be given to measures to assist employees who are unable, through length of service, to receive full maternity payments from UIF.

It is also recommended that the level of maternity payments should be increased. Olivier et al. (2011) recommend that maternity benefits should be no less than two-thirds of the woman's previous earnings to align maternity payments with international standards and to facilitate the ratification of ILO Maternity Protection Convention (183 of 2000). It has also been argued that the low rate of income replacement granted to women in South Africa during maternity leave forces many mothers to return to work before exhausting their leave entitlement (Dupper et al. 2000, 2001).

This debate on level of payments during maternity leave should include considerations on whether or not the current system of contributory social insurance is adequate for the purposes of maternity pay. In summary, some of the concerns emerging from the current system include the fact that:

- Many people in the informal economy and self-employed women are excluded from the benefits because they cannot contribute to the fund;
- Benefits are dependent on the length of contribution and in the case of maternity benefits it takes 2 years to accumulate the 17.32 week full entitlement; and
- Maternity benefits 'compete' with other benefits that can be accessed from the fund which means that if previous benefits have been accessed it may take more than 2 years to be able to access the full 17.32 week entitlement.

[5] Child support grants are provided to primary caregivers over the age of 16 in the amount of R270 per month (from October 2011) if they care for a child under the age of 18 years and if they pass a means test. According to the means test the caregiver's monthly income must not exceed R31,200 or, if married, their joint income must not exceed R62,400 per month. These grants have been criticised for being cumbersome in terms of application procedures, limited in their application and inadequate in terms of monetary payment and duration (Mpedi 2008; Lund 2009).

There are alternatives within the current system to increase both the coverage and benefits for maternity pay. Coverage may be increased through a system of voluntary participation (Mpedi 2008) and the level of benefits could be increased though increasing the employer and/or employee contribution to the fund or through increased contributions from the state into the fund (Olivier et al. 2011). Employers could be required by law to 'top up' the amount received by employees from UIF with the caution, however, that depending on the level of 'top up', this could work against promoting gender equality in the workplace. A further suggestion for consideration is for social assistance packages to support employees who do not fall within the ambit of UIF benefits for maternity leave either because they fall outside the legislation, or because they have not accumulated enough in the way of benefits or have exhausted their benefits. India has a system of providing this type of social support to marginalised sectors of employment whereby a tax is levied on the production, sale or export of specified goods to cater for the needs of those in the informal sector (Mpedi 2008).

There is also merit in the argument (see Olivier et al. 2011) that maternity payments should be removed altogether from the unemployment insurance scheme in its current form and be dealt with in a separate legislative provision. This would separate it from unemployment benefits, which have different considerations given that they apply in circumstances relating to a complete loss of employment and not a temporary absence.

These (and other) alternatives need to be debated with a view in improving the current deficiencies that exist in South Africa regarding maternity pay.

Paternity Leave

The importance of the presence of fathers at and after the birth of their children has been recognised, not only in terms of the bonding between father and child, but also for the support fathers can give to mothers after childbirth. Leave for fathers over the time of the birth of a child is provided to a very minimal extent in South Africa. There is no separate entitlement to paternity leave in South Africa. It forms part of the 3 days (5 days for domestic workers) that can be taken by an employee in terms of the BCEA as paid family responsibility leave for sickness of a child; birth of a child and/or death of a spouse or life partner, parent or adoptive parent, grandparent, child or adopted child, grandchild and/or sibling.

There are a number of problems with the combination of paternity leave with legislated family responsibility leave in its current form:

- It is only available to employees who work four or more days per week;
- It is only available to employees who have worked for longer than 4 months;
- It is not targeted at male employees—it is available to all employees (both male and female) and hence from a gender equality perspective it does not target men as fathers and the protection and encouragement of this role and

- The duration is too short. It is limited to 3 days per annum, which is reduced if it has already utilised for the other purposes for which it can be used (death, sickness, etc.).

The need to get men involved in fatherhood and care duties in general in South Africa has been highlighted (Morrell and Jewkes 2011; Department of Social Development 2011). Morrell and Richter (2006) note that most South African men do not seem especially interested in their children. "They seldom attend the births of their own, they don't always acknowledge that their children are their own, and they frequently fail to participate in their children's lives" (Morrell and Richter 2006:2). Nevertheless, it has been acknowledged that "fathers can make a major contribution to the health of South African society by caring for children and producing a new generation of South Africans for whom fathers will be significant by their presence rather than their absence" (Richter and Morrell 2006:6).

Smit's (2002) study of South African men has found that those who make use of paternity leave will not only be more involved in domestic task responsibilities and the rearing and care-taking of children, but will also be inclined to perform emotion work in the marriage leading to increased marital satisfaction.

The trend internationally is towards separate legislated paid paternity leave. It has been observed that:

> Overall, paternity leave provisions are becoming increasingly common, which may be an indicator of the growing importance attached to the presence of the father around the time of childbirth (International Labour Organisation 2012).

A number of countries in Africa (Algeria, Dijibouti, Kenya, Rwanda, Tanzania, Tunisia and Uganda) offer paid paternity leave ranging from 1 day (Tunisia) to 2 weeks in Kenya (International Labour Organisation 2012).

It is recommended that paternity leave be removed from the provision regulating family responsibility leave and that a separate paternity leave provision should be introduced in the BCEA. The duration of this leave should be considered in the context of other provisions (such as a parental leave provision, were this to be introduced—see discussion below) that provide leave for fathers to attend to childcare. It is also recommended that paternity leave be fully paid. The research from other countries indicates that men do not tend to take up their right to paternity leave to any great extent if the provision is unpaid or paid at low rates (Moss and O'Brien 2006; Whitehouse et al. 2007). The source of payment should mirror considerations regarding the funding of maternity pay and this has been highlighted for debate in the previous section.

Leave Available to Care for a Young Child (Parental Leave)

While maternity leave aims to protect working women during their pregnancy and recovery from childbirth, parental leave refers to a relatively long-term leave available to either parent, allowing them to take care of an infant or young child over a period of time usually following the maternity or paternity leave period (International Labour Organisation 2012).

Parental leave is encouraged in ILO Recommendations[6] and in EU Directives. Indeed, the trend in the EU and other industrialised economies, as well as in Central and Southern Europe (non-EU) and Commonwealth of Independent States countries is towards the provision of parental leave, and almost all these countries have some kind of parental or childcare leave provisions. Conversely, parental leave it is rather rare in developing countries and in less industrialised parts of the world (International Labour Organisation 2012). Two countries from Africa appear to offer parental leave—in Burkina Faso, male or female employees can request up to 6 months of unpaid leave to care for their children and in the case of illness, the leave period can be extended to 1 year. In Guinea, after the expiration of the 14-week maternity leave period, women may take an additional 9 months of unpaid leave. In some countries there is scope for flexibility on how and when to take this leave—in some cases it can be taken on a part-time basis, whether as a continuous period after maternity/paternity leave or is split over a period when the child is young (International Labour Organisation 2012).

In many countries parental leave is a shared entitlement between men and women although studies show that women are more likely than men to take it up (Whitehouse et al. 2007; Moss 2011), hence the introduction of a period of 'fathers only' parental leave in Norway which is lost if it is not used by the male parent. Studies also indicate that take-up rates by both parents can be low where parental leave is unpaid (Moss 2011).

With regard to payment during this period, Dupper et al. (2011) argue for a 'carers benefit' to be financed through a social insurance scheme providing also for maternity and adoption benefits and separated from the current unemployment insurance scheme. A 'carers benefit' would provide payments to employees who 'resign or suspend their employment for any *compelling family reason*'. This would include the purposes of taking care of children or to care for a terminally ill family member.

Parental leave is non-existent in South Africa and there is no legislative entitlement to it. Thus, employees who wish to continue to care for their children for any period of time after maternity leave will have to resign from employment or use their annual leave unless they are able to get consent for this type of leave from their employer (Dancaster and Baird 2008). It is recommended, therefore, that a separate provision regulating parental leave be introduced into the BCEA. There are a number of reasons for recommending the introduction of parental leave in South Africa:

---

[6] Recommendation No. 191 (accompanying Convention No. 183 on maternity protection) and Recommendation No. 165 (accompanying the Workers with Family Responsibilities Convention, 1981 (No. 156)) contain provisions on parental leave and the EU Directive on Parental Leave provides for no less than 3 months parental leave.

1. Parental leave encourages early childhood development by those shown to be most effective in providing this—namely, parents. This is particularly the case in a country like South Africa where state supported childcare services are limited;
2. The absence of any leave after maternity and/or paternity leave to care for young children may have the effect of women leaving the workplace to attend to this function. Kingdon and Knight (2004) note that that women in South Africa are more than twice as likely to resign from employment as men.
   "Working women may quit voluntarily for child-bearing and -rearing and, being usually the secondary income earners in the family, are also more likely than men to give up their work in case of family emergencies or migration of spouse" (Kingdon and Knight, 2004:203)
3. If fatherhood it to be encouraged and equal sharing of care is to be promoted then parental leave that is available as a shared entitlement, is one legislative measure to encourage this and
4. True equality of opportunity in employment, as defined by the ILO Discrimination (Employment and Occupation) Convention requires a work–family schema that permits workers to undertake their care responsibilities without loss of contact with the workforce. In circumstances where the bulk of care work is undertaken by women, failure to institute a scheme which permits job-protected time off from work to care for children is arguably at odds with commitments under this Convention (Murray 2004:20).

Questions regarding the duration and payment for this leave need to be debated at a national level.

Leave for Care Emergencies

Workers with care responsibilities may need to take time off to attend to unexpected care emergencies such as sudden illness of a child or dependent family member or the last minute unavailability of a substitute caregiver. This is different from anticipated and ongoing care such as the care of young children or those with special needs, elderly parents or someone infected with HIV and AIDS.

The need to consider revising the current legislated provision on family responsibility leave in terms of the removing the clause providing for family responsibility leave in the case of the birth of a child and the introduction of a separate provision regulating paternity leave has already been discussed above. In addition, it is recommended that in the context of care for leave emergencies the family responsibility leave provision is in need of revision. The reasons are as follows (Dancaster and Baird 2008):

1. Family responsibility leave in its current form is only for the birth or illness of a child. Accordingly, this leave is not available to attend to a sick adult dependent. Ironically, if the absence is to attend the death of an individual then the

scope of persons for whom it may be utilised is far wider: spouse or life partner, or their parent, adoptive parent, grandparent, child, adopted child, grandchild or sibling (Dancaster and Baird 2008). There is a need to examine whether or not family responsibility leave to attend to sick children should not be extended to include a broader range of dependents given the high prevalence of HIV and AIDS and the need for care for sick adult dependents[7] (Dancaster and Baird 2008:32).

2. Family responsibility leave is limited to time off to attend to birth, sickness and death only. In addition to the use of this leave for sickness and death, it is recommended that the provision be widened to include the utilisation of this leave for unexpected disruptions in care such as the failure of the substitute caregiver to arrive for work or unexpected incidents at school that require attendance by a caregiver. Given the widespread use of domestic workers as carers and the difficulties these employees face in terms of getting to and from work using the (sometimes unreliable) forms of public transport in South Africa, the widening of this provision to cover unexpected disruptions of this nature would be useful. Furthermore, the increase in strikes by teachers in primary and secondary schools has increased the need for parents to make emergency arrangements for children in these circumstances.

The Right to Request Flexible Working Arrangements

Flexible working arrangements can assist employees combine paid work and caregiving by allowing them to remain employed whilst making changes to their hours and/or place of work. There has been increasing recognition by governments towards the fact that specific legislation is required that grants employees the right to request flexible working arrangements from their employers. Hegewisch and Gornick (2008) reviewed statutory laws aimed at increasing workers ability to change working hours and arrangements in twenty high-income countries and notes that a large majority of these countries had introduced flexible working statutes. The United Kingdom, Australia and New Zealand are examples of three such countries that have introduced this legislation in the last 10 years as part of a number of measures to assist employees as caregivers.

The connection between flexible working arrangements in the context of assisting employees to combine work and care is evident in the recognition given to it in the Convention on Part-time Work. The Convention on Part-time Work requires that ‘laws and regulations that may prevent or discourage recourse to or acceptance of part-time work’ be reviewed to ‘facilitate access to productive and freely chosen part-time work which meets the needs of both employers and

[7] 55 of 1998.

workers' (Article 9). "The needs of workers with family responsibilities are explicitly recognised in the section requiring 'special attention, in employment policies' to specific groups including 'workers with family responsibilities' (Article 2(c)). The Convention further requires that 'where appropriate, measures shall be taken to ensure that the transfer from full-time to part-time work or vice versa is voluntary, in accordance with national law and practice' (Article 10)" (Murray 2004:21).

There are a number of reasons advanced for the adoption of this legislative right in these countries:

1. Existing anti-discrimination legislation has not been sufficient to assist employees advance this right and to place an obligation on employers to seriously consider employee requests to work flexibly (Smith 2006). As noted by Smith and Riley (2004:204) "any system of regulation that relies on traditionally disempowered individuals being able to navigate the legal system to enforce rights is inherently limited";
2. A positive law such as this one, not only places an obligation on employers to seriously consider employee requests to work flexibly, but also provides a (usually fairly simple) procedure for employees to claim it from their employer (Murray 2005);
3. Employee requested flexibility provides employees with care responsibilities a choice regarding the nature of their work arrangements, in some cases with a trade-off in income, and is increasingly being seen as part of a composite body of legislative measures to assist employees as caregivers.

Cohen and Dancaster (2009a, b) argue for a specific right to request flexible working arrangements in South African law. In doing so they consider the legislative framework that prohibits family responsibility discrimination in South Africa, namely the Employment Equity Act, (see foot note 7) and note that the South African experience has revealed that the legislative provision governing family responsibility discrimination remains grossly under-utilised and ineffective. Not a single family responsibility discrimination case involving a request for flexible working has been brought since the enactment of the Act (Cohen and Dancaster 2009a). They posit that this may be the result of the high costs of litigation, the difficulty in obtaining legal aid and that employees may be reluctant to engage in a 'naming, blaming and claiming' (Charlesworth 2005) process with difficult evidentiary requirements in showing discriminatory treatment and identifying an appropriate comparator. They also note that high unemployment rates in South Africa that make any job better than no job, discourages employees from jeopardising existing employment relationships with requests that involve a re-organisation of standardised working hours. In addition they point out the long entrenched societal practices and cultural norms around the 'ideal worker' and note the subtle gender assumptions and stereotyping of members of the judiciary.

Apart from the failings of anti-discrimination legislation to protect and advance this right in South Africa, there are additional arguments in favour of the introduction of this right:

1. Research on the characteristics of carers of people living with HIV and AIDS shows that some of the financial impact of caring is as a result of giving up work to care (Akintola 2004; Rajaraman et al. 2006). This break in employment, particularly in a country with high unemployment may be catastrophic in terms of trying to re-enter the labour force when the care demand ends. In such instances a reduction in working hours through flexible working arrangements, even though it results in lower income, may be preferable in that some income is maintained and so is labour force attachment;
2. Evidence from employer and employee surveys carried out after the introduction of this legislation in the UK point to its positive impact on employees and also indicate that employer's fears that they would be inundated with requests to work flexibly were unfounded (Holt and Granger 2005; Hayward et al. 2007);
3. Research among South African employers shows that they are not voluntarily implementing flexible working arrangements to assist employees as caregivers in formal policy provisions to any great extent (Dancaster 2012).

A brief consideration of this right in other countries is useful in considering its possible introduction in South African law. The policy motivations behind the right to request flexible working arrangements varies—in Germany the introduction of the general right to work part-time was motivated by considerations of job creation and affirmative action rather than work–care concerns (Jacobs and Schmidt 2001). In the United Kingdom, New Zealand and Australia the introduction of the right to request flexible working arrangements reflects government's commitment to supporting working families (Croucher and Kelliher 2005). Not surprising therefore, the target groups have varied with the German right being available to all employees irrespective of the reason for their request and the United Kingdom right being available to parents of children and more recently also to careers of adults in need of care.

There are also inter-country differences in terms of qualifications for use, both in terms of the size of the employer and employee duration of employment (Hegewisch and Gornick 2008). For instance, there are differences in terms of how often an employee may make such a request, the type of flexible working arrangements that may be requested, the procedure for the requests and basis on which employers can refuse such a request (Hegewisch and Gornick 2008). In the Netherlands employers are subject to the strongest test in denying a request and may only do so if there are 'serious countervailing reasons' and in Germany the refusal can be based on 'business or organisational reasons' but these need not be 'serious'. In the United Kingdom employers can refuse a request based on the burden of additional costs; detrimental effect on the ability to re-organise work among existing staff or to recruit additional staff; insufficiency of work during the period when the employee proposes to return to work and planned structural change. In all cases, changes result in a permanent alteration of the employment contract.

Conclusion

The role of the state in work–care integration, and specifically in the regulation of leave provisions that give employees more time to care has been on the increase in many countries, particularly in Europe (Moss and O'Brien 2006). Some of the different articulated rationales governing state policy on work and family include the need to support and strengthen families, to ensure that both paid and unpaid work are equally valued, to encourage the growth of employment generally by ensuring that those with care responsibilities are not lost to the workforce altogether, to improve the quality, as well as the quantity, of employment (this is a key objective of both the ILO and the EU) and/or to bolster the labour market's capacity in times of ageing populations and falling fertility rates (Murray 2004).

This chapter has argued for an increase in the regulation of work–care integration by the state in South Africa. Specific recommendations for legislative reform have been outlined with reference to comparative legislative provisions both in developed and developing nations. The discussion on legislative measures for work–care integration has highlighted the fact that, in terms of a comprehensive bundle of work–care leave provisions that incorporate maternity leave, adoption leave, paternity leave, parental leave and emergency care leave, South Africa has only one of these in its 'pure' form, namely maternity leave. Paternity leave is combined with emergency care leave and there are no legislative provisions for adoption leave or parental leave. It has also noted that the Employment Equity Act has not achieved much in the way of the advancement of employee's rights to work flexibly in circumstances involving family responsibility requirements despite the fact that the provision in the EEA on family responsibility discrimination and affirmative action provide potential avenues for employees to achieve flexible working arrangements in the context of care giving (Cohen and Dancaster 2009a).

There needs to be recognition on the part of the state that leaving work–care integration concerns to other actors such as employers and trade unions means that the burden of care remains essentially on females in households in South Africa. Evidence reveals that employers in South Africa are not improving on legislative minima regulating leave for care purposes to any great extent (Dancaster 2012) nor are South African trade unions bargaining over issues relating to gendered conditions to any great extent (Labour Research Service 2011). Unless there is political will on the part of government towards assisting employees with work–care integration and a commitment by employers to improving the way in which employees combine work and care, and unless the actors come together to discuss and debate issues affecting work–care integration in South Africa, the burden of combining work and care will continue to remain on those, primarily female, individual members in households.

References

Akintola, O. (2004). *Home-based care: A gendered analysis of informal caregiving for people living with HIV/AIDS in a semi-rural South African setting*. Doctoral Thesis, Health Economics and HIV/AIDS Research Division, University of KwaZuluNatal.

Charlesworth, S. (2005). Managing work and family in the 'shadow' of anti-discrimination law. *Law in Context, 23*(1), 104.

Cohen, T., & Dancaster, L. (2009a). The rights of employees with family responsibilities to request flexible working arrangements—the failings of the Employment Equity Act. In O. Dupper & C. Garbers (Eds.), *Equality in the workplace: Reflections from South Africa and beyond* (pp. 207–226). Cape Town: Juta.

Cohen, T., & Dancaster, L. (2009b). Family responsibility discrimination litigation—A non-starter? *Stellenbosch Law Review, 20*(2), 221–240.

Croucher, R., & Kelliher, C. (2005). The right to request flexible working in Britain: The law and organisational realities. *International Journal of Comparative Labour Law and Industrial Relations, 21*(3), 503–518.

Dancaster, L., & Baird, M. (2008). Workers with care responsibilities: Is work-family integration adequately addressed in South African labour law? *Industrial Law Journal including the Industrial Law Reports, 29*, 22–42.

Dancaster, L., & Cohen, T. (2010). Workers with family responsibilities: A comparative analysis to advocate for the legal right to request flexible working arrangements in South Africa. *South African Journal of Labour Relations, 34*(1), 31–45.

Dancaster, L. (2012). *State and employer involvement in work–care integration in South Africa.* Ph.D. Thesis. University of Sydney: Australia.

Department of Social Development. (2011). *Green paper on families. Promoting family life and strengthening families in South Africa.* Govt. Gazette no. 34657, 3 October 2011, 3–86.

Dupper, O. (2001). Maternity protection in South Africa: An international and comparative perspective (Part 1). *Stellenbosch Law Review, 12*, 421–438.

Dupper, O., Malherbe, K., Shipman, B., & Bolani, E. (2000). The case for increased reform of South African family and maternity benefits. *Democracy and Development, 4*(1), 27–41.

Dupper, O., Olivier, M., & Govindjee, A. (2011). Extending coverage of the unemployment insurance-system in South Africa. *Stellenbosch Law Review, 22*, 438–462.

Eddy, G., & Holborn, L. (2011). *First steps to healing the South African family*. Johannesburg: South African Institute of Race Relations.

Hayward, B., Fong, B., & Thornton, A. (2007). *The third work-life balance employer survey.* Department of Trade and Industry Employment Relations Research Series, No. 86.

Hegewisch, A., & Gornick, J. (2008). *Statutory routes to workplace flexibility in cross-national perspective*. http://www.iwpr.org/pdf/B258workplaceflex.pdf.

Holt, H., & Grainger, H. (2005). *Results of the second flexible working employee survey. Issue 39 of Employment Relations Research Series*. London: Department of Trade and Industry.

International Labour Organisation. (2012). *Maternity at work: A review of national legislation. Findings from the ILO database of conditions of work and employment laws* (2nd ed.). Geneva: International Labour Organisation.

Jacobs, A., & Schmidt, M. (2001). The right to part-time work: The Netherlands and Germany compared. *International Journal of Comparative Labour Law and Industrial Relations, 57*(3), 373–384.

Kingdon, G., & Knight, J. (2004). Race and the incidence of unemployment in South Africa. *Review of Development Economics, 8*, 198–222.

Labour Research Service. (2011). The trade union bargaining indicators report, 2011. *Bargaining Monitor, 25*(176), 1–43.

Lewis, J. (2006). Employment and care: The policy problem, gender equality and the issue of choice. *Journal of Comparative Policy Analysis: Research and Practice, 8*(2), 103–114.

Lund, F. (2009). *The Political and Social Economy of Care: South Africa*. Research report prepared for the United Nations Research Institute for Social Development (UNRISD). Geneva: UNRISD.

Morrell, R., & Richter, L. (2006). Introduction. In L. Richter & R. Morrell (Eds.), *Baba: Men and fatherhood in South Africa*. Cape Town: HSRC Press.

Morrell, R., & Jewkes, R. (2011). Carework and caring: A path to gender equitable practices among men in South Africa? *International Journal for Equity in Health, 10*, 17. doi:10.1186/1475-9276-10-17.

Moss, P. (2011). International review of leave policies and related research. In Moss, P. (Ed). *International network on leave policies and research*. http://www.leavenetwork.org. 2 May 2013.

Moss, P., & O'Brien, M. (2006). *International Review of Leave Policies and Related Research*. Employment Relations Research Series, No. 57. Department of Trade and Industry, United Kingdom.

Mpedi, L. G. (2008). *Pertinent social security issues in South Africa. Socio-economic rights project*. Cape Town: Community Law Centre, University of the Western Cape.

Murray, J. (2004*). International legal trends in the reconciliation of work and family life*. Report prepared for the ACTU's test case. http://www.actu.asn.au/public/papers/jill_murray. Accessed 28 September 2012.

Murray, J. (2005). Work and care: New legal mechanisms for adaptation. *Labour & Industry, 15*(3), 66–87.

Olivier, M., Dupper, O., & Govindjee, A. (2011). Redesigning the South African Unemployment Insurance Fund: Selected key policy and legal perspectives. *Stellenbosch Law Review, 22*, 396–425.

Rajaraman, D., Russell, S., & Heymann, J. (2006). HIV/AIDS, income loss and economic survival in Botswana. *AIDS Care, 18*, 656–662.

Richter, L., & Morrell, R. (Eds.). (2006). *Baba: Men and fatherhood in South Africa*. Cape Town: HSRC Press.

Smit, R. (2002). The changing role of the husband/father in the dual-earner family in South Africa. *Journal of Comparative Family Studies, 36*(1), 401–415.

Smith, B. (2006). Not the baby and the bathwater: Regulatory reform for equality laws to address work–family conflict. *Sydney Law Review* 689–694.

Smith, B., & Riley, J. (2004). Family-friendly work practices and the law. *Sydney Law Review, 26*, 395–426.

Whitehouse, G., Diamond, C., & Baird, M. (2007). Fathers' use of leave in Australia. *Community, Work & Family, 10*(4), 387–407.

Chapter 12
A Review of Work–Family Research in Sub-Saharan Africa

Zitha Mokomane and Desire Chilwane

Introduction

As stated at the begging of this book, the increasing academic and policy interest in the nexus between paid work and family life has led to an accumulation of a large body of literature on the subject. However, as Shaffer et al. (2011:221) assert, there is still "a disparate and fractured understanding of the dynamic interplay between work and family for those who live and work [in developing countries]" as the vast majority of studies on work–family interface have been done in the United States and other Western countries (Poelmans et al. 2003; Shaffer et al. 2011). In particular, while there have despite recent attempts to investigate work and family interface in other national and cultural contexts, paucity of African studies on the subject persists (Shaffer et al. 2011). The preceding 11 chapters have, however, shown that work–family conflict is as much an issue in sub-Saharan Africa as it is in other parts of the world where it has developed into a distinct sub-field of cross-disciplinary study (Rajadhyaksha and Smita 2004).

In illuminating some of the key challenges that sub-Saharan African workers who have family responsibilities face, the evidence presented and conclusions made by the preceding suggest that clear and distinct focus on work and family research in sub-Saharan Africa is outstanding given the socio-economic and demographic transformations taking place in the sub-region. The issue is also important against the background of increasing calls by international development organisations to pay more attention to it. For example, the United Nations Economic and Social Council's Resolution 2011/29 of 2011 on the "Preparations for an Observance of the 20th Anniversary of the International Year of the Family" has called on Member States to develop appropriate policies to address a number

Z. Mokomane (✉) · D. Chilwane
Human Sciences Research Council of South Africa, Pretoria, South Africa
e-mail: zmokomane@hsrc.ac.za

D. Chilwane
e-mail: deechilwane@yahoo.com

Z. Mokomane (ed.), *Work–Family Interface in Sub-Saharan Africa*,
International Perspectives on Social Policy, Administration, and Practice,
DOI: 10.1007/978-3-319-01237-7_12,

of family-related issues, including work–family balance, and to share good practices in those areas (United Nations 2012). Similarly, Article 16 of the 2008 Southern African Development Community (SADC)[1] Protocol on Gender and Development (SADC 2008) urges Members States to conduct studies "by 2015 and adopt policy measures to ease the burden of the multiple roles played by women", while in Article 27, 3(c) states that State parties shall, by 2015 "develop and implement policies and programmes to ensure appropriate recognition of the work carried by care givers, majority of whom are women…".

As a step towards responding to these and other similar calls, it is perhaps important to take stock of where sub-Saharan Africa stands in terms of work–family research, defined as "that which addresses the relationship between paid employment and commitments to kin" (Bardoel et al. 2008:317). The purpose of this chapter, therefore, is to conclude this book by presenting a summary and assessment of the sub-region's rudimentary research on the subject identifying the key issues and themes that have been explored thus far; identifying research gaps that remain; and offering suggestions for future research. The chapter draws from a broad brush stroke review of the literature conducted in 2011 as well as the conclusions made by the preceding 11 chapters.

Methodological Approach

The literature review on which the chapter is based followed to a large extent, the principles and processes of systematic reviews, defined as attempts to "deliver a meticulous summary of all the available primary research in response to a research question" (Clarke 2011:64). In particular, the review adopted the systematic procession from one stage to the other "with full transparency and explicitness about what research is to be critically evaluated and appraised, and using a protocol to guide the process" (Bardoel et al. 2008:317). It should be reiterated, however, that the literature review was not a full-fledged systematic review as all the processes of such reviews (see for example, Green et al. 2011) were not followed; the main aim was to give an *overview* of the sub-Saharan African literature on the subject.

Electronic literature searches—using the following keywords: work–life, work–life balance, work–family, and work–family conflict—were conducted between July and August 2011 in the following databases: African Journals Online, EBSCOhost, ISI Web of Science, Proquest, SABINET and the Sloan Work and Family Research Network. Studies were included in the literature review if they were published in English between 2000 and mid-August 2011 (inclusive);

[1] SADC is a regional economic community comprising of the following 15 Southern and East African countries: Angola, Botswana, Democratic Republic of Congo, Lesotho, Madagascar, Malawi, Mauritius, Mozambique, Namibia, South Africa, Swaziland, Seychelles, Tanzania, Zambia, and Zimbabwe.

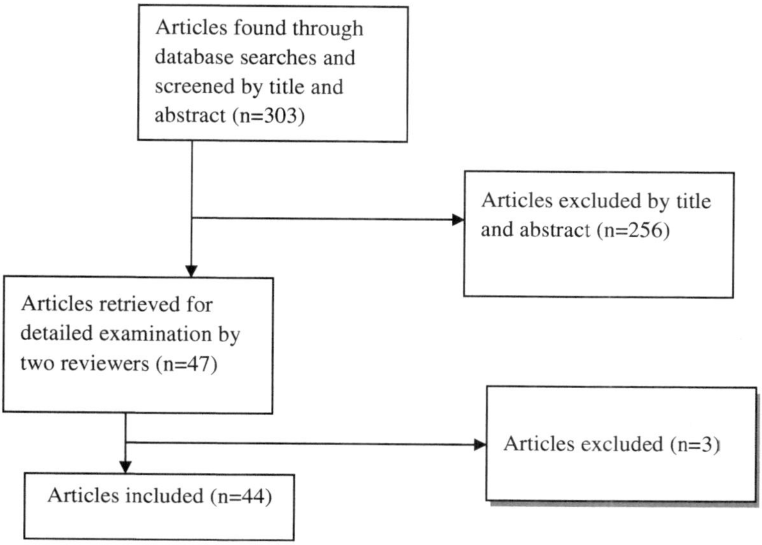

Fig. 12.1 Process followed in the selection of articles

published in a peer-reviewed journal; based on research conducted in an English-speaking sub-Saharan African country. While the focus of the preceding chapters was on *work–family,* the literature review included articles on 'work–life' as this concept is commonly used interchangeably with work–family in the literature.

A search of the databases using the above criteria identified 303 results (see Fig. 12.1). Of these 256 were excluded following viewing of the title and the abstract, as they clearly did not address the nexus between work–family or work–life issues. The full texts of the remaining 47 papers were retrieved for detailed and independent examination by two reviewers using a pre-designed eligibility sheet. This latter process excluded three articles as they did not meet the selection criteria, thus leaving 44 articles to be included in the review. The following data were extracted from each article: country within which the study took place; the work–family or work–life issue considered; and the study design and the data sources; results.

Results and Discussion

Geographical Focus

Consistent with Epie and Ituma's assertion in Chap. 3 that most of the existing African research on work–family interface has been carried out in South Africa, the majority (20) of the 44 articles that met the inclusion criteria for the literature review focused on South Africa. Fourteen were on Nigeria, three on Ghana, two on Botswana, while Kenya, Mauritius, Sudan and Tanzania each had one article focusing on them. There was one article that focused on the SADC region. All in all, therefore, only eight of the 52 sub-Saharan African countries (United Nations 2013) had work–family or work–life articles published on them in the 10 years between 2000 and 2011.

Themes

In a review of work–life research in Australia and New Zealand, Bardoel et al. (2008) grouped the themes emerging from the research two eight broad categories:

- *Organisation*: This theme includes articles that centre on organisational policies, programmes, strategies and support designed to alleviate employees' work–life or work–family conflict and to promote work–life and work–family balance;
- *Work*: This theme focuses on job characteristics and includes articles dealing with alternative work arrangements such as part-time-work, temporary work; the casualization of the workforce; and flexible work arrangements;
- *Occupations/industries* studies that address specific occupations and industries;
- *Government* articles addressing government policy and legislation, mostly related to childcare, maternity leave; parental leave and caregiving;
- *Health* articles in this theme address health outcomes of work–life and work–family conflict such as stress, burnout and other well-being related aspects;
- *Families* articles addressing family structure and children;
- *Gender* focus on gender differences in the experience of work–life or work–family conflict; and
- *Additional themes* any other themes addressing work–family and work–life issues.

Using this typology, the thematic analysis of the sub-Saharan research revealed that the largest proportion of the articles focused on themes related to occupations/industries and gender (Table 12.1). Within occupations/industries most of the papers explored the experiences and coping strategies of employees in different occupations and industries. The relatively higher number of papers focusing on women in academia is, perhaps, a reflection of the traditional view of academia as a "male field" in this part of the world. By the same token, the relatively high proportion of articles addressing gender can be explained by the historical conceptualisation of work–family balance as an issue of women with families engaged in paid employment (Bardoel et al. 2008). Topics addressed under all the other themes are also shown in Table 12.1.

Table 12.1 Themes identified work–family and work–life research in sub-Saharan, 2000-mid 2011

Occupations/industries	*12*
Women in academia	4
Breweries	1
Customer care	1
Management	1
Mining	1
Mixed industries (police service, earthmoving equipment, mining, nursing)	1
Nursing	1
Police service	1
Private organisations	1
Gender	*10*
Gender differences	2
Married women and work–family conflict	2
Women's work–life conflict and coping strategies	2
Women's work and breastfeeding	4
Organisation	*5*
Family-friendly workplaces	2
Organisational support	3
Families	*4*
Children home alone unsupervised	1
Dual-earner families	2
Working caregivers	1
Government	*4*
Breastfeeding policy	1
Parental leave policies	1
Work–life legislation	2
Health	*1*
Employees' health	1
Work	*1*
Tele-working	1
Additional themes	*8*
Employees' health	1
Measurement	2
Tele-working	1
Time use	2
Work–family conflict and voluntary turnover	2

Research Approaches: Conceptual Versus Empirical

Empirical and conceptual approaches are some of the most commonly employed in research where in the latter "an idea or concept is presented in the context of a broader body of knowledge to help clarify, explore, and expand understanding of the concept being presented" (Spencer 1988:271). Empirical research on the other hand is based on observations or measurements of phenomenon and thus derives

Table 12.2 Research methods used in work–family and work–life empirical research in sub-Saharan Africa, 2000-mid 2011

Methods	Number of articles
Quantitative	
Surveys	23
Secondary data analysis	4
Qualitative	
In-depth interviews	9
Mixed methods	4

conclusions from data-based research which is "capable of being verified" (Kumar 2008:8). Although empirical studies are often "considered to be the most powerful support possible for a given hypothesis" (Kumar 2008:8), conceptual research is also seen as an important method of analysis as it can assist "researchers develop awareness and understanding of the situation under scrutiny and to communicate this" (Bardoel et al. 2008:321).

Four of the 44 papers reviewed were found to be conceptual and revolved around government policy and legislation. Two of the papers were written by the same author and examined different aspects of the legal right to request flexible working arrangements in South Africa. Another paper was an examination of the National Breastfeeding Policy in Nigeria while the fourth one was a cross-country comparison of parental leave policies in SADC countries.

The large majority (40) of the articles examined were empirical and exclusively cross-sectional in design. The majority (27) of these papers used a quantitative methodology, while nine used a qualitative method and four used mixed methods, combining qualitative and quantitative approaches (Table 12.2). It is also clear from the table that there was a strong preference for surveys (23 articles). The remaining empirical studies used in-depth interviews, secondary data analysis and the combination of document reviews and in-depth interviews.

Journals of Publication

To the extent that "academic journals are one of the most important means of publishing and disseminating the results of academic research and scholarship" (Harvey et al. 2010:1), their quality is important not only as an indicator of academic productivity that can be linked to the tenure and promotion of the authors (Drago and Kashian 2003), but it is also important for readers in that high-quality journals publish more good articles which "are valuable to readers because they contain fewer bad articles that are costly to read but provide no benefit" (McCabe and Snyder 2004:17). Thus, recognising that the multidisciplinary nature and breadth of work–family and work–life research meant that there was no gauge for the quality and impact of academic journals in which work–family researchers

Table 12.3 Academic journals in which sub-Saharan African research on work–family and work–life appeared 2000-mid 2011

Journals	Number of articles
Acta Academiaa[a]	1
Acta Criminologica[a]	1
African Journal for the Psychological Study of Social issues[a]	1
African Journal of Business Management[a]	1
Agenda[a]	1
Child Abuse and Neglect[b]	1
Community Work & Family[b]	2
Eastern Africa Social Science Research Review[a]	1
Economic Development and Cultural Change[b]	1
European Journal of Scientific Research[b]	1
Gender and Behaviour[a]	2
Gender in Management [b]	1
Health Care for Women International [b]	2
IFE PsychologIA[a]	3
International Business Research[b]	1
International Journal of Human Sciences[b]	1
International Journal of Occupational Safety and Ergonomics[b]	1
Journal of Comparative Family Studies[b]	2
Journal of Diversity Management[b]	1
Journal of Human Ecology[b]	1
Journal of Social Development in Africa[a]	1
Personnel Psychology[b]	1
Population Studies[b]	1
Social Indicators Research[b]	1
South African Journal of Human Resources Management[a]	2
South African Journal of Labour Relations[a]	1
South African Journal of Industrial Psychology[a]	4
South African Journal of Psychology[a]	1
The International Business and Economics Research Journal[b]	1
The South African Journal of Economic and Management Sciences[a]	5

Note: [a] Africa-focus and [b] International focus

published Drago and Kashian (2003) mapped the terrain of work–family journals. On conclusion they recommended a set of 23 multidisciplinary core journals that demonstrate a commitment to work–family issues, and through which authors are likely to reach both researchers and policy-makers in the field thus "proving useful to researchers and [facilitating] further development of the field of work/family research" (Drago and Kashian 2003:510).

The review of literature revealed that the articles reviewed were published in 30 academic journals across numerous disciplines (Table 12.1). Although the articles were fairly split between Africa-focused journals (14) articles and internationally-focused journals (16 articles), only three were published in journals that appear in Drago and Kashian's core list: two were in *Community Work & Family* while one was in *Personnel Psychology* (Table 12.3). All in all, the distribution of the journals of publications was in line with the geographic focus of the studies in that journals with the most articles were the South African-based *The South African Journal of Economic and Management Sciences Labour* (five articles) and *South African Journal of Industrial Psychology* (four articles), as well as the Nigerian-based *IFE PsychologIA* which had three articles.

Limitations

This paper has provided *preliminary* insights into the dimensions of work–family and work–life research sub-Saharan Africa. These results should, however, be interpreted cautiously given the limitations of the literature review undertaken particularly: (1) the focus on English-speaking sub-Saharan Africa which undoubtedly left out any research which could have been done in francophone or Portuguese-speaking countries of the sub-region; (2) Reliance on a western-based model (Bardoel et al.) to identify themes. While this was necessitated by the paucity of African research on the subject, and hence lack of an appropriate conceptual framework, it means that some uniquely African themes are likely to have been left out. The review also omitted to examine the theoretical perspectives applied in the articles reviewed and the validity of research methods they used. There is therefore a need to re-affirm the conclusions of the review through more methodologically rigorous approaches. Nonetheless, the review provides valuable insights into the status of work–family research in sub-Saharan Africa.

Summary and Conclusion

Not withstanding the above limitations, taken together with the evidence presented in the preceding 11 chapters, the overall conclusion of this chapter and book is that work–family issues in sub-Saharan Africa require further and broader consideration. The introductory chapter, for example, highlighted various socioeconomic and demographic changes in the region that have implications for the reconciliation of work and family roles. These suggest that the nexus between paid employment and the demands of family and other life domains will increasingly become an important phenomenon and policy issue in most sub-Saharan African countries. This is affirmed by much of the empirical evidence provided in the other chapters. It is thus imperative for governments in the sub-region to elevate the issues surrounding work–family interface on their policy agendas.

It is however important for any mechanisms or policies that are adopted to be evidence-based and context-specific. As Korenman and Kaester (2005) caution, considerable care is needed before assuming that the more "family-friendly" policies and institutional arrangements present on western countries would be desirable for Africa. Indeed, the results of the literature review presented in this chapter, and the conclusions made by the preceding chapters identified major research gaps that require more in-depth interrogation and understanding as a first step towards designing and implementing work–family policies in sub-Saharan Africa.

To a large extent, these are in line with those previously identified by others such as Aryee (2005) and Mokomane (2009, 2013), and include the need to: establish how the changing family structure in the sub-region is interacting with workplace demands; explore time use patterns of household and family members; explore how changes in the labour market affect the capability of families to strike a balance between work and family responsibilities; determine the extent to which alternative working arrangements such as part-time work, temporary work, the casualisation of the workforce and flexible work arrangements can be feasible in sub-Saharan Africa; explore the sources and types of work–family conflict experienced by different types of workers including men, in sub-Saharan Africa; explore types of conflict that have the most influence on the well-being and productivity of sub-Saharan African workers and their families; determine the support mechanisms that are currently available for workers in different sub-Saharan African countries, and the gaps that exist between the needs of the workers and the existing support measures; study the gaps exist between the needs for workers and their families, and the existing labour legislations and employment policies.

It will also be worthwhile to elaborate, with more evidence, the themes explored in the four parts of this book. For example, by assessing the work–family fit[2] of sub-Saharan African workers in relation to that of their counterparts in both developed and other developing countries will affirm the extent to which work–family interface is an issue in the sub-region. This will be done through answering the questions such as: how do workers manage to combine their family responsibilities with paid employment?; how do they define and perceive their work burden?; and how do the definitions and perceptions differ between different types of employees?; Exploration of the workers' work–family fit will further illuminate other factors that underlie work–family conflict in the sub-region.

The third part of the book showed some of the social impact on the conflict. Research exploring the impact on other aspects of society including, *inter alia*, workplace productivity; employees' health; poverty reduction; and child health and development, is imperative. For example, to the extent that the survival of infants and children is directly related to, among others things, the environment in which the mothers live and work (Department of Social Development 2009; International Labour Organisation 2010), it will be interesting to examine the role that sub-Saharan Africa parents' poor access to supportive workplace policies has played a role in the sub-region's unsatisfactory progression towards the attainment of Millennium Development Goal 4, the target of which is to reduce child mortality (mortality in children under five years) by two-thirds, between 1990 and

---

[2] Work–family fit refers to an individual's overall assessment of how well she or he has been able to integrate paid work and family life (Hill et al. 2003).

2015. Recent indications are that while the global mortality rate for children under the age of five declined by a third between 1990 and 2009, the highest levels of under-five mortality continue to be found in sub-Saharan Africa. Here one in eight children die before the age of five, nearly twice the average in developing regions overall, and around 18 times the average in developed regions (United Nations 2011).

Overall, it is recommended that rather than continuing the current reliance of quantitative methodologies (Table 12.2) which, according to Bardoel et al. (2008:329), "runs the risk of masking anomalies and counter-intuitive findings" scholars should address the above research questions using quantitative and qualitative methods complementarily rather than as alternatives to each other. One value in this is that qualitative methods give the opportunity to probe into issues that would otherwise be difficult to obtain or explain from quantitative data only. Furthermore, in disseminating their results, it is important for sub-Saharan African scholars to aim to publish their work in academic journals that have demonstrated commitment to the field. This will not only ensure that African research is easily accessible to other work–family researchers and policymakers, but it will also facilitate the development of a work–family research community in the continent, and the participation of sub-Saharan African researchers in the global work–family and research community.

All in all, while some (for example, Cousins and Tang 2004; Van der Lippe et al. 2006) have argued that social policies have little or no effect in mitigating individuals' work–family conflict, the bulk of the research findings demonstrate that "taken as a whole ... national policies and institutional arrangements do make a difference and enhance to some extent the life balance of employed women and men" (Stier et al. 2012:278). It is to this end that the foregoing research agenda is worth pursuing so as to inform social policy-making in sub-Saharan Africa.

References

Aryee, S. (2005). The work–family interface in urban sub-Saharan Africa: A theoretical analysis. In S. Y. Peilmans (Ed.), *Work and family: An international research perspective*. Mahwah: Lawrence Erlbaum Associates.

Bardoel, E. A., De Cieri, H., & Santos, C. (2008). A review of work–life research in Australia and New Zealand. *Asia Pacific Journal of Human Resources, 46*(3), 316–333.

Clarke, J. (2011). What is a systematic review? *Evidence Based Nursing, 14*, 64. doi:10.1136/ebn.2011.0049.

Cousins, C., & Tang, N. (2004). Working time and work and family conflict in the Netherlands, Sweden and the UK. *Work, Employment & Society, 18*(3), 531–549.

Department of Social Development. (2009) *Review of the fifteen years of the International Conference Population and Development (ICPD) Programme of Action (POA) in the Southern African Development Community (SADC) Region*. Pretoria: Department of Social Development, Republic of South Arica.

Drago, R., & Kashian, R. (2003). Mapping the terrain of work/family journals. *Journal of Family Issues, 24*(4), 488–512.

Green, S., Higgins, J. P. T., Alderson, P., Clarke, M., Mulrow, C. D., & Oxman, A. D. (2011). Introduction. In J. P. T. Higgins & S. Green (Eds.), *Cochrane handbook for systematic reviews of interventions*. www.cochrane.org/training/cochrane-handbook. Accessed 3 May 2013.

Harvey, C., Kelly, A., Morris, H., & Rowlinson, M. (2010). *Academic journal quality guide version 4*. London: Association of Business Schools. www.myscp.org/pdf/ABS%202010%20Combined%20Journal%20Guide.pdf, 3 May 2013.

Hill, E. J., Hawkins, A. J., Märtinson, V., & Ferris, M. (2003). Studying "working fathers": Comparing fathers' and mothers' work–family conflict, fit, and adaptive strategies in a global high-tech company. *Fathering: A Journal of Theory, Research, and Practice about Men as Fathers, 1*(3), 239–261.

International Labour Organisation. (2010). *Maternity at work: A review of national legislation*. Geneva: International Labour Organization.

Korenman, S., & Kaester, R. (2005). Work–family mismatch and child well-being: A review of the economic research. In S. M. Bianchi, L. M. Casper, & R. B. King (Eds.), *Work, family, health and wellbeing*. Mahwah: Lawrence Erlbaum Associates.

Kumar, C. R. (2008). *Research methodology*. New Delhi: SB Nangia for APH Publishing Corporation.

McCabe, M. J., & Snyder, C. M. (2004). *A model of academic journal quality with applications to open-access journals*. http://papers.ssrn.com/sol3/papers.cfm?abstract_id=619264 Accessed 3 May 2013.

Mokomane, Z. (2009). *Work family conflict and gender equality in South Africa*. Paper presented at the 26th International Population Conference, Marrakech, Morocco, 28th September–2nd October.

Mokomane, Z. (2013). Socio-economic and demographic transformations in South Africa: Implications for work–family conflict and gender equality. In C. C. Wolhunter (Ed.), *South Africa in focus: Economic, political and social issues*. Nova Publishers.

Poelmans, S., Spector, P. E., Cooper, C. L., Allen, T. D., O'Driscoll, M., & Sanchez, J. I. (2003). A cross-national comparative study of work/family demands and resources. *International Journal of Cross Cultural Management, 3*(3), 275–288.

Rajadhyaksha, U., & Smita, S. (2004). Tracing a timeline of work and family research in India. *Economic and Political Weekly, XXXIX*(17), 1674–1680.

SADC. (2008). *Protocol on Gender and Development*. Gaborone: Southern African Development Community.

Shaffer, M. A., Joplin, J. R. W., & Hsu, Y. (2011). Expanding the boundaries of work—family research: A review and agenda for future research. *International Journal of Cross Cultural Management, 11*(2), 221–268.

Spencer, D. A. (1988). Conceptual frameworks for bibliographical education: Theory into practice: A book review. *Bulletin of the Medical Library Association, 76*(3), 277.

Stier, H., Lewin-Epstein, N., & Braun, M. (2012). Work–family conflict in comparative perspective: The role of social policies. *Research in Social Stratification and Mobility, 30*, 265–279.

United Nations. (2011). *Millennium development report, 2011*. New York: United Nations.

United Nations (2013) *Composition of macro geographical (continental) regions, geographical sub-regions, and selected economic and other groupings*. http://unstats.un.org/unsd/methods/m49/m49regin.htm Accessed 3 May 2013.

United Nations. (2012). *Report of the secretary-general on preparations for and observance of the twentieth anniversary of the international year of the family in 2014*. Geneva: General Assembly Economic and Social Council.

Van der Lippe, T., Jager, A., & Kops, Y. (2006). Combination pressure: The paid work–family balance of men and women in European countries. *Acta Sociologica, 49*, 303–319.

Index

Note: Page numbers followed by *f* and *t* indicate figures and tables respectively; notes are represented by n followed by note number

Z. Mokomane (ed.), *Work–Family Interface in Sub-Saharan Africa*,
International Perspectives on Social Policy, Administration, and Practice,
DOI: 10.1007/978-3-319-01237-7, © Springer International Publishing Switzerland 2014

O

P

MIX
Papier aus verantwortungsvollen Quellen
Paper from responsible sources
FSC® C105338

If you have any concerns about our products,
you can contact us on
ProductSafety@springernature.com

In case Publisher is established outside the EU,
the EU authorized representative is:
Springer Nature Customer Service Center GmbH
Europaplatz 3, 69115 Heidelberg, Germany

Printed by Libri Plureos GmbH
in Hamburg, Germany